MW00560157

KING OF DIAMONDS

Harry Winston,
The Definitive Biography
of an American Icon

By
RONALD WINSTON
& WILLIAM STADIEM

Skyhorse Publishing

For my wife and son.

Contents

CHAPTER ONE

Milk and Honey

A glass of milk was the leitmotif of my father's childhood. It wasn't whether the glass was half full or not, it was just about having any milk at all. My father, Harry Winston, loved to talk about how desperately poor and hungry he'd been as a child, and a full glass of milk represented not only the bounty of nature but also the love of his family. It also symbolized his thirst for wanting to build a business that would become renowned the world over.

My father would talk about his impoverished childhood over fine wine served in crystal goblets at the chef-and-butler-attended "high"table in our town house on 51st street off Fifth Avenue. His jewelry business, Harry Winston, Inc., occupied the first four floors. Our family lived on the fifth.

When I was very young, I had my own little dining table where I was served my favorite dish, vichyssoise, which I called "swish-swash." My table was always illuminated by candlelight, which somehow fascinated me. I detested bright lights. My English nurse, Miss Pender, and my Irish nanny, Rosie, both joked that I was very romantic.

When I was old enough to sit at the high table, I began hearing about milk and the czars and the pogroms and the Russian winters and the steerage crossings that were the experiences of my grandparents. Harry Winston was born poor in New York City, and he had grown up in what was still the Wild West of early twentieth-century Los Angeles. In addition to the Russian stories, he had cowboy stories, cops and robbers stories, and failed business stories. All of the stories burnished the legend of my father as a man who had transcended the quicksand of his own destiny and made something of himself.

As a little boy, I wasn't sure what to make of all this. We were living in splendor. My father seemed very grand, in bespoke suits, starched dickeys, and the priceless diamonds he often kept in his suit pockets and played with the way Arab men would caress and jiggle their worry beads. I first realized my father was famous when I heard his name on the radio on our annual winter holiday in Palm Beach in 1949. I was eight at the time.

"Harry Winston, the New York jeweler, has just bought the socialite Evalyn Walsh McLean estate for a staggering one million dollars. The purchase includes the world's greatest stone, the Hope Diamond, whose ominous curse has spelled tragedy for its various ill-fated owners," the newscaster intoned over the magic airwaves. Not "a" New York jeweler, but "the" New York jeweler. A million dollars in 1949 was a phantasmagoric sum, like a billion today. And the world's greatest diamond, which came with a curse, made a huge impression on me. It made my father more than just a dad. A lot more. It made him and the world of jewels, and the rich and famous who wore them, more than a little intimidating.

So I wasn't sure what to make of the milk story, the great metaphor for this mythology of poverty. I wasn't sure what to believe. How could I doubt my own father? Easy. Once, when I was even younger, my father was playing with me, holding me up, bouncing me around, having a wonderful time. Then, at the peak of my pleasure at being tossed up into the air, he dropped me, hard and fast, onto the rug. I wasn't really hurt, but I was shocked. I began to cry uncontrollably. "Never trust anyone in life," he told me. "Not even your own father." Although he was usually the soul of kindness to me, I never quite regained my equilibrium from that major life lesson.

Early on, my father tried his best to interest me in those precious stones in his pocket. I think I was three when he gave me my first lesson in gemology when he shook what seemed like an oddly colored gumball out of an envelope. "Son, I want you to remember this stone," he would say as if I would understand. "It's magnificent. It's a ten-carat Burmese ruby. Look at the color, pigeon blood. Slippery. Red. Juicy. Isn't it beautiful? Isn't it, son?" Beautiful? Pigeon blood? Yuck! What three-year-old wants to hear about pigeon blood?

Just like being dropped, the gem lessons, which came almost nightly, along with the milk lectures, made an impact on me, because these many years later, I can still summon these vivid images. I knew my father was a great man—and so did he. Normally reserved and understated, he sometimes could not help but be overwhelmed by his own mythology. "Afterall, how many Harry Winstons are there in the world?" he would often say. His dream was that I, and my brother Bruce, three years my junior, would go and work for him, with him, and create a dynasty that would rule the diamond world. "The three little Winstons," my father, who

3

acted like a giant but was barely five feet tall, would muse. "The three little Winstons."

But this little Winston had little if any interest in my father's big footsteps, apocryphal or otherwise. I was fascinated not by commerce, not even the grand commerce of my father, but by the science of my maternal grandfather, a distinguished and humanistic doctor of the old Viennese school.

Doctor Henry Fleischman, whom I called Winkie, would have reminded me of Sigmund Freud, if I had known who Freud was at the time. A specialist in treating unwell children, particularly those with rheumatic fever, Dr. F. had been the director of the Educational Alliance, a charity for underprivileged, mostly Jewish youngsters on the Lower East Side. I'll never forget his squealing hearing aid and his exhortation to "be kind to animals." As I got a little older, I took a special interest in his vast library of medical books, particularly those on female anatomy, things like *Diseases of the Female Urogenitary System*. which I managed to make off with. My father had already been warning me to never trust women. They were treacherous, he confided. They would get me into terrible trouble. Never trust your father. Never trust women. Whom *could* I trust?

I thought I could trust Grandfather Winkie, who wanted me to become a doctor, much to my father's chagrin. But even Winkie had trouble with the truth. He and my mother both told me that my grandmother had died long ago, run over outside Bergdorf Goodman by a car that had careened out of control. I later found out, however, that my grandmother had committed suicide when my mother was fifteen. Much later I learned that my grandmother's death might have been prevented had she not been turned away by Mount

Sinai Hospital. Mount Sinai was the German-Jewish pinnacle of medicine in New York, and the Winstons, or Weinsteins, which was their name then, were poor Russians who would lower the hospital's social tone. "Not our kind" was the shorthand for the anti-Semitism that overrode the Hippocratic oath at the time. But despite the truth of my grandmother's death being far more compelling, the Bergdorf fiction remained the official story.

Of course my grandmother would never have been run down outside Woolworth or McCrory's. It had to be first class. It had to be Bergdorf's, Bonwit's, or Saks. That was the league my family was in. The big league of luxe American retailing. After all, how many of my friends's fathers were immortalized in one of the hit songs of our childhood, "Diamonds Are a Girl's Best Friend," from the 1953 smash *Gentlemen Prefer Blondes*? In the film Marilyn Monroe coos, "Talk to me, Harry Winston. Tell me all about it," in her inimitable breathless voice.

While my father provided the fame and the wealth, my mother brought the class. Her name was Edna, and she was truly elegant, slender, a bit taller than my father, the embodiment of the glamour that my father was purveying. I remember the sound of her pearls clattering at night over my little crib as she came in to check on me after a night on the town. She was refined, educated, and born to wear the jewels my father created. As an only child to a widowed parent, she had surely been as overprotected as I, a perfect exemplar of the New York German Jew immortalized in the book *Our Crowd*. This was in dramatic opposition to the Russian Jew, my father's tribe, whose members came up on the mean streets of Essex and Rivington and Delancey on the Lower East Side.

Not that I had any real sense of a Jewish identity. Yes, my father would toss out occasional Yiddish phrases like gonif (thief) and meshuggener (nutcase), but to me these were just New York words, not Jewish ones. I went to the Christian Science Sunday School near our Scarsdale estate every weekend, and I went there with lots of children of prominent New Yorkers I later learned were Jewish, like the Revson boys of the cosmetics fortune. I wore a St. Christopher medal with my IDs on the back.

The only thing I remember from those Sunday school classes is hearing that the founder of Christian Science, Mary Baker Eddy, had been buried with a telephone in her casket. Somehow that made the creepy idea of dying a whole lot more palatable, and it made Christian Science seem very with-it, as religions went. What got me was the science, not the Christianity. My family did occasionally go to Passover seders at friends' homes, but my father was always impatient with the ceremonial why-is-this-night- different-from-all-other-nights stuff, wanting to get to the food part.

No, the only religion my father tried to inculcate in me as a young boy was the commitment to those mysterious sparkling diamonds and an ethic of ceaseless hard work. My father was like a whirling dervish: up at five thirty, back for dinner at eight. He never ate lunch, couldn't understand why anyone would eat when they could work. "What's the hurry, Dad?" I would sometimes ask him. He seemed offended by the question. "I have to go and make a living," he said, almost indignantly.

My father pushed me to take up running, which was an activity he loved. Not particularly athletic himself (though he was also an avid swimmer), he would brag about how much running he had done as a boy, running from one end of

Manhattan to the other, one end of Los Angeles to the other, which I believed until I found out how huge L.A. is. I ran with him around the estate in Scarsdale. "Pick your feet up! Pick your knees up!" He also insisted I become a Cub Scout. I hated it. Our butler had to chase me down and drag me to meetings.

On the indoor side, there were piano, dancing, and etiquette lessons. My parents took me to Europe before I was twelve. The idea was to make me a "gent," a gent who would one day take his place at Harry Winston. I was taken to Anderson & Sheppard, my father's Savile Row tailor, to dress me for the part, and plans were made to ship me off to the elite Swiss school Le Rosey to learn foreign languages and to make connections to the noble families of my classmates—all potential clients. "We have an international business," he would say, stressing the "we." I remained completely unsold. But I was aware, sometimes painfully, of how diamonds were my father's religion, passion, and obsession.

Sometimes I would see him sitting in one of his big leather chairs, holding, caressing, massaging a big shimmering, sparkling diamond as if it were something alive. He was totally focused, totally hypnotized, and totally absorbed, and that very absorption helped me get some idea of how precious these stones actually were. They were his treasure of the Sierra Madre, the much-sought after cache in the so-named, iconic 1948 film. I was too young to see it, but I remember the marquees on Broadway, and the title stuck in my mind every time I saw my father go into his trance fondling one of those magic stones. I was always fascinated by the fact that either he always had a gem in hand or I would hear the gentle tumbling of the loose gems he'd sift around in his pants pockets. And I always took note that it seemed ironic that a man with such rough, powerful fingers and hands worked in a rarefied world that revolved around such tiny, priceless things.

Whenever he'd reach out with his thick, stubby fingers, I'd flinch, because whenever he stroked my head, it hurt like the devil.

My father was also obsessed with never having his picture taken, or any of us having our picture taken. I honestly believe that, when my brother and I were young, he feared we would be kidnapped and held ransom for his most priceless jewels. He loved Rolls-Royces, but he wouldn't buy himself one. Instead, we "only" had a Packard, which was very grand and glamorous, but it was not a Rolls. We did have a liveried chauffeur, though, as father was a totally distracted driver, because he couldn't take his mind off work.

"Too flashy," he would say, telling another tall tale of being spat on during the Depression for driving a fancy car. He loved the sea too but wouldn't buy himself a yacht. He loved horseracing but wouldn't invest in a horse. He desperately wanted to be rich and famous, but he simultaneously hated conspicuous consumption or, I suspected, had trouble allowing himself to go all-in on pleasure.

Pleasure, you see, could get in the way of business. Hence his insistence on high leverage and low visibility. Still, for all my father's self-abnegation, Harry Winston was one of the best-known names in the country, synonymous with drop-dead wealth.

My father's wish to stay out of sight meant that my childhood exposure to the city and the culture that kids my own age enjoyed was pretty much off limits. Sometimes my aunt Dora, my father's only sister, would come over and take me out to Schrafft's, the famous candy shop, but that was as "street" as my life got. Dora, a doll-like Victorian woman who dyed her curly hair red and wore dresses with giant satin bows and square-toed shoes, gave me St. Exupéry's *The Little Prince* and always referred to me as her "little prince," and so I was, locked in my own castle, my father's realm. I had absolutely no idea what a wonderful and wicked metropolis lay outside our huge oak doors. I don't think I even descended into the subway until I was a teenager, and rarely even then. My idea of New York was the antiquities court of the Met, opening nights on Broadway, ice cream at Rumpelmayer's, toys at FAO Schwarz, and St. Patrick's Cathedral, which I could see from my bedroom window. Mean streets, no.

I was later amazed to learn that tiny, delicate Dora had once been a real frontierswoman, becoming the de facto materfamilias, the milk pourer, for my father and his father when my father's mother died young and the family made the pioneering move to Los Angeles to start a new life.

Once I was old enough to go to school, my mother kept me in Scarsdale during the week and sent me, by chauffeur, to Rye Country Day School, while my father stayed in Manhattan to work, work, work. Whenever I was in the city, we'd go to the great French restaurants like Le Pavillon or Cafe Chambord, or to places like the Colony or Quo Vadis or 21, where I was usually the only kid there. My parents always were seated in the front of the house, which I learned were the "A" tables, and my father seemed to know more of the patrons than the haughty maître d's.

Elegant women dripping in jewels and their tuxedo-wearing husbands would stop by our table, and my father would admire their taste and artfully flatter them, cultivating his clientele. My mother, too, knew how to make these people feel good, and she didn't seem to mind at all while the ladies fawned over my father. Instead of being jealous, she was proud of my father for having clients with last names like Whitney, Rockefeller, and Zeckendorf. Of course these names meant nothing to me as an overwhelmed little boy, but I learned to politely smile while my parents worked the room. Still, they were names I had heard on the radio, which was my lifeline to the outside world.

To my father's credit, he was never starstruck or allowed himself to be flattered or manipulated by the powerbrokers and celebrities he worked with. He would never gossip, never boast about his clientele. He was the model of discretion. He was known by the rich and famous as being someone they could trust, and they seemed to like that he never, ever pandered to them.

There were, however, two things that did impress my father. "He's a college man," he'd note about someone, with a great deal of admiration. "A college man." My father had never gone to college and yet understood how important a formal education was. He was also an admirer of anyone tall. "He's a six footer," my father would say to describe someone who towered over him.

My father also had a special fascination with and respect for the the maharajas of India, who, in the 1940s, when Europe was in ruins, were the richest men on earth. Their kingdoms had the most evocative names like Mysore, Indore, Hyderabad, Baroda, and Kashmir. The maharajas and their wives and retinues literally bathed in diamonds, and their man in New York was none other than my father. In 1947

India won its independence from Britain, but it remained a place of great imperial pomp and privilege. In return for each maharaja bringing his separate state into the new Indian federation, he was granted by the government something called the privilege of the privy purse, an annual grant based on the population of his realm. If the maharaja ruled over ten million people, he received ten million dollars, and this "grant" fed an appetite for diamonds and luxury.

One summer morning in Scarsdale, I discovered at our swimming pool a vision of something teleported from the banks of the Ganges. There was a dark, skinny man who looked just like Mahatma Gandhi, whom I had seen on the front pages of the newspapers, taking a bath in our big pool. I was so mystified by this image that I hid behind a giant Norway pine and viewed the ablutions as if they were those of a holy man bathing in holy water. The holy man turned out to be the secretary, a powerful post that didn't require typing, to one of the maharajas. Later that day, the maharaja himself came for lunch. First a whole contingent of cooks in turbans and saris arrived and transformed our kitchen with the scent of spices from the mysterious East. Then a long cavalcade of black Rolls-Royces streamed through our gates with the maharaja, his wife, his aides-de-camp, his armed bodyguards. The only thing missing were, I thought, the elephants. Later sitar players came, and white-coated bartenders poured tropical fruit drinks called Singapore Slings and Suffering Bastards that I would years later imbibe at Trader Vic's. It was the most fantastic afternoon of my young life, and one that would be repeated again and again and that led to my family's love of Indian food. The best curries in the city were served in the Pierre Grill, in the basement of the Pierre hotel, where we would go for an Indian feast at least once a week. I was thus dining on curry when my classmates were chowing down on hamburgers.

Aside from the great restaurants, my parents would take me to the theater, which was at its apogee in the postwar era. I saw Mary Martin in *South Pacific* and Julie Andrews in *The Boyfriend*, and then we listened to the records endlessly back at home until I knew every lyric. Even though I had been named after my mother's idol, the British actor Ronald Colman, I wasn't taken to the movies that often as a boy, and the opera, which bored my father more than Passover, almost never. Although we had one of the first televisions, in the late forties there wasn't that much to watch. Still, I became aware of television and movie stars and was surprised we never really met any among the very fast company my father kept. "Stars can't really afford diamonds," he said. "They're working on their houses."

If a few megastars like Elizabeth Taylor were ablaze in diamonds it was because her high-roller husbands like hotel heir Nicky Hilton or impresario Mike Todd had lavished them on her. If the notoriously penurious Cary Grant bought Barbara Hutton a diamond, it was with *her* money. Diamonds were for the big shots, at least Harry Winston diamonds.

I went along for the ride, but I was a kid who loved science, especially rocket science. By the time the Russians launched Sputnik in 1956 and I was fourteen, I, the Cold War baby, was as obsessed with science as my father was with diamonds. I knew I had found my calling, my future, and it wasn't catering to the high and the mighty, other than perhaps blowing up their (and *our*, as my father was very patriotic) enemies.

My interest in chemistry and combustion was more than merely a function of the times. It was a rebellion against the perfect order, the serenity, of my childhood. It was my need for action, for identity. It began with me raiding my parents' medicine chest and creating potions that I would bury in my secret places on the Scarsdale estate. I once burned a tree down, and back in the city I blew up a stove. My father woke up, calmly said to me, "Don't do that again," and went right back to sleep. Not heeding him, I then went on to blow up the chemistry lab of my new private school, Riverdale Country School, which was in a very soigné part of the Bronx over-looking the Hudson. I was in the ninth grade.

At that point we had outgrown the top floor of the town house and moved to a palatial apartment on Fifth Avenue overlooking Central Park. We lived at the Pierre for a year while our apartment was remodeled, and I had become the Eloise of that grand caravansary. I guess I liked being spoiled, but I didn't want my contemporaries to know it. Because I had heard whispers about myself as the "rich kid" in a school full of them, I insisted the chauffeur drop me off a few blocks away from the campus, so I could make a plebeian, pedes-trian entrance. It didn't help. So, in retaliation perhaps, I kept blowing things up at home and at school. If I had had my portrait painted, it would have been with a purple haze of chemical smoke around my head. Instead, my father had me photographed by a famous lensman, Yousuf Karsh, holding the Hope Diamond. That photo of the little boy with the big stone took pride of place in our living room. I cringed every time I looked at it.

At one point my parents grew so distressed at my mad sci-entist routine that they met with the principal of Riverdale to discuss sending me off to military school, which I equated with reform school. They shipped me to Europe for a summer at Le Rosey in Switzerland, the most exclusive boarding school on earth, which for me functioned as a halfway house. It was full of children of banana republic dictators, Middle Eastern potentates (the Shah of Iran went there), Asian billionaires, and heavily monied Eurotrash before the term was coined. The kids all spoke multiple languages, and their homes were so broken that they needed genealogical charts to figure out to whom they belonged. I found no chemists among the lot, no budding intellectuals, just a bunch of playboys in training. I hated it and literally kissed American soil when I got home. My parents knew I hated it, and mercifully, they didn't force me to go back. But being back home didn't stop my chemistry experiments; I just got better at them, achieving top grades, and eventually, I began to win national prizes. Outwardly my father beamed. Inside, he was in turmoil, for all he wanted was for me to join his business.

Eventually Harry Winston got his way. This is the story of how he got his wish and how *I* got his wish, and then I lost it.

Despite getting a stellar education at Harvard, it was clear that I wasn't going to win a Nobel Prize in chemistry. I might blow some big things up, sure, but I was smart enough to know I would never be a giant in the field. But perhaps I could make something of myself if I joined my father, who was undeniably a giant in his.

My father was the biggest mystery in my life, the little giant with the big glass of milk, the poster boy of poverty who became an icon of luxury. Who was he? Who was I? And what were these crystal compounds that came from deep within the earth and captivated us humans so profoundly? The intrigue of my father and the mysteries of his business began to call to me.

So I gave in to my father's dynastic imperative, albeit sometimes kicking and screaming. If I thought I was leaving the world of explosives behind, I was dead wrong. Once I committed to the family business, which appeared to be refined and utterly civilized, I found it was actually quite dangerous and adventurous. My old school friends took to calling the pampered little kid who once was the Eloise of the Pierre "Scarsdale Winston," in a play on "Indiana Jones," except I didn't get to carry a bullwhip. "We've got to toughen you up," my father would say time and again, promising, or was it threatening, to take me out of an environment best described not as "sheltered" but "protected."

I had no idea how much there was to be protected from in the diamond world: There were unscrupulous business rivals, treacherous colleagues, and powerful, vindictive clients. And then there was the actual buying of the great stones, which were mostly mined in Africa, a continent whose true darkness became known to me in my many adventures there. My father himself refused to go to Africa. Until he had his schism with the octopus-like South African diamond syndicate De Beers, he would get most of his noble African stones from them in London.

After Harry Winston boldly challenged and broke with De Beers, my father still stayed out of Africa, letting his trusted men in Antwerp and Geneva negotiate for him, while he held court on Fifth Avenue, at Claridge's in London, and at the Hôtel du Cap-Eden-Roc, in the south of France. My father had a major phobia about filth and disease. He had endured so much of it in his railroad-flat childhood, he felt that was enough for several lifetimes, and Africa to him represented the pinnacle of squalor and pestilence. I, on the other hand, had little contact with squalor and pestilence, other than some ill-fated *Animal House*–style road trips to women's colleges during my Harvard years. I wanted to find out what diamond mining was all about, nevermind that I'd seen too many John Wayne movies. I also had the romanticized notion that I couldn't send any of my men to any places I hadn't gone myself.

So off to the jungles, the steppes, and King Solomon's Mines I intrepidly went, cracking wise to my dubious friends that Scarsdale Winston was too young and restless to settle for a desk job. In the early 1990s I found myself in the major war zone of Angola, which, as luck would have it, is one of the major rough diamond zones of the world. Ever since Angola had thrown off Portugal's colonial yoke in the bloody revolution of 1975, capitalist America and communist Russia had waged a proxy war, killing more than a million, for the hearts and minds of this heartbreakingly beautiful and heartbreaking country on Africa's rugged Atlantic coast.

Despite his physical absence, Harry Winston was a seriously connected man in Africa, and through his connections, I had arranged an introduction, via our family friend Félix Houphouët-Boigny, the fearless anticommunist president of the Ivory Coast, to the equally fearless anticommunist Angolan Jonas Savimbi, who was involved in a to-the-death struggle with the Moscow-funded incumbent dos Santos dictatorship in Luanda, the capital. Savimbi needed arms to fight this war, and his best way to get them was to sell diamonds.

The faction that controlled the richest diamond mines in this potentially very rich country-in-shambles was called

UNITA and was led by Savimbi, one of the most colorful and charismatic revolutionaries this side of his role model Che Guevara. Dressed in radical chic trademark combat fatigues, pistol, and black beret, the powerfully built, brutal-looking Savimbi was actually brilliant and educated. He was known as "the Doctor," not only for his original medical studies in Lisbon, which he abandoned to get a PhD in politics in Geneva. Despite further studies and radicalization in Beijing, Savimbi, who had no problem selling diamonds to support his revolution, became the darling of the communist haters of the United States. The Reagan administration had given him $15 million in covert aid.

Getting to Savimbi required a dance called the African two-step. Step one involved a country with few diamonds, the Ivory Coast. Its president, Félix Houphouët-Boigny, both a Francophile and a French idol known as Le Vieux, was the longest surviving head of state in a continent not known for political longevity. He was a close friend of Savimbi. Boigny had personally decorated my father with La Rose d'Ivoire, the country's greatest honor to foreigners. Now it was time to call in the connection. I started with one of Dad's top men in Geneva, Urs Lindt, a member of the Lindt chocolate dynasty that did a huge business with Ivory Coast, the world's leading cocoa producer. Urs set up a meeting, and off to Abidjan I flew on this great adventure.

Abidjan was a very sophisticated, high-rise white city on the Atlantic Coast, considered the Paris of Africa. Boigny, educated in the French colonial system, had been a practicing doctor before turning to politics. Conversing with him in French, I found him charming and still powerfully vibrant in his late eighties. I could understand how France learned its bitter lesson from its own colonial disaster in Algeria that it was cheaper to bribe smart and cooperative strong men like Boigny than trying to administer these countries themselves. Boigny couldn't have been more helpful. He happily arranged my rendezvous with Jonas Savimbi.

To go into the Angola jungle war zone and Savimbi's base, I needed to assemble my own African team to guard the $6 million in cash we were bringing with us, as well as to guard the cache of rough diamonds that with luck would be the fruits of our negotiating labors. Through my Malta-based friend Steve Delia, a very cool security expert and soldier of fortune, I assembled a group of men worthy of the strike forces in the Idi Amin TV movie *Raid on Entebbe*. My chief commando was a Brit named Nish, a renowned parachutist who had rescued climbers stranded on Mount Everest. I had my "brains," Frank Rempelberg, the Antwerp "wizard of rough." And there I was in combat fatigues, my own version of Indiana Jones, Scarsdale Winston. Whoever thought the diamond trade was sedate and genteel was selling it short.

We assembled in Geneva and flew to Kinshasa, Zaire, where the legendary Ali-Foreman "rumble in the jungle" had been held. We had been told that Savimbi's people would be waiting to take us through customs, but nobody was there. We feared we had been stood up before we could even join the revolution. "We overslept," was the apology that came when the men finally arrived after a long night at the airport.

A grumpy mercenary Belgian pilot ferried us across the border into the Angolan jungle outpost of Ndulo, which was Savimbi's base, in an ancient cargo plane fitted with bolted-down tattered movie theater seats for the passengers. A caravan of jeeps topped with fifty-caliber machine guns awaited us and our six large duffel bags of cash on the dirt landing strip. "This is a war zone," Frank noted ominously. We were billeted, with those duffel bags always in our hands, in a bombed-out colonial dwelling.

I was a guest at Savimbi's plantation house, listening to Bach and dining on the best French fare one could expect in a jungle during a civil war. Speaking in French, Savimbi, a short, stocky man with a gravelly but cultured and mellifluous voice, lived up to his charisma, thanking us for coming and for our aid "to the cause," and flattering me for the Harry Winston reputation for honesty and fairness.

The biggest glitch of our get-acquainted dinner was when a rat scampering across a ceiling beam defecated on my *poulet roti*. "*Monsieur Winston, vous ne mangez pas. Y a-t-il un problème?*" Savimbi inquired, the perfect host. I quickly began shuffling my food around the plate, looking for an unadulterated morsel. "*Pas du tout, mon Général,*" I lied. "*Le poulet est magnifique. Et la sauce. Je suis ettoufée.*"

The next morning, we were able to see the shell craters in our lodgings that attested to the violence taking place there. Frank and I were taken back to the porticoed, once gracious main hacienda for coffee with Savimbi. He had been trained as a doctor before becoming a warrior, and there was something of the cloister still about him. A tape of classical music played softly in the background. He had lived on the lam for the last twenty years, but he didn't seem furtive at all, just totally cool. He spoke of the magical charm of the high savanna where we were located and its capacity to protect him from his far better armed communist adversaries. He saw the huge banana leaves of the plants that camouflaged the house as a kind of organic Kevlar, natural bulletproofing that would repel the fire of the dos Santos army. His dialogue was half mystic, half scientist, all courage. I found him very charismatic. I also found his talk of an imminent dos Santos assault more than a bit unnerving. I suggested we get to work.

Aides led us to another barracks workroom where under bare flickering light bulbs, twenty thousand carats of treasures dug from Angolan rivers were laid out like rock candy on bare tables of tropical wood. This was Angola's patrimony, and it would pay for its fight for freedom and democracy. That's what I was thinking about, not how they might look on Gwyneth Paltrow's neck or Oprah Winfrey's ears. With our loupes, tweezers, and scales, Frank and I spent hour after hour sorting the stones by size and quality. Every loud noise jarred us into thinking a new battle was erupting. We knew we had to work fast, a point underscored by the two generals in charge of the rebels' diamond business. "You must catch the cargo plane at dawn," one of them warned us. "We don't know when there will be another."

The generals were short and wiry and didn't look that different from the troops, except that the troops wore ratty uniforms and camouflage and weapons and garrison belts and the generals wore Adidas tracksuits and were unarmed. Less was more here. They could have been guys going to a pickup basketball game. Nonetheless, they were very shrewd and played their cards close to the vest. When Frank and I came up with our initial offer of $2 million for the cache, the lead general rolled his eyes in derision. "Come now," he said. "De Beers would do better than that." An hour or so later, they had gotten us up to the full $6 million we had brought, and the deal was sealed. Of course, there was nothing to stop the generals from slitting our throats and keeping all the money for themselves, nothing except the word and honor of Jonas Savimbi. That was our mystical Kevlar, and it worked. We would be back, and they knew it.

We packed up all the diamonds in glassine envelopes sealed with Scotch tape, and made the trade of three hundred pounds of hundred-dollar bills for a very few pounds of stones. Such was the value of these diamonds, although there was nothing like the Hope or the Star of India among them. Lots of good stones, but nothing exceptional, which was defined as over fourteen carats. Still, those few pounds of gems were worth $7 million retail. We went back to our lodgings and waited out the dawn lying awake on our cots. The cargo plane arrived, and away from Ndulo we rose into the blazing and rising African sun. It was the first of about fifteen trips over the next few years that netted us $35 million to $45 million profit.

There were many ways to die in these African adventures, but I never thought one could be at the hands of one of my own people. Our paratrooper Nish was an excellent, formidable security man, the perfect protector in a war zone. Alas, Nish went to prison for attempting to murder his wife. Through a CIA contact in Washington, who had a deep black book of soldiers of fortune, I found a replacement. His name was Clark Blumner, based in Colorado. He was a handsome six-foot-four Rambo type in his late thirties. In the interest of secrecy, I had him meet me offshore, in Geneva, at a hotel, La Réserve. The first night, over drinks, I was quite impressed, at least with his movie-star appearance. The next morning, however, I had a rude awakening when I arose to Clark there in my room, pointing a gun at my head. "Bang! Bang!" he said with a demonic laugh.

"I'm already awake," I said, deadpan.

"You need to be alert," Clark warned me, though I wasn't sure about whom or what. "You never know what can happen." Later that day, when I went to our Swiss executive Michel Pitteloud to assemble the millions we were planning to bring to Angola from our Swiss account, Michel seemed upset. "Who the hell is that guy? Michel asked. "Did you know he smuggled guns into Switzerland?" Well, I knew he had a gun that morning, but it turned out that he had another which he brought as an undeclared weapon (highly illegal) into Michel's gun club. I realized I had a real mercenary on my team.

Nonetheless, I refused to abort. Four months after my first visit, we proceeded once more on the long trip to Savimbi's base in Ndulo, loaded with our bags of money. I never realized how heavy all those hundred-dollar bills could be. We were there for four days, during which Clark Blumner was MIA for one of them. I later found out he had gone out with Savimbi's men to lay deterrent mines on the derricks in the rich oil fields in the area that Savimbi controlled. It seemed like Clark, soldier of fortune that he was, was interested in joining Savimbi's army—if the price was right.

Three months later we reassembled in Geneva for another mission to Africa. When Clark joined us from Colorado, he was "scratching like a hound." He bragged he had gotten a social disease from a local *fille de joie*. This time I introduced Clark to Urs Lindt and Albano Bochatay, who ran the Geneva Winston office. They were both horrified and later separately warned me, "Don't go back to Africa with this man. He will kill you." I took their advice. That night, at the Italian restaurant at La Réserve, I told Clark, who was giddily excited about our trip, that I was scrapping the entire mission. Nothing personal, plus I paid him in full anyway. But it was more than this payday that mattered to him. "How can you do this to me?" he asked menacingly. "You're ruining my reputation." I had images of Clark taking Frank Rempelberg and me out into the wilds of Ndulo, killing us both and absconding with the cash.

Canceling the trip was money well spent. A few months later Steve Delia was available, and he came with Frank and me for the remainder of the trips, each of which was greatly profitable both for Harry Winston and for Jonas Savimbi, who used income from us to finance his war for Angola until 1994, when he was forced to accept the peace terms dictated by his communist-backed enemy dos Santos. Savimbi was never one to give up, waging a guerrilla war against government troops and becoming a "galloping ghost" legend who survived over a dozen assassination attempts and had been reported dead by the world press fifteen times. His real end finally came in 2002, in a firefight that took fifteen gunshot wounds from head to toe to kill him. Clark Blumner was never heard from again.

Out of Africa, I discovered that diamonds could be deadly hazardous in countless ways, none of which had come to mind when I was a little boy marveling at the maharajas and Marilyn Monroe. Just as I ventured into the heart of darkness in Africa, I ventured into the equally stygian heart of darkness in Hollywood, if Hollywood can be said to have a heart of any sort. There was a terribly sinister side to all that glamour, and the blackest widows of all could be the successors to Marilyn, world-famous sirens behind the call of diamonds. For better or for worse, I must confess that I was the one behind "the red carpet syndrome," wherein movie stars are lent priceless jewelry to wear at the Oscars, the Golden Globes, premieres, wherever publicity is to be found. My father might, on rare occasions, have lent jewels to his dearest customers for special events, mostly in hopes that they would love them so much that they would buy them.

By the time my father had gotten me on board his crystal ship, celebrities, and mostly those of cinema, had become the chief currency of the promotional realm. A product of my own times, I was as wowed by these celluloid fantasies as anyone else and came up with the lend-lease gambit. If diamonds were a girl's best friend, why couldn't these famous girls, by the same sparkling token, become Harry Winston's best friends? And so they did. Diamonds, if only for a night, were an offer that no woman, star or civilian, could refuse. The stars all lined up to play dress up, like little girls playing in their mothers' closests. Yet diamonds can make people do crazy things, and since most stars are a little crazy to begin with, when crazy people do crazy things, the situations can be explosive.

Nothing could have seemed more tranquil, however, than the idyllic May day in Manhattan in 1993, when my office suggested, as a goodwill gesture, that I personally drop off the jewelry to Sharon Stone that she was going to wear for an appearance on *Larry King Live*. Sharon, whom I had not met, had worn our jewels several times in the last year and always loved doing it, I was told. Millions of people all over the CNN world would watch Larry King fawn over the beauty of Sharon and, hopefully, her blockbuster jewels, which Sharon, in return for making the most indelible impression, would beam and blush and credit Harry Winston. Some tycoon in

Des Moines, or Dubai, for that matter, might see the treasures and think, *That sort of thing would be perfect for my wife,* and to Harry Winston he would come. Or maybe it would be another star who would be the prospective customer. Unlike in my father's day, the stars were now making untold millions. They didn't need the Aga Khan to buy them diamonds anymore. They were the new royalty.

I was looking forward to seeing this instant legend in person. Sharon Stone was at the height of her post–*Basic Instinct* (1992) glory, her flashiness making her the sexiest woman on screen. Putting $500,000 worth of necklace and earrings into my briefcase, and eschewing bodyguards on this perfect day, I walked the lush, tree-shaded blocks from my home in the East 70s to Sharon's hotel, the Mark on East 77th Street and Madison, the heart of the coiffed, coutured, and bejeweled Upper East Side. The Mark, like the Carlyle across the street, was the hotel Hollywood stars liked to stay at when they were pretending they were classy, sophisticated Gothamites. When they were just being stars, before everything moved down to Soho and beyond, they would stay at the Plaza or the Waldorf.

I called Sharon's suite from the lobby and spoke to an assistant, who told me "Miss Stone" would be ready in a few minutes, so I cooled my heels until the summons upstairs finally came. Entering Sharon's suite was like entering the ground, or cosmetics, floor of Saks Fifth Avenue. I was overwhelmed by the blast of perfume. A female assistant led me through the living room, with its views over the rooftops and spires of Manhattan, into the bedroom, or should I say boudoir, which was filled with flowers and packed with no fewer than five more assistants. Behind them all was Sharon, who rose from her dressing table, shook my hand, led me to her bed, or at least the foot thereof, where I supposed my audience would be taking place.

Sharon was less tall, but more charming, than I had expected. She was indeed beautiful, professionally so, with those all-American Ford Model bones and that angelic blonde hair. But I had read that she had clawed her way to the top, a hard decade of B-movies and broken promises, and I could see she wasn't some ingenue but a seasoned pro savoring her long-awaited close-up. Speaking of which, I got right to the point, removing the necklace from my briefcase and then from its Harry Winston lambskin carrying case. I felt like a messenger boy.

"You put it on, Ron," she purred to me. "You do it." And she underscored the request by leaning forward in her clingy, low-cut designer sundress, and providing me with an above- the-waist version of her famous *Basic Instinct* flash-dance, except she drew out this moment until I acceded and strung the jewels around her swan-like neck. At that steamy Hollywood instant, I saw yesterday and tomorrow, heaven and earth, all at once, while the phalanx of assistants did a Greek chorus of oohs and aahs. Sharon got up to admire her-self for a short eternity in the vanity mirror, while assistants fluttered around her. Finally, she smiled. It was a big smile. I took it as my cue to give her the earrings, but she waved them away. The necklace, the $400,000 necklace, was "enough," she said. "I don't need those," she waved dismissively at the gems in my hand.

We chatted a bit about the new movie she was promoting, *Sliver*, a voyeuristic thriller from the fevered pen of *Basic Instinct* scribe Joe Eszterhas, about a lonely book editor in a narrow high-rise and her overheated suitors, Tom Berenger and William Baldwin. Sharon, who had been marooned in bimboland for so long, loved playing brainy types, writers, editors, East Side women, women at the Mark, even if these ladies were actually bimbos in Prada rather than Frederick's. Sharon's dream had come true, and part of it was wearing Harry Winston. Finally, the audience ended. I admit I was fairly speechless, though I realized that with Sharon, even men like Henry Kissinger tended to let her do the talking. She walked me through the suite and gave me a firm handshake at the door. Her last words were, "Don't worry, Ron. I'll be sure to mention you on Larry King." Once I left her perfumed suite and was brought back down to earth by the bus fumes of Madison Avenue, I realized that I hadn't asked her to sign anything acknowledging receipt of the jewels. I called the office, thinking I should go back. "She's Sharon Stone," I was told. "Where is she going to go?" One of the perks of being a big star was not having to sign for anything.

As it turned out, Sharon Stone did not mention Harry Winston on *Larry King Live*. Larry didn't notice our beautiful $400,000 necklace, and Sharon didn't push it on him. But I wouldn't have known this, because neither I nor anyone else in our office had watched the show. It only came to my attention when our New York office began getting calls from our Beverly Hills office asking for Gemological Institute of America authentication certificates for the jewels in the necklace we had loaned to Sharon. Why, we wondered. The office found out that Sharon needed the certificates to purchase insurance for the necklace. Why, again, we wondered, until, to our enormous chagrin, we discovered that the necklace had never been returned to us at all. Such was our total trust in stars. Of course Sharon was a busy woman. How easy it would be to put the necklace in the jewelry box and forget it.

But such was not the case. Sharon had absolutely zero intention of ever returning the necklace. When my office called her to mention her oversight, one of her many assistants conveyed Sharon's decisive declaration that she owned the necklace, that it was hers in return for her appearance on *Larry King Live*. That would have been pretty nice work, even by Hollywood standards, a $400,000 treasure for simply wearing something for an hour. Then we got a tape of the show, and the insult of not being mentioned was added to the injury of our purloined necklace. Our lawyers began writing threatening letters.

Finally, Sharon returned the necklace, but that was only the beginning of this lurid tale. No sooner was the necklace received than Sharon's attorneys commenced a $12 million lawsuit against Harry Winston for breach of contract and assorted related atrocities. The idea here was that she and I had concluded a verbal agreement at the Mark, witnessed by all of her assistants, that I had promised her that she would be the worldwide "face of Harry Winston" and that the necklace would be a token of my esteem, a down payment on a much larger payout. No matter that there wasn't one word of this multimillion-dollar pact on paper. The assistants saw it, Sharon said it, and who would dare doubt the word of the hottest female star in show business? What followed was a surreal battle involving celebrity greed and megalomania, and the power of diamonds to bring out the worst in us, waged both in the courts and the tabloids. I did get off one early bon mot; I said I was planning to sue Sharon's pants off, but I wasn't sure she had any. Neither the guerrillas of Africa nor the gorillas of Hollywood were able to get the better of Harry Winston.

CHAPTER TWO

Into the West

In the mid-1960s, when I was in my mid-twenties, America was in the honeymoon stage of its thrall to the mystique of Southern California. This California dream, of the new Disneyland, of surfing in winter, of driving a T-bird convertible down the Sunset Strip, of the Beach Boys and Gidget and Sinatra's Rat Pack cavorting in the Palm Springs sun, was every bit as powerful, as magnetic to my peers as the shining dream of America itself was to my father's father and his peers back in the frozen depths of czarist Russia. But I myself was fairly indifferent to California, and it wasn't for the media's lack of promotion. I was unimpressed probably because my father was unimpressed. Harry Winston never opened a store in Beverly Hills, which he could have easily done at the height of his fame and at the height of the cinema world's conspicuous consumption of jewels. He never even took his family to Disneyland, never even mentioned California.

Yet Harry Winston had been to the Golden West, at the very beginning of the California Dream. And he found it, if not a nightmare, not the stuff Harry Winston's dreams were made of. I never even learned he had lived in California until the sixties, and I was fairly amazed that he hadn't stayed. He had never spoken about it, but his silence, amid the increasingly deafening national buzz that California was *the* place to be, was especially curious to me. In the late fifties both the Dodgers and the Giants had left New York for California, which said a great deal about that state's siren call. But my father had been there on the ground floor. He could have owned the place. Or could he?

As I would learn, Harry Winston, who would one day be Mister New York, had come to Los Angeles in 1910, when he was fourteen. He left in 1918 and came back to New York City, when he was twenty-two. When I was twenty-two, I was still in the cloister that was Harvard. My father, on the other hand, had gone coast to coast, had scrambled with the pioneers in the still-wild West, had served in the Great War, had endured terrible family tragedy, and was very much a man, his own man, albeit not the man he wanted to be.

"There was nothing there," my father, when pressed, said of Los Angeles. "There was no money. No money to be made." But what about oranges, oil? What about the movies? "Los Angeles was a hick town." And so my father's word trumped that of Walt Disney, who, incidentally, was his friend. My father took our family to Europe, to Paris, to Geneva, to the Côte d'Azur, but never to California. To my knowledge he never once went back to California after he left. Did he see it as a Sodom that would turn him to salt if he looked back? He just never returned, not even for the movie stars who in truth represented only a drop in the gilded bucket of tycoons, royalty, and Arabian Nights that was Harry Winston. If Marilyn

31

Monroe wanted Harry Winston to talk to her, she would have to come to New York.

But why did my father go there to begin with? Or his father? It seemed quite incongruous for a poor Russian Jewish watch and jewelry man to be in the Wild West, or whatever it was, at the turn of the century. Given my father's constant expounding on how terribly poor and hungry he was as a child, my image was of the family huddling in a tiny and stygian Lower East Side tenement, not basking under palm trees in the brilliant California sun. Dark, frock-coated Jews among cowboys and Indians thus became the new image in my head, and it was almost comical, Chaplinesque long before Chaplin's *The Gold Rush* of 1925.

But my father was not comedy material. He was very proper, very dignified, very imperial, urbane but not particularly urban, more like a cattle baron in big sky country. In fact, there was something distinctly western, if not wild, about him, the little Alan Ladd in *Shane*. He had zero New York accent, no trace of the shtetl. He was cool, he was a gambler, he was fearless. I could see him striding into a saloon and walking out with everyone's holdings. Was that something he learned in California? It certainly wasn't from Delancey Street. But Harry Winston, westerner, was still a deeply curious concept. How did it happen?

It all started in the Wild East that was Russia in the late nineteenth century. My grandfather Jacob Weinstein came from a modest-sized town with the immodest name of Starokostyantyniv, about two hundred miles west of Kiev in what is now Ukraine, not far from the nuclear wasteland of Chernobyl. I went there a few years ago, and the name seemed larger than the village, whose most lasting impression was its indifference to any amenities whatsoever. The concept of toilet paper there was alien, even with a translator in tow. On the roads were more donkey carts than big rigs. "Staro" was in an agrarian zone of sorts, the site of vast Soviet-era collective farms, rye fields and wheat fields that could have been Kansas. But Kansas never had the pogroms, the Russian word for "riots," that had driven my grandfather and millions of other oppressed Jews like him to the New World.

My father rarely spoke about his own father specifically, but rather in a general context of extreme adversity that of course reflected nobly on my own father for having transcended it.

Harry Winston spoke frequently of the frozen Russian winters, winters that quenched the ambitions of the likes of Napoleon and Hitler, but somehow not the Winstons. He spoke of the oppression of the czar; the most oppressive element that struck a chord in me was the idea that young Jewish boys could be drafted into the imperial army at twelve and forced to serve for twenty-five years, all that in a life span that, by the actuarial tables of the time, didn't last much beyond forty. This was a brilliant case of state-sponsored institutional genocide, to turn the despised Jews into cannon fodder.

The great reformist czar Alexander II, who freed the millions of serfs, also cut the conscription term in half, to twelve years, which was scant consolation to the young Jacob Weinstein, born in 1864, and even less so when Alexander was assassinated in 1881 and a Jew was blamed as the brains of the populist, democracy-craving, aristocracy-despising conspiracy that led to his death. A decade of violent pogroms began. Although my father once said the Weinsteins were descended from a long line of rabbis, my father, who was anything but devout, or even religious, explained his secularity as an inheritance from his father, whom he described as a "freethinker." Unlike all the other Staroites, Jacob didn't keep kosher, didn't go to temple, worshipping instead at the altar of health and fitness, eating whole grains and fresh fruits and vegetables, although God knows where they got them in the Russian winters. He was surely much more worried about being drafted than being persecuted for his faith.

My father liked to describe how the Weinstein house had a secret tunnel that went directly down to the river and afforded a secret flight to waiting little getaway boats to escape the conscriptors or marauders, whoever came first. He made the Weinsteins' existence in Staro sound like *Stalag 17*. When I visited the town, I did see the lazy Sluch River, a meandering stream that coursed through the village. I never found the family abode. Nor were there any Jews left in a town that in my grandfather's era contained maybe ten thousand of them, or 50 percent of the local population. They all spoke Yiddish, and they all intermarried, and they all either fled or were killed by czars or later by Joseph Stalin. What seemed so peaceful was in fact a ghost town decimated by successive reigns of terror.

Through it all, however, Jacob Weinstein wed local girl Jennie Harivman, or Hurriman, or, as the immigration rolls listed it, Harriman. Jennie was obviously no relation to the American railway czars the Harrimans, who gave us the great statesman Averell Harriman, whose ambassador to France, ex-playgirl wife Pamela did happen to be one of my father's clients. My own middle name, Harivman, is one of the myriad spellings of my grandmother's maiden name, and it represented one of the rare instances of my father's paying tangible homage to his heritage. A social-climbing arriviste would have played the Harriman card and created the illusion that his progeny were the descendants of barons (albeit robber barons) and not rabbis.

What a difference an "r" could have made. But my father, despite the pomp and ceremony of his clientele, was anything but pretentious, and anything but dishonest.

Things were so bad and bloody in the late 1880s that Jacob saw no choice but to get out of Dodge. Jacob's odyssey through the Pale of Settlement; changing his name, maybe several times to deceive his draft board; sleeping in the forests; evading Russian troops, even the conscripted Jewish ones who would sell out a brother for a bounty, had to have been a harrowing adventure. He probably caught a ship in Bremen or Hamburg or even perhaps Genoa, depending upon the zigs and zags of his evasions. He arrived, alone, at Ellis Island in 1890. The Statue of Liberty had to have been the most beautiful woman Jacob had ever seen. Jacob left behind in Staro his young wife, Jennie and their two baby boys, Charles and Stanley, who somehow made it to America, surely with the help of friends, less than a year later. My aunt Dora was born in Manhattan in 1891, my father five years later. Or maybe five, as the records from this tsunami of displaced humanity are muddled at best, and often frankly contradictory. Whatever, the man who became Harry Winston always celebrated his birthday on March 1.

In the Weinsteins' first years in New York there was neither the cause nor wherewithal for celebration. I remember my uncle Stanley, whose birth certificate called him Samuel, describing how he rang in the twentieth century. He was twelve on New Year's Eve, 1899, and he was so poor that all he could do was go outside and beat a lamppost with a stick to greet 1900.

Still, the family was enjoying some upward mobility, for a 1901 New York City business directory lists Jacob Weinstein as retailer of watches and jewelry, with a business address of 930 Columbus Avenue and a home address of 275 W. 114th Street. The store was just on the edge of Morningside Heights and the spectacular new classical campus of Columbia University, which had moved uptown to a site overlooking the Hudson from the land that later became Rockefeller Center. Designed by the uberarchitects of the era, McKim, Mead & White, the Columbia neighborhood was known as the "Acropolis of America" and was light-years, especially in terms of light and air, from the fetid tenements of the Lower East Side where the Weinsteins' fellow countrymen were jammed ten to a room.

Furthermore, the 114th Street address, while below Columbia down the steep slopes of Morningside Park in what would become Black Harlem, was at the time in Jewish Harlem. It was a very desirable address, a bucolic suburb, the Scarsdale of its era, made very convenient by the extension of the new IRT subway line to 145th Street. So desirable seemed Harlem, however, that real estate speculators and contractors overbuilt new apartment houses, which at first offered slashed rents to families like the Weinsteins. But later, when there weren't enough Weinsteins to fill the flats, the speculators began renting to Blacks, first the prosperous but later also the poor, arriving in increasing numbers from a South still deeply depressed by the Civil War. The concept of "white flight" would begin, including that of my own family, whose new address became 60 W. 106th Street, still technically Harlem but closer to downtown and to the "division street" that 96th Street would become, separating Blacks from whites in the Manhattan of the years ahead.

My grandfather's mobility, and move northward, may have been in part a function of necessity. He had developed a severe asthma-like respiratory condition, perhaps from the Russian winters or the miseries of his escape therefrom. Whatever the cause, it necessitated he leave the miasma of the Lower East Side for the more salubrious breezes of the Hudson. The move would benefit his wife, Jennie, too, who suffered from heart disease, perhaps brought on from a childhood bout of scarlet fever, which was endemic at the time. Both conditions could have gotten them sent home by the authorities at Ellis Island, but the doctors there were so overwhelmed that if Jacob wasn't coughing and Jennie wasn't gasping, the medical men waved them through.

Whether Jacob had been in the jewelry or watch business back in Staro is unknown. Prosperous Jewish families were there, the baker and mill owner being the leader of the community, and others who may have been flush from bounties turning malingering Jews into the military. But Staro didn't strike me as a big jewelry town. Jacob Weinstein did strike me as a man of great resourcefulness. If he could get out of Russia, he could get into business, and so he did. His first known job was as an apprentice to a jeweler and watchmaker on the Lower East Side. The name of the establishment, Walkowisky and Mann, conjures up criminal images of rum-running and the Mann Act, but apparently it was a house of some repute. Two years later, Jacob was out and on his own. His store on Columbus was called Jacob Weinstein Jeweler. For all this enterprise, this freethinker had the heart of a Bolshevik, and capitalism was not his passion. "Your possessions will possess you," was a Jacobean precept that my father often repeated, even as he amassed one of the largest caches of jewelry in the history of wealth.

My father never spoke of a halcyon childhood in Manhattan. The only pleasant memory he shared was that of swimming with friends in the Hudson, diving off the rocks where the George Washington Bridge would be built in 1927. It sounded like a scene from the Dead End Kids serial. It was more than coincidental that he became an avid and fine swimmer and spent his adult summers diving off the world's most exclusive rocks at the Hôtel du Cap in the south of France. He never spoke about going to the Museum of Natural History, or the Yiddish theater, or the Bronx Zoo, or the bright lights of Broadway, or even sledding in Central Park. All he talked about was running, running from one end of Manhattan to the other and surely not stopping to savor the wonderful sights of the upwardly thrusting metropolis, with its amazing skyscrapers and teeming, diverse population. He was his father's runner, his messenger boy, going down to the diamond district that was then near Wall Street and coming back up to Morningside Heights with modest treasures and cuckoo clocks for his father to sell. He was too poor to take the subway or the streetcar.

My father quickly developed confidence that he had a special talent for jewels. On one of his early journeys, he spotted in a pawnshop a tray of junk jewelry with the sign TAKE YOUR PICK—25 Cents. A ring set with a green stone caught his eye and his heart. He parted with his hard-earned quarter, then took the bauble back uptown to flaunt it to his father. Harry knew he had something, and he was right. Two days later Jacob sold what turned out to be a very genuine, two-carat emerald for the then-princely sum of $800. Talk about return on investment. My father was hooked on jewelry, and on himself, for his eagle eye, the stuff carnival wizards were made of, but with a vastly greater upside than guessing ages and weights. Harry Weinstein never stopped running, didn't want to. Who knew what the next pawn shop might bring.

Because education was then compulsory only up to age twelve, my father probably went to work full-time by that tender age, if not earlier. You grew up fast in those days.

Before his uptown-downtown runs, Jacob had dispatched Harry to do all the family errands, mother Jennie being too frail to do them and Aunt Dora taking on the maternal role. My father would thus be dispatched to buy the fruits and vegetables and the cheap protein of organ meat. My father liked to recount, often over prime steaks at Twenty-One, how he bought liver for two cents a pound, slipping in and out of the butcher's back door so as not to embarrass the higher-paying customers of the better cuts. Harry's older brothers Charles and Stanley may have begun their careers working for their father, but at some point they left the old-fashioned field of jewelry for the burgeoning business of electricity, opening their own lighting-fixtures shop and leaving little Harry as his father's right-hand man, his only man. Although my father spoke a bit of Yiddish, which had been the language of the father and the lingua franca of a jewelry trade dominated by eastern European Jews, Jewish religion and culture played an indiscernible part in his young life. To my knowledge, neither he nor his brothers were bar mitzvahed. The religion of the Weinsteins was work, endless, relentless work.

How much that work paid off is hard to determine, for another factor was involved, that of health. As far as my grandparents were concerned the air off the Hudson in upper

Manhattan may not have been as foul as that of downtown but still wasn't fair by any means. Ever since the gold rush in the 1840s and 1850s, the New York tabloids had written about the sunshiny, desert-arid Eden of wealth and health that was California. The citrus explosion was another form of gold. The orange crates festooned with images of white Spanish missions surrounded by palm trees under the bluest of skies could not help but stir imagination and wanderlust. California seemed as far and opposite from the Russia of Jacob Weinstein as any place could ever be, as magnetic as Russia was repulsive.

Now the transcontinental railways had made this Eden a dream that could come true, a four- or five-day journey with steam heat and in-car toilets, without monthslong trips around Cape Horn, or through the jungles of Panama, or with wagon trains and wild Indians. San Francisco had been one of the world's greatest and most fabled boomtowns, and even the devastating 1906 earthquake was unable to extinguish the fantasy. Now Los Angeles, seen in the aftermath of the quake as a rock of relative geological stability, came into public focus as the next palmy, sunny American boomtown, an earthly paradise with no czars and no coughs. The notion must have had great appeal to Jacob Weinstein, who obviously had no fear of travel or of uprooting himself. He had left Russia for one safe heaven. Now he would leave New York for an even more heavenly one. In 1909 he took his daughter Dora *in loco maternis* and boarded a westbound train to establish a beachhead in the Golden State.

With Charles and Stanley on their own in business and traveling much of the time, Jacob's departure left Harry alone with his mother Jennie. According to the 1910 federal census, they moved out of the 106th Street apartment into a rooming house across the street, owned by a Swiss couple, the Messers. The husband, Rudolphe Messer, worked as a butler. There were six other lodgers there, including Stanley, still known as "Samuel." Charles was living on his own, and at some point Stanley moved in with him. The census listed Harry as a "clerk" in a real estate office, about which no more is known, other than that my father did have an inordinate interest in real estate and would go on to own two of the great addresses in Manhattan and Scarsdale, respectively.

Despite the time Harry and Jennie must have spent alone with each other, my father basically had nothing to say about his ostensibly beloved mother, other than, "She worked like a slave. She worked so hard." That was his standard refrain about everything in his youth: work, work, and more work. Did Jennie sing him lullabies, read him nursery rhymes, regale him with tales of the old country? What did she cook for him? What were her specialties? We have one very faded picture of her, at the very end of her life. When Harry Winston *didn't* speak, people didn't dare ask. My father, the soul of discretion, as much about his own identity as those of his famous clients, kept his own counsel about his past. Surely he loved his mother, but when I found out the horrible circumstances in which he lost her, I somehow understood that this too was a kind of love that dare not speak its name. My father rarely displayed emotion; the tragedy of his mother may have filled his emotional quota for a lifetime.

Talking to my other relatives over time, I gathered that my grandmother had probably contracted scarlet fever as a girl in Russia and continued to labor under its effects throughout her adulthood. She was said to have "dropsy," a term of the time that indicated edema, a swelling of the extremities caused by the failure of the heart to pump adequately. Sometime after my grandfather departed for the West, my grandmother got very sick, and, with his uncles away, my father was left with the responsibility of caring for her. It must have been awful, for the idea was that as soon as Jacob would send for them they would go to the promised land and live healthily ever after. Thus Jennie's illness was a race against time, a race that time was winning. There were no telephones, a super luxury at that time, and it isn't clear that Harry had any way to reach his father except by telegraph. So the little boy, or little man, as he actually was, was totally on his own.

My father did tell me that at one point he tried to get his mother into Mount Sinai Hospital on Fifth Avenue, the greatest hospital in the city, founded by the German Jewish aristocracy that dominated Jewish life and Jewish charity. Alas, that charity did not extend to poor Russian Jews like the Weinsteins. "Not our kind," I could hear the administrators of this grand institution, which had been founded in the 1850s under the name Jews' Hospital, cluck disapprovingly as they turned Jennie, and my father, away. Perhaps the doctors in the emergency department examined my mother and said she was beyond hope. But even if they did, they did not offer her a bed to die in. Jews' Hospital indeed! Was there no brotherhood in faith? What was in a name? Rebuffed by his "own people" my father took his poor mother to St. Luke's Hospital, across from Columbia. He may have had to take her to the charity ward. This Christian institution took Jennie in, but they could not save her. She died and was buried on the same day, in a shabby Jewish cemetery paid for by a "burial society" that my father had been paying fifty cents a year for, in anticipation of this miserable eventuality.

There was no known ceremony. My father may have been alone at his mother's grave. He may have had to shoulder this ordeal all by himself. He was fourteen. It was October 1910. The weather at the time was warm, Indian summer, California weather, the weather that my grandfather was counting on to keep his wife alive. Jennie was only forty-four. Being rejected by Mount Sinai was one of the defining moments in my father's life. Small wonder my father put little stock in religion. Small wonder he worked like a dog, to be rich, to be respectable, as rich and respectable as the Loebs and the Schiffs and the Warburgs, the German Jewish dynasties who had built Mount Sinai and were catered to there. My father didn't want his loved ones, or himself, to die in the street. That would be one of the most awful fears of all. In another great irony, when my own mother got sick, again way too early in any life that might be considered fair, my father, then rich and famous, donated a fortune to Mount Sinai, the very hospital that had so cruelly rejected him and his mother, to try to save his wife's life. And once again, while Mount Sinai took his money, it committed so many grievous errors that it might as well have turned him away a second time. Whether he was Harry Weinstein or Harry Winston didn't seem to matter. The results were equally heartbreaking.

Within months, if not weeks, of his mother's death, Harry Weinstein, only fourteen, set out by himself on a cross-country train to join his father and sister in the promised land of California. He surely couldn't have felt that nostalgic about leaving behind a New York he barely knew outside of its pawn shops and lesser jewelers and watchmakers. New York had wounded him profoundly by taking his mother from him. Still, it had to be with great trepidation that he entered the vast glass and iron shed that was Commodore Vanderbilt's original Grand Central Depot to take his first train journey across the unknown continent. The largest interior space in the Americas, the depot, which would be replaced by the terminal in 1913, soared one hundred feet tall and could accommodate a hundred trains. The smoke, the noise, the crowds, must have been overwhelming.

Nor was my father's journey west that much more comfortable than that on a wagon train. He had no money to speak of and hence was unable to afford one of the luxury Limiteds to Chicago, like the Broadway or the Twentieth Century, from which he could connect to something like the all-Pullman Los Angeles Limited, and reach the city of angels having slept like one, cosseted by courtly porters, fed the finest foods, and arriving in less than four days. That was how the Mount Sinai people traveled, unless they had their own private railway cars. Instead, my father surely took the slow locals, sleeping on hard seats, feeding himself on jelly sandwiches and tinned sardines and boiled eggs and bananas as he saw America through the coal-smudged train windows for the first time.

Whether he stopped in Atchison, Topeka, and Santa Fe, or Denver and Reno, depended on where the cheapest ticket would have taken him. Regardless, he seemed to have arrived in Los Angeles no later than April 1910 (he was listed on the census taken there and then) and thus had crossed the Rockies at the end of winter. He was fearful of an avalanche, a fear borne of a February 1910 railway disaster in Washington's Cascade Mountains when two Great Northern trains got stuck in a blizzard and were swept away by an avalanche and hurled hundreds of feet into the ravine below. About a hundred people died, hundreds more were injured, and the Wellington Disaster, as it was known after the nearby station, soon became known as the *Titanic* of the rails.

Harry Weinstein, rattled and hungry, made it to Los Angeles and staggered off the train into the burning sun and fragrant flowers at the new Santa Fe station near the downtown where his father had set up shop. Grand Central it was not. Los Angeles was then a boomtown with a population of three hundred thousand, which was triple what it had been just a decade earlier. Compared to 1910 Manhattan, which had a population of 2.3 million, and greater New York, which had a population of over 5 million, L.A. was still a fast-growing small town. Harry Weinstein could see some tallish buildings as he got off the train, ten, maybe fifteen Romanesque or Beaux Arts towers of ten stories or more, but nothing like the Manhattan range of spectacular skyscrapers rising twenty, thirty, forty stories or more into the heavens, like the new 1909 Metropolitan Life tower, which, at seven hundred feet, was the tallest in the world, with a clockface that dwarfed that of Big Ben. New York was big time, Los Angeles bush league. There was simply no comparison.

But comparison perhaps was not the point. New York was a real city, the ultimate city. Los Angeles was a health resort in the process of becoming a city, one day one of the ultimate cities, although Harry Weinstein would have never believed that at the time. What was at stake here was a matter of life and death. New York had killed Jennie. Jacob felt it would have killed him as well had he not gotten out. Tall buildings and big money didn't matter to my free-thinking grandfather. But little Harry, still high on his big emerald score, was all about business, big business, and nothing about Los Angeles, except for the snowcapped San Gabriel Mountains looming above the city, seemed very big at all.

As with most aspects of his past, at least his past before becoming famous, my father spoke very little about California, and of that little, all in the negative, despite L.A.'s many positives. There was huge railway money (Huntington), oil money (Doheny), newspaper money (Otis), real estate money (Griffith, Kinney), and citrus money. There was a huge amount of retirement money as well, particularly in Pasadena, which had become something of a nonhumid Palm Beach, or a desert Newport, where eastern *Social Register* types and multimillionaires like David Gamble of Procter & Gamble had come to live in snobby Eastern high style in craftsman-style mansions designed by the cutting-edge architectural firm of Greene and Greene. These people could afford jewels, major jewels. There was indeed money here, though it wasn't yet coming his family's way.

Yet it couldn't have been because of a lack of trying. The only real artifact from my father's California odyssey is a photograph from 1910 of opening day at the Jacob Weinstein jewelry store at 528 East Fifth Street in the heart of what was then and now downtown Los Angeles. There is Jacob Weinstein, resplendent in a black morning coat, a white vest, and a silk cravat holding court before three well-stocked glittering glass cases of rings, watches, and trinkets. A case of clocks dominates one wall behind him. With his black hair slicked back, his eyes piercing and all-knowing, Jacob has the air of an imperious headwaiter of the most exclusive restaurant in any town. For a man supposedly short of breath, he looks hale and hearty and cocky indeed, ready to take on the world. He could be ruling the floor at Tiffany on Fifth Avenue in New York, not sweeping the floor on Fifth Street in Los Angeles. That sweeping was obviously done in great haste before the photograph was taken, because there are mop marks on the floor and evidence of dust, something that would have irked my father, who was a major germ and dust phobe.

Ah, my father. There he is across the floor, looking like a Gainsborough painting, a tiny, perfect featured aristocrat in his own black morning coat, white cuffs perfectly displayed, as he rests his chin on his hand atop the treasure of jewels beneath him. He is holding court in this modest shop, just as he would someday hold court in the palaces of the world, and he seems to know exactly what his destiny will be. In this photo, he exudes a quiet, almost mystical serenity that things, however awful they might have been for him, were going to get better, and amazingly so. And then, in the center of the shot, between son and father, is Dora, the new maternal anchor of the family, her curls perfectly coiffed, bracelets on her arms, wearing a long dress and little black boots, the little Russian girl of the golden West. She looks exactly like a doll and exactly as she did sixty years later when she doted on me.

Because the census gives no residence address for the Weinsteins for their first four years in Los Angeles, it may be surmised they lived above their store. The store in the photograph may have been their second one in this same location, as there is some evidence Jacob's first establishment was on the back of this same building, facing what might be called an alley, but which was actually a fairly busy lane. The premises in the photograph had before been occupied by a restaurant whose proprietor was one Mister Ishikawa, a representative of a wave of Japanese immigration to the West Coast that xenophobic nativist politicians—wishing to keep, or rather *make*, California Anglo-Saxon—soon pruned in the bud. Fifteen years later my father, flush and living the high life of the Roaring Twenties in the Sherry-Netherland Hotel on Fifth Avenue, employed a live-in and liveried Japanese valet, which was the height of fashion for gentleman playboys of the Jazz Age. The valet's name was "Ishi," very premonitorily, as the name means "stone" in Japanese. My father spoke of him with great nostalgia. Could this Ishi of Fifth Avenue have been the same Ishikawa of Fifth Street?

The coincidence sounds Dickensian, yet unlikely alliances and continuities did tend to occur in my father's life. For instance, one of Jacob Weinstein's neighbors at 424 South Broadway (a name which surely made my father homesick) in what was then something of a jewelry district was a diamond importer named Daniel Wolkowisky, who was the Wolkowisky to whom Jacob apprenticed at his first job in the New World. Daniel, who had an inventory valued at nearly $1 million and later had a salesroom in the shopping arcade of the posh Alexandria Hotel, whose ads described it as the Waldorf Astoria of Los Angeles, was definitely a player in the business. He was able to open doors for the Weinsteins and certainly supply them with goods to sell. He may have even been the prime mover in enticing Jacob to move out to California. This Wolkowisky did, however, eventually sour on selling jewels. A later census finds him as a gentleman asparagus farmer in the San Fernando Valley, where he had lured the Weinsteins to come live.

As I would learn from my father, connections were made to be kept. If Jacob Weinstein could reconnect with Daniel Walkowisky across a decade and a continent, Harry Weinstein could surely make the same kind of long-standing, bicoastal connection with a man named Ishi.

Harry Weinstein, who loved to run, may have felt very constrained by the twenty-square-block radius of the business world of downtown Los Angeles. This was before the automobile made Los Angeles a hundred suburbs in search of a city. In 1910, for Harry there was literally nowhere to run, except to estate sales, auctions, and bankruptcies and to pawn shops and wholesale jewelers looking for something to buy, which would become something to sell. But the diamond in the rough that he might expect to find in New York was one in a million in Los Angeles.

For such a small city, Jacob Weinstein had a lot of competition. The Los Angeles Times was filled with advertisements for jewelers claiming to have been in business ten to fifteen years, going back to Los Angeles's pueblo days. Oddly enough, when Jacob arrived, many of these venerable establishments were going out of business, which wasn't very auspicious. After a huge distress sale, where "everything must go," said venerable institution would reopen in a new location "due to overwhelming popular demand." Maybe that's how the jewelry business ran in a boomtown, but it certainly didn't inspire the impeccable confidence that Harry Weinstein used to create Harry Winston. The business, L.A.-style, was rife with the sale of fraudulent goods, judging from the many prosecutions of unscrupulous operators reported in the press. Fake jewelry auctions were so rampant that bills were presented in the state legislature to try to regulate them, though with no particular results.

Until recently Fifth Street has been one of America's worst skid rows, a cesspool of addicts, unhoused people, and mental patients dumped by heartless hospitals. It has been a scene out of the Depression. Even the police, in a city notorious for its law enforcement brutality, didn't go there on foot. In my father's day, Fifth Street was no Fifth Avenue, but it wasn't the Bowery either, although the city's "tenderloin" or red-light district of burlesque houses, bordellos, and patent medicine shops selling male potency elixirs was only a few blocks away. Teenager Harry Winston was the right age to be tempted by such diversions, but he never recalled or shared any youthful indiscretions, and whether this was due to his unwavering sense of discretion or to the fact that he'd behaved impeccably is anyone's guess.

My father did recount, with revulsion, having watched a poor Mexican woman give birth in the back of one of the "Red Car" trolleys, of Los Angeles's public transportation system, which he used every day. He told that story numerous times, and it stuck in my head, as it had stuck in his. Was that a symbol of Los Angeles's primitivism? Did that put him off sex? Did that quell his raging hormones or deter him from taking advantage of all the temptations to be found in this boomtown? Aside from that image of naked motherhood on that streetcar, neither love nor lust was part of my father's California chapter. Nor did he ever tell me that the street parallel to East Fifth Street was called Winston Street, undoubtedly the source of his new, WASPy, and patrician name. Growing up, I had assumed that any Jew with the name Winston was originally Weinstein, that it was sort of an automatic Americanization for those eager to assimilate. But I was wrong: Harry Weinstein's "Winston" had a very distinct provenance.

Although there was a Concordia Club downtown for prominent Jewish families barred from joining clubs established by and for old-guard Gold Rush aristocrats, most of whom resided away from downtown in Pasadena, there was no great Jewish family among the Huntingtons and Dohenys who could be said to be one of Los Angeles's leading dynasties. That would not happen until the 1920s with the rise of the film industry. There were no Warburgs and Belmonts like in New York, or even Fleishhackers and Strausses like in San Francisco. Despite its Mediterranean feel, the spirit of Los Angeles was closer to small-town Iowa. The majority of the population had indeed come from the Midwest and maintained solid, stolid, Christian middle-American values. Small wonder that Harry Weinstein felt like a stranger. Jews were a distinct minority, as other as Chinese immigrants or African Americans, who also began arriving from the South when my family did. The jewelry Jews, most of whom were orthodox and wore frock coats and tallises, must have seemed particularly alien in the California sunshine, and alien even to my grandfather and father.

Just as in Russia, where radical, pre-Bolshevik Jews were blamed for the assassination of the czar, here in California, Jews were suspected, if not outright indicted, as the radical brains behind a terrifying series of nearly a hundred timed dynamite bombings of new downtown office buildings, which was part of a campaign of labor unrest that pitted workers agitating to unionize against the city establishment. These explosions were taking place almost weekly when my father arrived from New York. The earthly paradise he may have expected turned out to be a war zone and may have contributed to my father's disinclination to the Golden State. Labor's reign of terror culminated with the bombing of the *Los Angeles*

Times headquarters, which was very near the Weinstein store. Twenty people were killed, and many more were injured.

The eminent lawyer Clarence Darrow, who would find later fame in the twenties in the Leopold and Loeb murder case and the Scopes evolution trial, came west to defend the accused masterminds, who weren't Jews at all but two Irish brothers named MacNamara who were leaders of the iron-workers' union. Darrow lost the trial, but the brothers' prison terms were reduced in view that the inflammable printing ink on the *Times'* premises made the catastrophe far more cata-strophic than the brothers intended. It was a triumph for the *Times'* archconservative owner, General Harrison Gray Otis, but it established a police-state tone to the so-called easy life of Southern California that could have only put my father off further.

To Harry Weinstein, Los Angeles seemed like a hick town, and a deadly one at that. Instead of the theaters of Broadway, the main downtown amusements, before the invasion of the movie palaces to come, were a water world called Chutes Park, featuring a fifty-foot near-vertical plunge slide, and the nearby Alligator Farm, where inge-niously trained huge leaping lizards did plunges à deux down their own steep slides and children could ride bare-back on these inexplicably docile creatures. The adjacent ostrich farm was a big hit as well, and the three parks con-stituted the Disneyland of the period. Harry might have also ridden one of the Red Cars out to the beach in Santa Monica, with its long amusement park pier. For all his love of swimming, he never mentioned once dipping a toe into the blue Pacific. He probably was too busy helping his father mind the store.

Nevertheless, there were people, big people, who made an impression on the undoubtedly impressionable young Harry Weinstein. One of the these was Henry Huntington, probably the most influential and high-living of the Los Angeles tycoons. Huntington's lifestyle influenced that of William Randolph Hearst, creator of San Simeon and inspiration for *Citizen Kane*. If Huntington could inflame the imagination of Hearst, he surely could do the same for Weinstein. Huntington was known as the Trolley King, the president of the Pacific Electric Company, the largest electric street railway transit system in the world.

The heart of Huntington's trolley lines, which went from the orange groves of Riverside to the beaches of Newport, was the Romanesque quasi-skyscraper Pacific Electric Building, a few blocks from the Weinstein store, which was a combination of New York's Port Authority Terminal, the Woolworth Building, and the Racquet Club, all under one massive beaux arts roof. The epicurean Jonathan Club, of which Huntington was president, sat atop the structure, while Huntington maintained a sort of Hugh Hefnerian bachelor pad within the ornate, servant-filled club. On one hand, the Red Cars for my father were a symbol of poverty, of nakedness, of destitution and desperation, as exemplified by the woman giving birth on a streetcar. On the other, they were the symbol of wealth, of modernity, of power, as seen in Henry Huntington in the sky atop the Pacific Electric Building.

Huntington's main residence was a Versailles-like palace on his ranch in nearby San Marino, the largest home in California, before Hearst Castle was built. But Huntington was no philistine. He owned a Gutenberg Bible, one of the world's premier libraries of English Renaissance books, and an unparalleled collection of English art—the best of Gainsborough, Constable, and Reynolds—assembled by Lord Duveen, the leading art dealer in the world. Plus his wife Arabella had a collection of jewels and diamonds befitting the woman considered the Queen of California. The family life of the Hungtintons was rife with drama and scandal. Before marrying Henry, Arabella had been the wife of Henry's uncle Collis, one of the transcontinental railway's "Big Four" fathers of the Golden Spike, the others being Leland Stanford, Charles Crocker, and Mark Hopkins. These transplanted easterners had come to California during the gold rush, created the Southern Pacific, and basically owned California. They were the robber barons of the West.

But even before landing Huntington Number One, Arabella had a past. A Virginia adventuress whose first husband, a riverboat gambler and scoundrel, loved her and left her, Arabella made her way to New York and connived and seduced her way into becoming Collis's mistress. Lust in this case eventually led to love, or at least marriage. She had a son, but no one was sure whether he was the issue of Collis or of the gambler. In any event, Arabella gave her boy Archer the right name—Huntington—and Archer went on to a distinguished academic career as a Hispanic Scholar, founding the regal museum of the Hispanic Society of America on Manhattan's Upper Broadway. When Collis died in 1900, Arabella, who hated California even more than my father did, moved to Paris and the attendant gaiety and sophistication America's arguably richest woman so deserved. But her nephew Henry, his uncle's chief heir, had fancied her for years and wooed her back to the West by building his own Versailles-in-the-palms as their love nest. They wed in 1913, and their romance was one of the highest-profile love affairs in American society. My father couldn't help but notice and be dazzled by Arabella's jewels, which she proudly modeled in every photograph taken of her.

I'm not sure my father ever saw the great Arabella Huntington in the flesh, even at a glance, but he did see the wife of another member of the Big Four, and that encounter was one of the seminal events of his young life, one that he never stopped talking about well into his eighties. He talked about this more than anything else that happened to him in California, and I'm convinced it made him want to be the man he became. This sighting took place in 1915, on my father's first trip to San Francisco with his father. I believe they'd gone up to attend the opera. My dad was dazzled by the Nob Hill wealth and the New York–level luxury of the stores on Market Street, all vastly more lavish than what he was used to in Los Angeles. My grandfather adored the opera. He bought the cheapest tickets he could find, to stand in the stalls. Perhaps the opera was *Aida* because of the pomp and ceremony of the whole experience, and no opera was more pompous than *Aida*. What made an impression on my father was the grand entrance, not of Aida herself, but of Mrs. Charles Crocker, like Arabella Huntington, one of the railway baronesses.

Mrs. Crocker, then in her seventies, sat in her exclusive box, very much the Empress of San Francisco. The emblem of her power was a multistrand pearl necklace of the most voluptuous proportion, its splendor shimmering in the reflection of the footlights. My father later found out, among the jewelers he asked (for he had become obsessed with that moment), all the details of the legendary piece; the seven-rope extravaganza weighed fourteen pounds. If anything was a choker, this was it. Although my father would be a diamond man, *the* diamond man, the pearls to him had an ineffable sensuality. Mrs. Crocker's pearls were not cultured; that process wasn't invented until the 1930s, by Mikimoto in Japan. Otherwise, my father might have become the pearl man, for he often went on and on about how women delighted in pearls, and how men delighted in giving them, conjuring up the image of rolling the strands over a woman's nude flesh. And then he would stop, before he got too carried away.

In any event, Mrs. Crocker, and Mrs. Huntington, came to symbolize to my father the ultimate in feminine glamour and bejeweled extravagance. These were the clients he dreamed of serving, of adorning, of making him rich and powerful. The Big Four was his fantasy, a fantasy forged in the standing room of that San Francisco opera house when my father was barely twenty and barely solvent. The fantasy came true when Arabella Huntington died in 1924. Barely a decade after hustling cuckoo clocks in the Tenderloin, Harry Weinstein, now Winston, bought Arabella's entire jewelry estate for a staggering $1.2 million, one of the biggest coups of all time.

To finance his purchase of the Huntington estate, my father turned to another California connection he had made in those humble days on Fifth Street. This was Amadeo Peter "A. P." Giannini, founder of the Bank of Italy, which became the colossus Bank of America. HW met APG when Giannini opened one of his branch banks right around the corner from the Weinstein store. Giannini took pride in bringing banking, formerly a service to big business and big men, to the "little fellow," as Giannini called him, a man like Jacob Weinstein. Perhaps my father went in for his father to seek a business loan and met the humble mogul. The two had a lot in common.

Both were American-born sons of immigrants. Both worked in the family business, Giannini's being produce. Both had lost a parent at a young age. Giannini's father had been brutally murdered by one of his ranch hands in a dispute over one dollar.

Out of that tragic dollar, an institution was born. The first Bank of Italy opened in 1904 in a former saloon in San Francisco. Giannini survived the 1906 earthquake by settting up his bank on a plank and two barrels and made loans to all comers, when the establishment banks said no. In doing so, he was taking banking back to its Italian roots. The word *banco* meant an outdoor bench, from which moneylenders would dispense their often-usurious favors. Giannini's pride was that every earthquake loan he made, always at fair rates, was repaid. Giannini became a true folk hero, not the least to my father, who treasured his friendship and would call on it in the future, when his future turned bright.

Speaking of ranch hands, one of the reasons my father, or his father, was not taking out bigger loans from Giannini was illuminated in an anecdote my father told about his Los Angeles jewelry days. A ranch hand came in and wanted to buy a ring for his wife. "You're too poor to waste money on jewelry," my grandfather told the prospective customer. "Go buy food or something you *need*." As opposed to something you *want*, which was the essence of my father's success. You could take Jacob out of Russia, but you couldn't take Russia out of Jacob, not the latent Trotskyite part.

Weinstein and Son, the name of the business, endured, but it didn't seem to shine. In 1915 the family made a big move, up the block on Fifth Street to Number 110, right on the corner of Main Street, which was everything its name implied, the main drag of downtown. That relocation indicated a certain prosperity, as the family's move from above the store to the ostensible graciousness of their first single-family home, whose address was 1518½ Winfield Street, Panorama City, in the newly settled San Fernando Valley. The valley was over the hills of Hollywood, through the Cahuenga Pass.

Until the reservoir that brought it water from the Owens Valley in 1910 and the Huntington electric trolleys that connected it to civilization in 1913, this valley was a desert wasteland. Now it was the cornerstone of the California Dream for poor dreamers who wanted a home of their own. Real estate developers went wild exploiting this fantasy, and endless tracts of wooden bungalows went up overnight. Maybe Jacob was following Daniel Walkowisky into the asparagus fields, or maybe he just wanted to be somewhere even warmer and drier than downtown, which could be cold and damp in winter. The key point here is that what had lured Jacob west was health more than wealth. What mattered were his lungs, not his wallet, although my father surely felt otherwise and must have been terribly frustrated by the waste of the three hours spent commuting each day, especially when he had business to do.

The experiment in rusticity lasted a year. In 1916, the Weinsteins moved back over the hill to 2506½ Raymond Avenue, about three miles from the store (as opposed to thirty from the valley), in a pleasant, leafy neighborhood of Victorian homes near what was becoming the campus of the University of Southern California. But by 1917 Jacob Weinstein and Son was no longer listed in the Los Angeles city directory. That's because the boom in population my grandfather was banking on in L.A. just didn't pan out: though the population tripled in the decade from 1900 to 1910, the next decade only saw 50 percent growth.

Jacob was back in New York, living again in Harlem just below Morningside Heights, and with a new store uptown in Harlem at 1348 St. Nicholas Avenue, not far from where my father's beloved Yankee Stadium would one day be built, just across the East River, in 1923. Weather or not, Jacob had come home.

My father, however, stayed behind. In 1916 he was twenty years old. World War I was raging in Europe. The *Lusitania* had been sunk the year before, killing 125 Americans, making it harder and harder for President Woodrow Wilson to justify his isolationist stance. A draft was instituted; millions of men were being called up. Despite his petite size, Harry Weinstein fully expected to be summoned to the ranks. He was prime military material, and I'm sure he dreaded the idea. Maybe he thought it would be easier to hide out in California and evade the draft board. That was one explanation why his next known address was 993 3rd Street in San Bernardino. That address was the location of a sprawling three-story caravansary called the Planet Hotel. It sounds like a bad B movie, a man on the run holing up in some flophouse in godforsaken San Berdoo, the butt of endless Jimmy Durante jokes, hiding out from the Feds. But there was, as always, likely to be a method behind this seeming madness on the part of my father.

Ultimately, Uncle Sam came calling. Whether Harry Weinstein served his country, how, and where, are all questions to which no answers are available, as a great number of Army records from World War I were destroyed in a fire some years ago. However, I always knew my father not to be a fabulist. If he said he served, I'm sure he did. I wish I knew more. What I do know is that Harry Weinstein appeared on no public records whatsoever from the time of his days at the Planet Hotel in 1917 to his reemergence in a 1921 New York City business directory as "Harry Winston," proprietor of the Premier Diamond Company at the redoubtable address of 535 Fifth Avenue.

The war ended in 1918. As George M. Cohan sang, "I won't be there til it's over, over there," and I doubt my father went "over there." If he had he would have found that a tale worth telling. More likely, he served his country in California, and the war was over sooner than anyone thought, hence he never had the chance to be dispatched to the Western Front. He probably stayed in the Golden West, and he probably played out his hand in the Inland Empire and Imperial Valley until he realized that the Arabella Huntingtons of the world were a lot easier to find on Park Avenue, Back Bay, the Main Line, and other social enclaves of the East than in the citrus groves and asparagus fields. There was money, for sure, in California, but it simply wasn't accessible to Harry Weinstein of Fifth Street. Harry Winston of Fifth Avenue would be a different story.

I recall my Uncle Stanley's wife telling me how impressed she was when little Harry showed up at their door the first time he came back to New York. He only had thirty-six dollars in his pocket, he told them, and he needed a place to stay. But despite his lack of resources, there was a new confidence, a saloon swagger, a man-of-the-world aura about him. My aunt described this new Harry as a fashion plate, resplendent in a Norfolk jacket, that belted, pleated hunting coat made a de rigueur fashion item by the Prince of Wales, who had worn it at his Norfolk stately home. He also looked taller. Stanley's wife, confused by Harry's new stature, was nonplussed. Then she noticed his feet. Harry was wearing elevator shoes. To look at Harry, she might have thought he had been with the naval attaché in London or Dover, not peeling potatoes at Fort Ord. He looked dapper, cosmopolitan, ready to take on the world. Having taken Horace Greeley's advice to "Go West, young man, go West," Harry Weinstein had decided to follow his own contrarian instincts and reverse course. My father had seen America. Now he was ready to take on the world.

CHAPTER THREE

Designing Harry Winston

When my father left New York City in 1910, it was the capital of America. When he returned in 1919, it was the capital of the world. If he had thought Los Angeles was a hick town when he was there, he must not have been able to comprehend its provinciality once he saw the Big Apple with new eyes. Now, skyscrapers shot up sixty, seventy stories, all over Manhattan, the most beautiful being the Woolworth Building, "the cathedral of commerce." Midtown had come into its own, and, aside from the finance center that was Wall Street, the city's finest stores had all migrated uptown to Fifth Avenue. This commercial diaspora included the diamond dealers, once ghettoized on Maiden Lane, now grandly ensconced on Fifth above the Flatiron Building at 23rd Street.

The Great White Way was virtually unrecognizable to my father, as the theaters, and the restaurants and nightclubs that swam in their wake, had also moved above Times Square. A Frenchman named Georges Claude in 1915 had invented neon lighting, and the result was a sea of King Kongian advertising signs that turned night into day. The great restaurants, known as "lobster palaces," like Rector's and Delmonico's, which my family was too poor to even get hungry about, also moved uptown, but the chief nexus between diamonds and Broadway was the Ziegfeld Follies and its re-creation of the chorus girl as gold digger. Chorus girls, in the tawdry days of burlesque, were glorified prostitutes, but Ziegfeld, in creating the proto-Vegas vaudeville-nightclubs that were the Follies, took that chorus girl, slimmed her down, stretched her up, and made her glamorously untouchable.

As the comics character Dixie Dugan observed, the idea of the Ziegfeld girl was to "be cool and look hot." Ziegfeld girls were the supermodels of their day, and the best way for socialites and tycoons to get into these girls' dressing rooms and hearts was with expensive jewelry. The biggest smash play in my father's first year back in New York was Avery Hopwood's *The Gold Diggers*, which enshrined this phenomenon. It was a tribute to the emergence of the liberated woman (the Nineteenth Amendment, giving women universal suffrage, was passed the next year) , and back then "gold digger" was a term of honor rather than opprobrium. It was considered totally cool to get rich by being beautiful.

The gold the girls were digging for was gems, and my father must have been inspired and exhilarated by this. Before, the only women with jewels were the superrich, the "400" of Astors and Vanderbilts, or Crockers and Huntingtons, depending on your coast. But now diamonds could be every girl's best friend, providing she was nearly six feet tall and could balance one of Ziegfeld's trademark six-foot headdresses for hours, posing half naked in high heels. If she could, the democratization of wealth was at hand, as those Astors and Vanderbilts laid on the jewels and increasingly married beneath themselves.

My father in those days was as hungry as any chorus girl. He made up for his lack of height with more drive than Ziegfeld himself. Ziegfeld was born in Chicago, the son of successful German immigrants who ran a music school. He thus started his career with a leg up. My father, on the other hand, created himself out of whole cloth, very similarly to three other tiny Russian Jews who became American giants in the 1920s: Irving Berlin, the greatest song writer of the age; Al Jolson, the greatest singer; and Walter Winchell, the great columnist who, more than anyone else, created the legend that was Broadway. Harry Weinstein may have been half a head even smaller than Israel Baline, Asa Hesselson, and Walter Weinshel, but he shared their singlemindedness and ruthless determination to re-create themselves into something grand and something their parents would have never possibly believed that they could be.

But the diminutive immigrant Jew my father most identified with was the "other Harry," Harry Houdini. Houdini actually lived in a Harlem brownstone at 278 W. 113th Street while my father's family was living at 275 W 114th Street. The two Harrys were only a block apart, though my father was just a little boy and Houdini had just returned from conquering Europe as the Handcuff King, and would soon conquer America as the greatest escape artist of all time.

Surely the Weinsteins were aware of their most famous neighbor, and my father may have developed a special pride based on this proximity. But they had other things in common. Houdini had changed his name, from Erich Weiss. He had grown up in the West, Wisconsin to be precise (anything across the Hudson counted as "the West" in those days), where his father had gone as a circuit-riding rabbi. Even though my father surely admired Irving Berlin's feat of marrying "up," to one of the richest socialite heiresses in America (Elin Mackay, the daughter of Clarence Mackay, the Telegraph King), his days in the rugged West made him especially impressed by Houdini's amazing physicality, something songwriters and journalists could not generally boast. (Winchell was famous for packing loaded guns and trolling for public enemies with his best friend J. Edgar Hoover.) But Harry Houdini, whose first job was as a lowly but observant locksmith's apprentice and who had started his performing life as a trapeze artist, was an inspiration to Harry Weinstein. That a poor rabbi's son could go this far was proof of America's endless opportunities. Plus my father adored magic. Back in New York, it was time to work his own.

"Harry, Harry darling," I remember him saying to himself over dinner in our Fifth Avenue apartment. "Harry, Harry darling." That was his prelude to holding forth, usually on the triumphs of the day, but sometimes on the obstacles of the past, during the Weinstein days. We were then in our grand Fifth Avenue apartment. It was quite dramatic. The sun would be setting behind the western canyon wall of Central Park West. My mother would call us to dinner. My brother Bruce and I would be seated on opposite sides of the sixteenth-century Dutch antique dinner table. My mother had her back to Fifth Avenue and the window. The view of lush, green Central Park was reserved for my father.

Because he never paused for lunch, he was always ravenous at dinner. He ate the chef-prepared meal with great gusto and speed. Because he invariably finished before the rest of us, he took the occasion to regale us with tales of great jewels and great people, occasioned, naturally, by his own great labors and great brilliance. "Harry, Harry darling," he would say in self-regard. And he would always close the dinner lecture with, "After all, how many Harry Winstons are there in this world?" Would Houdini have made such a grandiose statement? Would Napoleon? Maybe Louis XIV. Whenever my father uttered the phrase, the table would go silent. Such a comment could wreak havoc on a fragile, vulnerable adolescent ego. I felt bruised. My brother, I think, was crushed. Harry, darling, indeed. How could you? I would later read Shelley's poem "Ozymandias": "Look on my wonders, oh, ye mortals, and despair." This might have been my father's mantra. And yes, he had done it, all by himself, fame and fortune and a perfect view of Central Park. But his bragging, his constant self-aggrandizement did a terrible number on us kids.

One of Harry's most-told comeback stories was how, in 1920, his first full year back in New York, he was completely cleaned out in a robbery. The first thing Harry Weinstein had done upon arrival was to change his name to Winston and to christen his new firm the Premier Diamond Company. The second was to get his own office, at 535 Fifth Avenue, near the current diamond wholesale district of 47th Street, but decades before the wholesalers had moved there from downtown's Maiden Lane. His father Jacob had started another small retail jewelry shop up near Morningside Heights, but Jacob Weinstein *and Sons* it was not to be.

Harry was going to be his own man, and he was going to be a rich man. And apparently he was, in barely a year. He had assembled $45,000 worth of stones in his office vault, worth close to $600,000 in 2023 dollars. But, in a case of beginner's bad luck, he lost all of it.

Harry had been doing business for four months with William Greenburg, a former Maiden Lane commission jewelry salesman who was thirty-nine, married with a sick wife, and living on West 93rd Street. Greenburg was becoming a diamond broker and, to that end, had taken several parcels of the diamonds my father had bought and showed them to prospective buyers as a middleman. Greenburg's last check to my father, for the then-huge sum of $10,400, had been returned for insufficient funds, but my father relied on his instincts that Greenburg would make good. On April 20, 1920, Greenburg had come to Harry saying that he had a hot prospect, an out-of-town buyer. Harry gave him goods worth a whopping $24,400 "on memo," which meant that Greenburg's authority was only to show the stones and return to Harry with an offer, which he could take or leave. If he accepted the offer, Greenberg would bring him a check, hopefully a good one.

The next day Greenberg came back to Harry and told him that the buyer was even hotter than he had thought. Harry gave Greenburg another $10,000 of diamonds on memo. My father must have been feeling expansive, for at the same time Greenberg was pitching him, another diamond broker named Joseph Riskin was in the office trying to sell Harry a parcel of diamonds for $4,600. Greenberg saw the stones and said he could sell these too. So, Harry took them on memo from Riskin and passed them to Greenberg. On April 23, a Friday, Greenburg got still another $1,300 diamond haul from Harry. On Saturday, the Sabbath, Greenberg dropped back into Premier to assure Harry that he expected his deals to close on

Monday, with a big written offer for Harry. That big Monday never came. Greenberg disappeared.

Harry went to the police, swore out a complaint, filing an inventory of the three thousand unset stones and three pieces of fine jewelry, with a total value of $45,000. The police offered a reward of $500 for Greenburg's arrest. It didn't seem like a big deal to them, not in this era of Al Capone, "Mad Dog" Coll, and Legs Diamond. Prohibition had just commenced. This was the decade of the speakeasy and of the gangster bootleggers running them. Jewelry theft, big as it was to my father, was small potatoes. The police report did note that Greenburg had a brother who was a pawnbroker, a major clue that somehow achieved no results. On June 28, a grand jury indicted Greenburg, in absentia, for grand larceny, first degree.

Nothing more was heard of Greenburg that summer, until August 1, when he was arrested in my father's office. Greenburg was cuffed, then taken down to the infamous "Tombs," the jail in lower Manhattan. Bail was set at $40,000, later reduced to $15,000. It was noted in the documents that Harry Winston's name be withheld from the press, as "the shock might kill his sick father."

The trial began on December 27, 1920, right after what must have been a very blue Christmas for my father. Greenburg's lawyer tried to get the case dismissed on grounds of "incompetent and insufficient evidence" and that in fact, no real crime had been committed but that what was at hand was nothing but a civil dispute, which was not uncommon in the jewel trade. Despite his lawyer's pleas, Greenburg was convicted in February 1921. Despite a letter signed by nine of the jurors asking for leniency on account of Greenburg's sick wife, the judge sentenced him to eight years in Sing Sing, the infamous prison "up the river," in Ossining, New York.

In 1929, records show that Greenburg had been released and was running a radio store. My father, never one to forget a debt, or a wrong, apparently found him and sued him, though all he got was a few thousand dollars.

But all was not lost. Their shared misfortune seemed to have cemented a bond of lifetime friendship with fellow victim Joseph Riskin, who might be considered the hard-luck kid of the diamond business. Riskin, a Russian émigré a decade older than my father, was frequently in the *New York Times* in the twenties as the victim of spectacular robberies. In 1922 he was robbed twice, once near Maiden Lane, another, of $25,000 in gems, in his 522 Fifth Avenue office by a safe-cracker. In 1926 Riskin was robbed on a train with two fellow jewelers. The haul was a staggering $500,000, but the gems were quickly recovered. The next year he was in the headlines again, for having been defrauded by another jeweler for $8,000. The bottom line was that getting your name in the papers was great for business. Riskin moved up Fifth Avenue to grand quarters.

The next time Riskin was in the news was on the society pages, in 1933, for marrying Mona Fox, daughter of William Fox, founder of 20th Century Fox, at the Fox palazzo in Miami. Mona had ambitions to become a jewelry designer, and Riskin obviously played well to them. He moved to Hollywood and opened a prestigious jewelry store near the then-fabled corner of Hollywood and Vine and lived nearby in the most glamorous apartment house in filmdom, the El Royale on Rossmore. Alas, Riskin, began having paranoid delusions and was taken back to New York to be institutionalized at the chic

West Hill Sanitarium in Riverdale, the Bronx, next door to my high school, and where my father faithfully visited him for decades. Convinced people were out to poison him, Riskin ate nothing but hard-boiled eggs, which he insisted on peeling himself. The sanitarium closed in 1961, and Riskin was moved to another facility, where he died in 1975.

A lesser man, totally wiped out as young Harry Winston had been, would have taken a job, but my father's self-fantasy would simply not condone his working for someone else.

Certainly, the job offers were there. He knew lots of people, through his endless running around, and no one who met him didn't think he was brilliant and driven. But he was too brilliant to play by anyone else's rules. Moving into a ratty single-room occupancy residential hotel on the Upper West Side, he spent the next couple of years doing small deals, with small loans, but never thinking small. His epiphany came with the advent of the thoroughly modern, slender, half-dressed, tomboyish flapper as the female symbol of the Jazz Age. The socialite dowager was out.

The epitome of this sea change was Queen Mary of England herself. The wife of King George, Mary of Teck (the name to her Saxon roots) had instituted, during World War I, an austerity drive at Buckingham Palace to convey the stiff-upper-lip approach to her subjects. At the end of the war, her youngest son, "little Johnnie," died at the tender age of thirteen. Even though she was obsessed with jewelry and had one of the greatest collections of any royal, she knew it would be in bad taste to glitter like a chandelier while the lights of Europe were dim and, especially, while she was mourning the loss of her son. So she took off her famous "dog collars," and her unadorned regal simplicity turned her into a beloved global figure. Other fashionistas of the day—on both sides of the Atlantic—followed suit.

Dog collars circled the neck four or five times, and each orbit contained dozens of carats of diamonds, often totaling fifty or more. Woman of wealth, the well born, and the well wed, all wanted to be both "queenly," à la Mary, and contemporary, à la Zelda Fitzgerald, wife of Scott, the poet laureate of all the modern madness. So they tossed these dog collars away, along with their tiaras and stomachers and corsages. Whole museums of Victorian and Edwardian ornaments were as obsolete as a brougham up against a Bugatti, and all this "antique" jewelry created a terrible bear market, into which dived my father, picking up treasures for pennies on the carat. The Premier Diamond Company then became something of a jewelry "chop shop." My father would stay up all night, taking dog collars apart, removing the gems from their ostentatious settings and soaking them in acid. Years later as a boy obsessed with chemistry, I worked with these same acids and saw how volcanic they could be. I wonder what passersby thought walking up Fifth Avenue and seeing giant plumes of smoke erupting from my father's windows.

The method to my mad scientist father's seeming madness was to remove these stones and have them recut. He would take a tasteful, understated "old mine" cut (with high tops and small tables, which, in diamond jargon, means the large flat surface on the top of the stone) and do a new "brilliant" cut, which would create more facets and more sparkle. Then he would have the stones remounted in much lighter, more stylish contemporary settings. He wasn't a cutter or a setter himself, but he knew all the right men for the job. The result was jazzy jewelry for the Jazz Age, and the man to see for that kind of jazz became Harry Winston.

Harry thus began haunting estate sales the way a dipsomaniac would haunt speakeasies. Of course, one couldn't do the estate circuit without funding, and Harry had spent years cultivating banking connections. As he always told me, the three keys to his success were knowledge, courage, and the ability to finance. Without the latter, however, the smartest, gutsiest diamond man would be nowhere. Harry had friends at the progressive New Netherland Bank, which had extended purchasing credits to him for his early deals. The bank, which stood on the corner of Fifth Avenue and 34th Street, across from where the Empire State Building would soon be built, was in the new retail district. It prided itself on cutting-edge banking that the stuffy Wall Street monoliths could not provide. For example, the bank in 1913 was unique in starting its own woman's banking floor, closed to men, where "gold diggers" from the Follies could come and stash their loot. It was these women who were the ultimate market for Harry Winston's diamonds, and it is not surprising the bank was open to his highly speculative needs.

The bank was dominated by the very social, very powerful Fleischmann family, whose yeast had made it one of the great fortunes in New York. (These were different Fleischmanns from Dad's in-laws-to-be, the Fleischmans.) The Fleischmanns understood upper crust, they collected jewels themselves, and, unusually for an establishment clan, they liked taking chances. Raoul Fleischmann, who played poker with a colorful reporter named Harold Ross as part of a gambling group called the Thanatopsis Literary and Inside Straight Club, staked Ross to the $25,000 that started the *New*

Yorker magazine. Likewise, Raoul's cousin Udo Fleischmann, vice president of the New Netherland Bank, was intrigued with the little gambler from California and his encyclopedic knowledge of gems. New Netherland would provide an ever-increasing line of credit.

To build that line, and to rebuild his post-Greenberg business, Harry Winston began running once again, running to estate sales, running to other dealers, then running up and down Fifth Avenue selling his new-cut diamonds to the luxury emporia of that magic stretch from 34th to 57th Streets. He would march up and down that gauntlet of luxe, like the General Sherman of jewelry, sometimes twice a day. Along the way, there were fifteen to twenty jewelry stores he would call on. There was Kahn, and Jacques, and Bestor, great names then, all gone after the Crash. There was Gattle, across from St. Patrick's Cathedral and the brand-new (in 1924) Saks Fifth Avenue, whose most famous client, Enrico Caruso, figured prominently in its otherwise discreet advertising. There was Black, Starr & Frost, Manhattan's most venerable jeweler, whose seven moves uptown since its founding on lower Broadway in 1810, from Murray Street to Prince Street, then 28th, 39th, and finally 48th, sounded like a subway line and reflected the northward migration of retail commerce.

Forming Harry Winston's perception of how he himself would become rich and live accordingly thereafter was the success story of Dreicer & Co., Fifth Avenue's grandest Jewish jeweler, as opposed to its grandest foreign jeweler, Cartier, or its grandest WASP jeweler, Tiffany, which was so blatantly anti-Semitic that my father did not call on it directly but offered his wares through a WASPy intermediary named Mr. Proudfoot and paid a WASPy broker with the equally haughty name of Mr. Snigert 2 percent to close the Tiffany deals. For all its exclusion, however, my father didn't want to be Tiffany. If he wanted to be anyone, it was Dreicer.

Jacob and Gittel Dreicer had come to America as Orthodox Polish-Jewish immigrants after the Civil War in 1868, armed with a large sum of Confederate dollars they had acquired before their journey and had no idea was worthless. That was about the only mistake the Dreicers would make. Jacob Dreicer also brought with him an inventory of precious stones, and Gittel, for whom jewelry had been her hobby and passion in the Old World, proved a valuable business partner for Jacob in the New World. Gittel actually became a lapidary who cut the firm's stones, and, as they prospered, the Dreicers took annual trips back to Europe in search of bargains from newly deposed royalty, or destitute aristocracy, in those revolutionary times. They took with them their son Michael, who became perhaps the world's leading expert on pearls, and sold one of his masterpieces to a Philadelphia financier for $1.5 million, the most expensive pearl necklace in history. The firm moved uptown from a rented cellar on Lexington Avenue to a noble emporium at 292 Fifth Avenue, at 30th Street and next to a branch of Delmonico's, the most exclusive of the city's restaurants and where Jacob ate each day with the Gotham power elite, always with a case of jewels to show the swells as gifts for their wives and girlfriends.

Jacob was thus considered instrumental in the education of the New York aristocracy about gems and their investment potential.

The Dreicers became millionaires and moved to a mansion on the corner of 78th Street and Fifth Avenue. Once Fifth Avenue below 57th Street had gone commercial, Upper Fifth, above 57th, was known as Millionaires' Row, and the Dreicers were charter members of the big club, the Astor-Vanderbilt society who bought their jewels from them. The Dreicers were considered above reproach, with one glaring exception. In 1914 they made the front page of the *New York Times* in a scandal that illustrated how jewelry could be one of the glaring excesses in what was emerging as an age of excess. Represented by the super WASP firm of Sullivan & Cromwell, which did the legal work for the new Panama Canal, they sued another WASP scion named George Quintard, heir to an iron ore fortune, for $55,000 (about $1.6 million in 2023) for jewels he unknowingly bought for gold diggers while he was heavily under the influence.

No one else tried to make excuses for their purchases from Dreicer. Son Michael Dreicer lived as large as any heir in the city, minus the alcohol, on Fifth Avenue across from the Metropolitan Museum and at Deepdale, the forty-three-acre former William K. Vanderbilt estate, which was the one of the most palatial residences on Long Island. Alas, when Michael died suddenly at fifty-three, Jacob went into shock and died himself a few weeks later.

Then there was Cartier, which was so French, so snobbish, so *raffiné*, that my father must have thought he was on another planet, if not merely another continent, when he came to call. Founded in Paris in 1847 by Louis-François Cartier, the house, which by the turn of the century was known as "the jeweler of kings, the king of jewelers" made its first royal connection by designing pieces for Princess Mathilde, cousin of Napoleon. Louis had three grandsons who would carve up the world.

The first of these was Louis-Joseph, a genius who pioneered the use of platinum in designs that became the hallmark of art deco, invented the "invisible setting," developed the signature panther icon, and created the first modern wristwatch, the Santos-Dumont, named for his friend the Lindberghian Brazilian aviator. Brother Jacques would open the London office and build the bridge to the maharajas of India, a bridge my father would later cross countless times and rebuild as his own. And then there was Pierre, who opened Cartier New York and made a huge splash by selling the Hope Diamond to *Washington Post* heiress Evalyn Walsh McLean. Again, my father would follow in these giant footsteps by buying the Hope himself and donating it to the Smithsonian. But in his own infancy as a dealer, he felt blessed and privileged just to set foot in the Cartier marble mansion on Fifth and 52nd, an urban palais Pierre had acquired in a 1916 trade for a million-dollar string of pearls from the Florida railroad millionaire Morton Plant, who felt Fifth Avenue was getting too congested for his rustic taste.

Last and most, there was Tiffany & Co., which was then located on Fifth and 37th Street. These headquarters were a McKim, Mead & White–designed exact replica of the sixteenth-century Palazzo Grimani, on Venice's Grand Canal. So arrogant was Tiffany that the store had no name at all on the outside. Its trademark clock and statue of Atlas above it had been moved from the previous emporium at Union Square. Inside was as noble as out, with purple marble pillars and a super modern ceiling made of that new (in 1905) metal aluminum. There were huge Tiffany-made silver chandeliers. The teak walls, inlaid with polished steel and brass, also had a silver finish. The entire place reeked of precious metal, which, of course, was precisely the idea.

Tiffany was the biggest of the big. Founded downtown on Broadway and Warren Street, near City Hall, in 1837 by two

Connecticut prep school friends, Charles Tiffany and John Young, the store made its initial mark by selling Chinese and Japanese novelties the owners acquired from sailors at the nearby South Street docks. The partners did so well in a booming New York economy that they took on a third partner to fund sending the unmarried Young (Tiffany had married Young's sister) to Europe and thus be able to boast that they were the only store in Manhattan with its own representative abroad. Young's first success was a line of very authentic-looking fake diamonds called Palais Royale, which did so well that the partners decided to sell *real* diamonds. Soon, imported watches, clocks, and other baubles were added to the booming silverware department, not to mention hair and skin products, toiletries, and a large stock of horse and dog whips. In short, Tiffany's was a fancy general store, with no real focus.

The focus came in 1848, when Young arrived in Paris in the midst of a revolution against Louis Philippe, one that drove down the price of diamonds among the nervous nobility by over 50 percent. Somehow, in all the tumult and without any really adequate papers of provenance, Young was able to buy Tiffany's first crown jewels, plus lots of others from the *nouveau pauvre* aristocracy. The French government was too much in disarray to claim that Tiffany had unlawfully come into the royal treasure. The next year, 1849, was a very good year for the firm, for that was the year of the gold rush, when countless new fortunes were created, fortunes that needed to be burnished by owning the jewels of Marie Antoinette.

Tiffany founded a Paris branch to supply the spiraling demand. Charles Tiffany turned out to be a master of public relations, arrogating all the credit for the French coup to himself, as well as upstaging national events, like making a silver horse and carriage as the most elaborate wedding gift for the nuptials of the world's most famous romantic midgets, P. T. Barnum's Tom Thumb and Lavinia Warren, and giving silver swords to the victorious generals of the Union Army after the Civil War. Eventually, Tiffany bought out his two partners and made the store's name solely his own.

The ostentatious fortunes amassed by the robber barons after the Civil War, the creation of the new-money New York high society and "the 400" who could fit into Mrs. Astor's ballroom, played directly into Charles Tiffany's sticky fingers. These men, and their jewel-obsessed wives, were the least price-sensitive elite the world had ever seen, and Tiffany's was where they spent their mad money. It was a history lesson not at all lost on my father, for history was now repeating itself. The raging bull stock market of the Roaring Twenties was creating more millionaires than ever, and even more need for ostentation and luxury than the Gilded Age itself. Diamond Jim Bradys were being churned out like Model Ts. My father didn't just want a piece of the action; Harry darling that he was, he wanted *all* the action. One day he would challenge Tiffany, that mighty fortress that had no use for him. Just give Harry darling a chance. Just give him time.

The other lesson my father learned from Tiffany was the art of making a store more than a store. Tiffany was itself something of a museum, its most famous centerpiece exhibit being the Tiffany Diamond, the largest and most perfect canary diamond ever mined. The Tiffany, as it became known, was discovered at the Kimberley Mine in South Africa in 1877. Its original weight was 287 carats. When cut, it weighed 124 carats. Charles Tiffany paid $18,000 for it.

By the twenties it was worth millions, but it was never, ever for sale. That was the Tiffany style, and that unbuyable stone was worth millions more in free publicity.

And yet here was Harry darling, a poor guy who not long before was totally wiped out, fully expecting to eat at Tiffany's high table of commerce. Was it hubris of the most insane, suicidal sort? It seemed like it, yet he miraculously pulled it off. Harry darling became Ozymandias, the King of Diamonds. He saw Tiffany as hidebound, a dinosaur that he could easily outmaneuver. No Jews? He got WASPs to front for him. Then there was Tiffany's snobby policy against buying secondhand diamonds, which was exactly what my father's estate business was all about. No problem. He had the old jewels cut so brilliantly that his fronts, Proudfoot and Swigert, were able to sell them as new ones, and old fogy Tiffany couldn't tell the difference and became one of his prime customers, without it even knowing with whom it was dealing.

His first bold step toward the throne was his maiden sally into the world-class blue chip estate business. In 1925 the most buzzed-about estate of the year was that of Rebecca Darlington Stoddard, of New Haven, Connecticut. The late Mrs. Stoddard was from old and big Pittsburgh iron and steel money. Her husband, Major Louis Stoddard, a major clubman, was president of the United States Polo Association and captain of the 1914 team that had beaten England for the world championship. My father somehow decided this estate had to be his, even though every other diamond dealer in the country wanted it as well. He went to Udo Fleischmann at New Netherland Bank, and told him his grand scheme, and Fleischmann decided to aid and abet him. Fleischmann gave my father a flattering letter of introduction, and my father took the New Haven Railroad north to Yale country and the Stoddard estate, Ten Acres.

The bank letter got little Harry through the big door to appraise the estate, after which he somehow got an audience with the major himself and got his attention by offering him a cool million for the lot. Before the major could say a word and possibly dismiss him, my father raised his bid by $200,000, as long as the major would give him six months to conclude the transaction. The major, for all his class, did not regard such lucre as filthy and readily agreed, teaching my father another life lesson that no matter how rich and grand people might seem, there was no such thing as enough when it came to money. In a Herculean six-month effort to place the jewels with an assortment of connoisseurs, collectors, and dealers, my father sold the entire lot, and for a total of $1.2 million, $50,000 more than he had promised the major. Harry Winston had just reaped a profit of $125,000. In 1925, my father was suddenly and wildly rich beyond anyone's dreams, except his own.

But Harry Winston was hardly one to rest on his new laurels. He knew that to get into the big leagues, he would have to constantly top himself. He began writing letters to the top dogs of the *Social Register* looking for estates to buy. He contacted the trusts and estates departments of all the great law firms, like Cravath, Sullivan & Cromwell, White & Case, and Lord, Day & Lord, offering his services. He pitched himself to Morgan, Chase, and all the major banks.

Then, in 1926, the sweetest of all possible opportunities came his way. The "golden op" had arisen with the 1924 death of one of the great California dowagers who had forged his dreams of wealth and fame, Arabella Huntington. By 1926 her philanthropist son and heir, Archer, was thinking of putting his mother's immense jewelry collection on the market. The pièce de résistance was a five-foot necklace of 160 perfect pearls that had cost Arabella $1 million to have made. It was ironic that she had gone blind by the time it was ready for her.

Of course, my father had to have it, along with the rest of the estate. It was his way of settling his score with California and the Wild West. Getting Huntington would also put Harry squarely and definitively in the Tiffany league. It wasn't easy. For one, Archer Huntington had been adopted, and his actual father was a riverboat gambler, and Archer had inherited all of his birth father's card-playing skills. At six feet four, he towered several heads above Harry Winston. He must have assumed the little jeweler who had come to appraise the glittering treasures was easy to intimidate, sitting him in a low chair with a high back in his bank's vault while Archer stalked around him. "Please sit down," my father said to the giant. "It's difficult enough to see you." Then, establishing his authority, he announced that he had to leave at ten to noon, sharp, so there was no time to dawdle.

In any event, Archer Huntington saw my father meant business. Still, the gambler emerged when my father asked if he could take a diamond bracelet upstairs into the sunlight for a clearer examination. Sure, but it will add $10,000 to the price, if you do, Huntington goaded him. My father called the big man's bluff and went upstairs. He determined that the bracelet was worth far more than Huntington was asking, even with the inspection premium. In the end, my father offered over $1.5 million for the whole lot, and Archer said yes.

Now all my father had to do was pay for it all. And this time, Udo Fleischmann, his man at New Netherland, was away in Europe. Harry had to appear before the stern board of directors, who took one look at this apple-cheeked Tom Thumb and assumed he was a messenger boy for the titan Winston. "Go back and tell your boss that unless he appears before us in person, there can be no conclusion to this transaction." "But I *am* the boss," he told the disbelieving board. Somehow he convinced them that he was, in fact, *the* Harry Winston, and they gave him the money.

Accordingly, my father found himself a front man, a tall man, a man of the West, a "judge" of the wild frontier, a man trustees and lawyers and tycoons would sit up and listen to. It didn't matter that this John Wayne–like frontiersman, Judge Garbey, as he was known, was actually a Jewish son of Russian immigrants, just like my father, and was originally named Harry Garbarsky. He had grown up in Colorado and had worked as an itinerant jewelry peddler in the West before coming to New York in 1918 and moving into the Hotel Longacre, with his seventy-nine-year-old widowed mother, not far from my father's office on Fifth Avenue. Garbey stayed in the jewel trade, and the trade being a small world, somehow met my father, who took to him, especially as a fellow "westerner." Judge Garbey was twenty years older than my father, making him fiftyish, which gave him seniority. More important, he was a foot taller than my father, which gave him size. And he had developed a Western mystique, especially with the "judge" business that evoked Wyatt Earp and Bat Masterson and drew New Yorkers to him.

The judge maintained my father's ties to the West. It was he who had first alerted my father to the Lucky Baldwin estate.

E. J. Baldwin was one of California's leading, and most colorful, pioneers. His most famous quote, regarding California real estate, was "Hell, we're *giving* away the land. What we're *selling* is the climate."

Baldwin was constantly hit by paternity suits, often from underage mothers. He won some, lost some, and stayed rich enough to breed three Kentucky Derby winners and to amass another amazing West Coast jewel collection, including the renowned Lucky Baldwin twenty-five-carat pigeon-blood ruby. My father had seen the ruby and some of the other Baldwin gems as a boy in Los Angeles, when they were being cleaned by a friend of his father. He remembered them so vividly he could describe to me, late in life, every facet. Jewels brought out the artist in my father. Lucky Baldwin himself died in 1909, but Garbey had had his eyes on the estate for years and trained my father's eyes on it as well. It finally came on the market when Baldwin's playgirl daughter Clara died in 1929. Together, the big judge in front and the little king behind, they got it.

Rich, for sure, and en route to being famous, my father was able, gradually, to put aside his feelings of inadequacy about his lack of height, education, and sophistication and begin to enjoy the fabulous party that was the 1920s. He had alternated between SRO hotels and bunking with his brother Stanley during Stanley's interregnum bachelorhood. Stanley had married and divorced, remarried and redivorced in rapid succession, and had a son Bobby, whom my father adored and often babysat while Stanley, a tallish, sleek, dapper European-style ladies' man, would go out on the town in search of more conquests. Stanley's amorous triumphs surely added to Harry's insecurities. It was thus a good thing for my father that the money rolled in and he moved out. Where he moved was the pinnacle of Manhattan bachelorhood, the Sherry-Netherland, then a residential hotel and apartment skyscraper in the French chateau style right on the prime corner of 59th and Fifth overlooking the Plaza and Central Park. This is when the "new" Harry Winston hired as his own personal valet and chef a crack manservant named Ishi, who may well have been the same Ishi he knew from his California days.

What my father did with women is something he never discussed, certainly not in front of my mother. Certainly as a young rich bachelor in the Sherry-Netherland who possessed, if not dominated, the commodity that may have been considered the ultimate aphrodisiac, I would have thought that Harry Winston could have been as big a playboy as Lucky Baldwin. Yet I know, from his elevator shoes to his using Judge Garbey as his front, that he was obsessed about his size, and plagued by it, unlike the endless little Napoleon playboys of the age, such as the microscopic Broadway showman Billy Rose, who never dated a woman less than a foot taller than he. Ziegfeld had made his fame and fortune playing on such height disparities, hiring only Amazonian chorus girls who stoked the fantasies of his "little big man" clientele.

My father occasionally mentioned going to the Follies. I'm sure he enjoyed many a dawn at Ziegfeld's Follies spinoff, the Midnight Frolic, a supernightclub famous for its glass walkway where the giant chorines would dance and strut directly over the customers' heads. The most famous production number here had the chorus girls, clad only in a few colored balloons, parade among the audience, while the men would use their Havana cigars to pop the balloons. To prevent the swells from getting sore hands from all the clapping, Ziegfeld invented little wooden hammers for the men to bang out their appreciation. There was also a five-dollar cover charge, which was unprecedented for its time.

My father also went to the most famous of all the speakeasies, Texas Guinan's, as all the rich and famous of the era did. If the Ziegfeld extravaganzas were the Vegas of the time, Guinan's was the Studio 54. There was no better place on earth for Harry Winston to find prospective clients, prospective estates. Mary Louise Cecilia Guinan, the star of the 1921 silent film *Code of the West*, the first movie cowgirl, was a regular. Scribes like Walter Winchell and Damon Runyon sat in corner booths, jotting down all the celebrity gossip. Irving Berlin loved the place, and George Gershwin would play the piano, just for fun. Perhaps my father first met Gershwin there. In any event, he seems to have developed a serious crush on Gershwin's gamine sister, Frankie. He spoke about her all his life.

For all his exposure to chorus girls and gold diggers, my father never could see himself as a Valentino. He was a tiny Jewish boy not that far removed from the ghetto, and his business dealings and social encounters with the Major Stoddards and Archer Huntingtons of the world must have been highly disorienting. Despite his new wealth and valet at the Sherry, he would trek uptown to Riverside Drive every Friday night to spend time with his father, Jacob, and Aunt Dora and nephew Bobby, the three of whom he would take to dinner at Schrafft's, Dora's favorite restaurant. After dinner, Dora would serve Jacob some hot water, which hopefully would soothe his racking, and worsening, asthmatic gasps and ease him into sleep. My father then would bid his family goodnight and walk from 86th and Riverside down Broadway to Central Park South and across to the Sherry.

A girl like Frankie Gershwin would have made an ideal wife for my father, who at thirty-one was more than old enough in 1926, now that he had "arrived," to think about starting a family. Frankie was the perfect bridge between past and present, tradition and abandon. Even before he hit the Stoddard and Huntington mother lodes, Harry Winston had been looking for love, surely to please his father, if not himself. He had tried the traditional Jewish route, the *Shidduch*, or matchmaker, like Dolly Levi in *Hello, Dolly!* But those kind of fix-ups were terribly short on romance. My aunt Lillian, Stanley's second wife and a long-stemmed showgirl herself, had regaled me with tales of the brothers' elegantly wild parties at the Sherry, when Stanley was between marriages. Stanley was Harry's sexual Judge Garbey, a showgirl wrangler who invited the biggest and boldest Ziegfeld girls to the Ishi-catered festivities. There were huge bouquets of flowers and vintage wines and champagnes bootlegged from France. There were no college girls, Lillian noted, in these bacchanals. Those proper Smith and Wellesley types were way beyond the Winston reach; they had usually been betrothed to their brothers' roommates at Yale or Princeton by the time they graduated. Only "college men," as my father so respectfully referred to them, got the flapper coeds. A man, even a rich man, like Harry Winston, would have to settle for gold diggers.

And yet he couldn't do that. For him, beauty was not its own reward. Small wonder then that he was smitten by Frances Gershwin.

Frances was born in New York in 1906, ten years after her oldest brother Ira, eight after George. Their father, Morris, was an entrepreneur who owned Turkish baths, restaurants, and a billiard parlor, many of which eventually failed. Still, the family lived far more comfortably than the Jacob Weinsteins and had a maid, though they too lived on the Upper West Side. The matriarch, Rose, was obsessed with diamonds, and whenever Morris's ventures turned a profit, she would invest it in jewelry. The financial panics of 1893 and 1907 had destroyed her confidence in banks, not to mention the stock market. When times were hard, she hocked the jewels to support the family. So it makes sense that Mother Gershwin would find Harry Winston an eminently eligible suitor for her only daughter, who instead married the man who would become a billionaire by inventing Kodachrome. That, it turned out, was the best thing that ever happened to Harry Winston. And to me.

CHAPTER FOUR

The Player

With the stock market crash and the shocking end to the nonstop party that was the Roaring Twenties, 1929 goes down as one of the very worst years in American history, up there with those war-starting years of 1861, 1941, and 2001. For my father, 1929 was even more of an annus horribilis, for it was also the year he lost his father. Yet he never looked back to the end of the 1920s with anger or remorse. Instead, he regarded it as something of a coming of age for himself, an adult bar mitzvah; he was thirty-three in 1929, though still looking like a kid and still needing Judge Garbey to front for him. In the decade ahead, Harry Winston would truly grow up, getting even more serious about his business and more serious about his life. And it took his own twin towers of the death of his father and the death of Wall Street to turn him in the right direction.

In September 1929, just a couple of months after his father's death and just a month before the crash and panic, Harry Winston, in classic Roaring Twenties extravagance, sailed for Europe on the *Leviathan*. The huge and luxurious ship, the art deco pride of the American merchant fleet, was something of the *Titanic* of its day. And there my father was, the king of the sea, on his first trip abroad. With him was his best friend, Al Greenspan, a self-made, or rather self-making, young textile mogul who, aside from his early success with the miracle fiber rayon, had something that my father deeply admired, prized, and probably coveted: a Columbia degree, which spelled academic exclusivity in New York just as Harvard did in Boston.

I'm sure my father enjoyed having such a brainy friend, whose Austrian family background of great books and Strauss waltzes and Sacher torte were light-years from the Weinstein hardscrabble legacy of progroms, fear, and rationed milk. It was Al Greenspan who suggested my father join him in Europe, to salve the trauma of Jacob's death. Al's task couldn't have been easy, given my father's "we never close" workaholism. But Al had a bit of catnip up his sleeve in the persona of a fellow tony child of Austria: my mother-to-be, whom Al knew was also going to be in Europe that September. Al knew my father fancied her but was very slow in declaring his interest. This trip was designed to have Cupid hit Harry's heart.

My father and mother had first met, Hitchcock style, as strangers on a train. He was going down to Atlantic City, which in the 1920s was an elegant seaside resort, a sort of American Deauville, with a world-famous boardwalk and luxury hotels with grandiose names like the Breakers, the Blenheim, the Traymore. But Harry wasn't going down to New Jersey to take the sun and sea breezes. There was always a method to his madness, and in this instance it was the major jewelry auctions that were held there periodically. My father was taking the Pennsylvania Railroad from Penn Station with his other good friend Henry Baker, the courtly son of Hyman Baker, a Manhattan real estate tycoon. Henry, like Al Greenspan, was a college man with a coveted Columbia degree. He wasn't a German Jew, as all non-Russian Jews were known, like Al, but his Petrograd-born father's great wealth gave Henry a certain easy charm that my driven father surely admired. On the train, Henry spotted a lovely but pale and wan young lady entering the parlor car with a distinguished older gentleman. "I know them," Henry said with a grin to Harry. "You've got to meet her," he continued, who apparently was something of a matchmaker, as well as a ladies' man himself. At first Harry shyly begged off.

But Henry, ever the Dolly Levi, could not bear to let the match remain unmade. "She's just your type," he insisted and dragged Harry up to the front of the car to "shake hands, that's all." Henry assumed that just one shake was all it would take. Perhaps my father was intimidated by his future father-in-law, who, given the tenor of the times, might have been the yound lady's suger daddy. Henry hadn't bothered to say.

As my father recounted the encounter to me time and again, the gentleman was intimidatingly dressed in a somber gray three-piece suit, embellished with a shimmering gray pearl stickpin. Whether father or philanderer, this was one man Harry didn't want to cross. The young lady in question was in her early twenties and wearing a then height-of-fashion cloche hat that cosseted her mane of chestnut brown hair. He noted that she wore a loose-fitting blouse and a pleated mid-length skirt. She didn't seem like a flapper who had danced the night away, but she did look as tired as one. Her head was propped against the open, gritty train window.

Recognizing Henry, the man stood up. He was a big man, nearly six feet tall. Harry must have been even more intimidated. He also proved to be a college man, as Harry found out when Henry introduced him as "*Doctor* Fleischman," who was with his daughter, Edna. I assume my father was relieved that he wasn't going to have to compete with this giant for Edna's attentions. However, she didn't seem in the mood for romance. Edna was green as a peridot, he told me in a jargon only he could use. The peridot was one of my father's least-favorite stones in the pantheon of gems. Edna had just had a tonsillectomy at a downtown Manhattan hospital, her father explained. The good doctor, and good father, was taking his baby down to Atlantic City to recuperate.

Somehow my mother-to-be, through her nausea and vertigo, gave my father-to-be a wan smile that transfixed him for life. He told me it was a warmth and energy that he never heretofore had seen. He never forgot her first words to him: "You must excuse me. I'm not myself right now." Such were the makings of true love. My father, who rarely discussed his feelings, described to me how smitten he was. He went back to his seat on the train, lost in thought. He said he began to daydream of great diamonds; even in his most romantic throes, he thought of diamonds, big stones, legendary stones like the Cullinan, the Hope, the Koh-i-Noor, and stones that had not yet been discovered, stones that *he*, Harry Winston, would acquire, stones that would make him famous.

Somehow, by meeting Edna, Harry Winston had an epiphany; it was one thing to be rich. He was already rich. But it was another to be famous, to be the King of Diamonds. But he was still basically a backroom wholesaler. He wanted to *be* Tiffany, Cartier, Black, Starr, not just *sell* to them. And he suddenly realized the way to do it was not to get bigger estates, but to get bigger diamonds, giant diamonds, the diamonds of kings, the diamonds that would make a king out of Harry Winston. In the last few years new diamond fields had been discovered in Southern Africa, in the earth, on the beaches, beaches that were literally paved with diamonds. Big diamonds made big news, and Harry Winston, on seeing Edna, somehow flashed on those big diamonds and also saw himself on the front pages, up in lights.

But in those fevered diamond daydreams Harry Winston now saw this young woman tinted green by anesthesia and began to reconsider the emptiness, loneliness, of his life as a single man, a very wealthy man. Through the array of diamonds he saw her face floating, reflecting, scintillating. With this frisson came an inspiration: this Edna one day might be *his* Edna. She would be his muse; big rocks would be his grail.

And then he woke up and went back to work. Harry was here to unload the jewels he had been unable to sell to the great diamond emporia on Fifth Avenue. The local outfits weren't exactly the dregs; Harry Winston didn't do dregs. Whatever, he would call on all of them.

Harry and Henry checked into the Traymore, which was the queen of the Boardwalk, while the Fleischmans went to the President, a cut below. Henry had told Harry that Dr. Fleischman was an academic who ran the Educational Alliance on East Broadway near Chinatown, a wonderful charity for immigrants, mostly Jewish, immigrants like Jacob Weinstein. Dr. Fleischman specialized in treating ill and disabled children. He achieved local renown by establishing first-floor classes for rheumatic-fever patients, whom all other schools forced to wheeze their way up the stairs. Recalling his father's own wheezing, Harry Winston was touched. Henry kept talking Edna up, stoking my father's interest. She had already been to Europe five times, Henry said. She was very sophisticated.

Dr. Fleischman, Henry Baker told my father, was actually born in London, which only added to his aura of worldliness. His father had been an international grain merchant. They were an old Vienna family, Henry stressed, which conjured up images of Freud. I recently discovered an old, tattered photograph of my mother and her father, seated together. The good doctor's hair is neatly combed and my mother, impeccably dressed, smiles at him serenely. They were, clearly, very close. I found this picture in my late father's belongings, and based on its condition, it must have been one that he looked at frequently.

All those trips to Europe were father and daughter. She was an only child. My father complained that when they were dating, Edna called the doctor at least three times over the course of an evening. He recalled once visiting Edna and the doctor after he had gone for a horseback ride in Central Park. When Edna brought out a tea tray, the doctor leaped up to take the tray from her delicate hands. He wouldn't let her do *anything*. My father boldly took charge and put the tray back in Edna's hands so she could finish serving. "She can handle it," he told the doctor, who never interfered that way again. Still, until her father, whom my father loved and admired and in fact referred to as "Dad," passed away in the early 1960s, Dr. Fleischman and my mother remained extremely close, often to the annoyance of my father, who found it all too much, if not unnatural.

When Edna's mother died in 1921, the party line was that she'd been hit by a car while shopping on Fifth Avenue. The truth, I would learn, was suicide, which obviously raises questions about my maternal grandfather, as does the fact that the vaunted medical school in Chicago, the Illinois Medical College, where he got his supposedly prestigious degree, had been closed down by the state as a mail-order diploma mill. Maybe that's why the doctor didn't practice medicine.

Still, "Winkie" as I called him, was brilliant, and with his wall of medical books, my grandfather will always be a doctor to me. What else was there?

Egged on by Henry, and fortified by a few drinks, Harry called the President Hotel to make a date for that evening. The doctor shot him down. Edna was too tired. She had already gone to bed. But my father never stopped at no and won the doctor's consent for the three of them to spend the next evening together.

The next night was Saturday, the big night in Atlantic City, when *le tout* East Coast dressed up in black tie for the auctions. The late Diamond Jim Brady had helped put the event on the map, and the new generation of social high rollers turned out in force. Harry Winston loved seeing society's Pavlovian response to diamonds, especially *his* diamonds. He knew he was in the right business at the right time. Before fetching the Fleischmans, he and Henry went sea-bathing. Then at five, leaving Henry to be with his own hot date for the evening, Harry went to his rendezvous with destiny. He told me how he picked up Edna and the doctor in a bicycle rickshaw, in which the three of them jammed into the wicker sedan chair and rode up and down the miles-long Boardwalk, past the Steel Pier with its legendary diving horses, and the newer Million Dollar Pier with its endless electric circus of arcades.

What did they talk about? Diamonds, of course. Harry regaled them with stories of his arcane big business. Although the doctor held his counsel, he was probably wondering who this tiny, uneducated, boastful *businessman* was who fancied his beloved daughter. He may have stayed silent, but Edna asked questions, lots of questions. If anyone was the opposite of her father, it was Harry Winston. And it seemed as if opposites did, indeed, attract. Harry stopped the rickshaw to buy Edna some saltwater taffy, then took the Fleischmans for a lavish dinner at the Knife and Fork Inn, which was the Maxim's of Atlantic City.

During dinner, fortified by smuggled champagne, Harry continued to hold forth about the Huntingtons and the Baldwins and the Main Liners and the other society types who were in his thrall. Edna kept asking questions, the ample bodice of her formal gown rising and falling as she drank in what turned out to be an intoxicating ether of New Jersey's ocean breezes and my father's hot air. Harry was transfixed by Edna's dark complexion, her full lips, her patrician, aquiline nose, her luminous, mysterious smile. Plus she was *Jewish.* Jacob Weinstein would surely approve.

After dinner, they went to Harold Brandt's auction house. Brandt's trademark line was "I do things I can't even tell my mother," but the truth behind the show was that he was involved in several merchandise kiting schemes for which he did time. Brandt was the P. T. Barnum of the diamond trade, and to him every buyer was a sucker, just like the patrons at Texas Guinan's. After each auction, Brandt would approach certain big buyers with the promise that, if they were patient, he could double their money on the jewels they had purchased. So they would pay him for the jewels and leave them with him, leading to all sorts of scams that did not enhance the integrity profile of my father's trade.

What mattered most this night was Edna's curiosity about the proceedings, a genuine aesthetic feeling for the beauty of diamonds. Most men would have proposed on the spot. But not Harry Winston. The morning after this enchanted evening, Harry bid his adieus. "Got to go. Got to make a living," as he would say to our family a million times. Edna and her father stayed on another week. Harry did not send flowers.

Edna's fantasies toward Harry Winston, such as they were, became an endless exercise in delayed gratification. He would take Edna out to Delmonico's and then for ice cream at Rumpelmayer's, and then, rather than taking her back to his suite at the Sherry-Netherland, he'd take her to his office to check on the diamonds he was soaking in acid. Perhaps my mother seemed so pure, so innocent, so perfect, that my father was putting her on a pedestal, saving her for *something*, a wedding day in another galaxy perhaps.

My mother was certainly hooked on diamonds and on the king-to-be. Mother had gone to college briefly and didn't have a job, other than attending to her father, as my Aunt Dora had attended to hers. But she lived in her father's world of books and music and art and had enough culture for any man, certainly my busy, busy father. She would often drop by the Winston office during the day just to see the new treasures my father had acquired in his estate dealings. She was genuinely interested, and that, to my father, was the real turn-on. But he was way too distracted, blinded by the light of the stones, to commit to anything vaguely serious.

"Dismiss it from your mind," was one of my father's mantras. Moving on was something my father always did. He could make the past, the unpleasant past, evaporate like the morning dew. He never visited the family burial plot except to inter his brother and sister. Underlaying all this selective amnesia was Harry Winston's total denial of death, even when it struck his own family. So it was with the death of his father.

Perhaps Edna had given Harry emotional support during Jacob's protracted illness, just when they were getting to know one another. He certainly shared the news of Jacob's death in one of his rare, terse missives, which he sent to Edna while she was summering in Europe with her father. But emotions, at least those depths of feeling not connected to diamonds, were rare to my father. Everything was connected to diamonds, including his reveries regarding Edna. So, when Al Greenspan persuaded Harry to go abroad with him in 1929, Edna's presence there may have been one lure, but the prospect of seeing diamonds in one of their natural habitats, the royal precincts of the Old World, were surely another.

My father was in Europe for two main reasons, to move past his grief, and to explore the Old World. The European sophisticates really *understood* jewels the way no one in America did, no one except Harry Winston. He visited the museums and palaces that contained the treasures he dreamed of one day owning and selling.

My father went by himself, or actually with Al Greenspan, to the glamorous Norman resort of Deauville at the height of its glamorous racing season, its last before the Crash. The September my father arrived, the *New York Times* reported sightings of the likes of Gloria Swanson; the Duc de Nemours; the banking Schiffs of Manhattan; the Main Line Wideners of Philadelphia, who gave Harvard its main library; plus several maharajas and maharanees, all dripping in jewels. Unintimidated, Harry, who may have been forced to show his passport to prove he was old enough to enter the casino, loved to boast to me how he stepped right up to the baccarat table and proceeded to win 2023's equivalent of almost $870,000, $50,000 in French francs. It may have been beginner's luck, but what luck it was, and it hooked my father on France and its casino-resorts of Deauville and Cannes, as well as Monte Carlo, for the rest of his life. When my father hit the jackpot and counted the money, he fainted dead away.

And then there was London. It wasn't all Westminster Abbey, the Tower, Big Ben. First stop for Harry Winston had to be a visit to the heart of the world rough (i.e., uncut) diamond trade at Hatton Gardens, not far from the city of London, where all the gentlemen wore striped suits and bowlers and carried furled umbrellas. Even though the leafy two-block warren of jewelry stores that comprised Hatton Gardens was in the shadow of St. Paul's Cathedral, the gentlemen there would never be mistaken for the Anglican elite of the city's ruling banks and solicitors. No, Hatton Gardens was London's answer to Maiden Lane, but far more traditional, overrun with orthodox Jews in their yarmulkes and dark frock coats. For centuries Jews had dominated the diamond trade, and many of the Jews my father saw in London were visiting from the diamond cutting centers of Antwerp and Amsterdam.

The dealers and cutters of Hatton Gardens were an artifact of the Jacob Weinstein past. Many were rich enough, but to Harry Winston they were small time. What did interest Harry was around the corner at 17 Charterhouse Street, just across from the Smithfield Meat Market. At 17 Charterhouse was a heavily guarded sprawling Victorian structure whose wide verandas gave it a colonial, tropical feel that obviously was intended to evoke the balmy Transvaal rather than icy, foggy London. This was the home of De Beers's Diamond Trading Company, which held a monopoly over all the treasures of the mines of Africa. If it was a rough diamond, the Diamond Trading Company pretty much controlled it. It was the world's biggest monopoly, and its ruler was a man named Ernest Oppenheimer. Oppenheimer was the reigning King of Diamonds, and, while in London, he was of far greater interest to my father than England's King George V across town in Buckingham Place.

"Jews are diamonds," Ernest Oppenheimer was quoted as saying. My father, for all his disdain for religion, was still very proud about who and what he was, and he therefore took great inspiration in the fact that Oppenheimer was a Jew, and that still another Jew, Barney Barnato, was, in a previous generation, the chief contender to the diamond throne. These were good precedents for the ascent that Harry Winston was planning.

The modern jewelry business really dates back only to 1867, when huge numbers of diamonds were discovered in South Africa, and a massive rush began from all over the world, a rush that continued for decades and made the California gold rush of 1849 look sedate. Diamonds were first discovered in India around 800 BCE, and for centuries most diamonds came from there, most notably the diamond fields of Golconda, which made the ruling Nizams of Hyderabad, who controlled the fields, synonymous with magisterial wealth. Some of the most famous great stones, the stones that Harry Winston wanted to become synonymous with, like the Hope, the Koh-i-Noor, and the Great Mogul, were all from India and were the diamonds that became the vogue of the courts of Europe, starting in the Renaissance. The dukes and princes wanted to live like maharajas, and diamonds became the ultimate universal status symbol.

By 1725, even before the royalty of Europe began to be played out, the diamond fields of India were largely depleted. In that year Brazil became the new India, with diamonds discovered in the state of Minas Gerais ("General Mines"). By the mid-1850s, Brazil's output was dwindling, and that's when South Africa came up with the mother lode. De Beers, which became the shorthand for the South African diamond monopoly, was simply the name of a farmer on whose property one of the key diamond mines was dug. Other mines were Kimberley and the Premier Mine, renamed Cullinan, for the world's largest diamond, which was mounted in the royal scepter of the British crown jewels, to which my father made a pilgrimage on that first trip to London. It must have been a religious experience for him.

Speaking of religious experiences, the first king of modern diamonds, the man who fought it out with Barney Barnato, a onetime boxer (and music hall magician as well), for control of the treasures of South Africa, was the son of a clergyman. This was Cecil Rhodes, whose decades long grudge match with Barnato was a classic struggle of Jew versus Christian, outsider versus establishment, underdog versus top dog. It was a battle that my father refought countless times, especially when he became big enough to actually challenge De Beers. He identified with Barney Barnato, much in the way he identified with that other tough magician Harry Houdini. They were all incredibly gutsy little guys who started with nothing and wanted everything. They were all masters of self-promotion, and they were all among the greatest risk-takers in history.

Cecil Rhodes, who won it all, hardly seemed like the risk-taking, swashbuckling type one associates with the greediest treasure hunt in history. The sickly son of an Anglican priest in Hertfordshire, Rhodes, who was born in 1853, was sent to South Africa to live with his older brother, who had a cotton farm there. With the discovery of diamonds, however, it became impossible to keep young Cecil down on the farm, not after he'd seen Kimberley and its vast open pit of fortune. But he didn't strike it rich, not at first. Instead he went home to England to attend Oxford, whose liberal education produced in Rhodes a rabid racist and imperialist of the then-current "white man's burden" school. He even felt America should be reconquered and recolonized. At Oxford, Rhodes, who would never marry, also developed a passion for bright, handsome young men, sound-mind-and-sound-body types for whom he would establish his famed Rhodes Scholarships to attend his alma mater.

Returning to South Africa, Rhodes began purchasing mining claims in the De Beers diamond mine. But what initially made him rich was importing from England the pumps to get the water out of the increasingly flooded digs. The more floods, the more money Rhodes made, the more claims he would buy up. The concept of monopoly was sweet music to him. But it wasn't just greed. Rhodes had a logic behind his grasp, the logic that order was necessary and that, without order, the nascent diamond business would collapse.

The miners, or, more accurately, their semi-enslaved native laborers, would dig into what was known as the "yellow ground." This was the top layer of the volcanic matrix, or lava "pipe," known as kimberlite (named after Kimberley) that contained the diamonds. The yellow ground was quickly exhausted. Beneath it lay a much harder, rocklike substrata known as the "blue ground," which yielded even more diamonds. As the prospectors dug down scores of feet into the blue ground, small footpaths were necessary to allow each miner access to his plot. This mining scheme would have worked fine if each miner extracted the precious rock at the same pace, creating, if you will, a level playing field. But some miners went deeper and faster than others. High walls of rock often loomed over neighboring tracts, and cave-ins were rampant. The more efficient operators were penalized, sometimes at the cost of their lives, for digging walls too high in relation to their rivals.

What Cecil Rhodes did was buy up the claims from the caved mining pits. The De Beers mine would eventually be worked as a single mine with one owner. Then a unified development scheme, with the most modern engineering methods, would proceed. Likewise, Rhodes noted, that if too many diamonds were discovered, an unregulated system would see desperate miners all dumping their gems on the market at once and thereby lowering prices. But if Rhodes controlled the source, he could also control the flow, and, most important, the price of the goods.

It was a brilliant idea, but not necessarily an original one. Not far away, at the Kimberley mine, the richer of the two great pipes on the De Beers farmland, Barney Barnato was attempting to create his own monopoly. Born Barnett Isaacs in London's Cheapside Jewish ghetto in 1852, a year before Rhodes, but on the same day, Barnato changed his name (as would Houdini and Winston) when he joined his brother Harry in a magic-comedy act in London vaudeville. Barney's father Isaac Isaacs (he had an uncle named Joel Joel) was a peddler on Petticoat Lane, and Barney, having washed out in vaudeville, washed up in South Africa for the diamond rush to peddle fake Havana cigars to the newly rich prospectors always eager to light up a stogie to celebrate their finds. Barnato frequently ran into Rhodes at the pubs (Rhodes was a lush), although never at the bordellos, which Barnato loved and which were an indispensable aspect of the boom times.

Eventually Barnato sold enough cigars for his own grub-stake, which he expanded by buying up collapsing claims. By the mid-1880s he was the biggest claimsman at Kimberley. All he needed to control the pit was a block of claims owned by a French company to make Kimberley his. But Rhodes, too, wanted Kimberley; he wanted it all, and he despised Barnato, who was anything but Rhodes Scholar material, not to mention a Jew. A vicious multiyear bidding war ensued, during which Rhodes ironically got the multimillion-dollar backing of other hated Jews, the Rothschilds, to acquire the French claims. Rhodes won.

Eventually Rhodes bought Barnato out; his check to him for his assets in the Kimberley mine of £5.5 million was the largest check ever written at the time. Rhodes merged the two great mines into De Beers Consolidated Mines, Ltd., and went on to take over much of Southern Africa. Barnato made another fortune in gold, but it was never enough. He wanted to be King of Diamonds, and he never recovered from his failure. In 1897 on a trip back to London he committed suicide by jumping overboard. Rhodes himself died in 1902 from a heart attack brought on by a spurious lawsuit brought by an ambitious

Polish princess claiming that he had promised to marry her. Anyone who knew Rhodes knew this forerunner of a sexual harassment action was a shakedown, but the shame of it, and the risk of exposing his true inclinations, were too much for him.

Just as Barney Barnato sold cigars to get to diamonds, the father of the next King of Diamonds was a cigar merchant, and a Jew as well. Ernest Oppenheimer was from a large family in a small town near Frankfurt. When Ernest was born in 1880, Fritz Hirschhorn, a cousin of his, had already left Germany for the South African diamond rush and had gotten rich. Hirschhorn set up two of Ernest's older brothers in still another relative's diamond firm, Dunkelsbuhler, and at sixteen Ernest was sent to the firm's London office to work as a diamond sorter. Ernest, like my father, was more impressed by the elegant gents in the city than by the unpolished diamond men of Hatton Gardens. His role model was Rothschild, not Barnato, and Ernest became a naturalized British citizen.

Like my father, Ernest was tiny, barely five feet tall, and like my father, he had enormous ambition. When Ernest was twenty-two in 1902, Dunkelsbuhler sent him down to Barnato-land to run the firm's Kimberley office. He lived, like a proper English gent, in the mansion of cousin Hirschhorn, who would soon become a director of De Beers and a manager of "the syndicate," a group of major diamond buyers, including Dunkelsbuhler, which bought the entire De Beers output and then sold it in smaller lots to the diamond cutters of Amsterdam and Antwerp, who in turn eventually sold the stones to Tiffany, Cartier, and other retail outlets.

With all his excellent family ties, Ernest was considered an eligible catch, and accordingly in 1906 found an equally eligible Jewish heiress to wed, May Pollak, the daughter of the president of the London Stock Exchange. Ernest brought his bride back to the Cape, where he immersed himself in politics. In 1912 he became mayor of Kimberley. Ernest was a pillar of society, until World War I broke out, when he was branded in this English colony with two irons, one as a German, two as a Jew. Mobs stormed Kimberley torching homes and stores and attacking people. The Oppenheimer home was a prime target. The police protected Ernest long enough for him to organize an escape to London, via Capetown. But the mob caught him before he could get away. They stoned him, cutting up his face. His life was saved only by his taking refuge in a convent, where the nuns shamed the mob into submission. Ernest got himself and his family to England, vowing never again to see the Cape and raising his two sons as Anglicans.

Never say never. After the war, the now totally Anglicized Oppenheimer, who would be knighted by the king in 1921, could not resist the lure of the power he would have in South Africa. He came back to run a J. P. Morgan–financed gold mining concern that was named Anglo American Corporation South Africa. But for all the gold on earth, Oppenheimer couldn't resist the lure of diamonds. In the postwar realignment, South Africa was awarded the former German colony of South West Africa, today called Namibia, which was rich in the alluvial diamond fields controlled by nine different German companies. The deserted wide sand beaches of this territory were magically carpeted with diamonds, no digging necessary. It was a fortune hunter's Garden of Eden. Oppenheimer's new Anglo American devoured the German diamond firms, which expected to be nationalized and felt lucky for what little they got. Oppenheimer decorated his new Johannesburg offices with regal portraits of himself and always referred to himself with the royal "we."

Oppenheimer's idol was Napoleon, but it might as well have been Cecil Rhodes, whose monopolistic imperative Sir Ernest inherited and expanded. The German alluvial fields in southwest Africa, now Namibia, had been discovered in 1908. Diamonds were also found in the Congo in 1913, in Portuguese Angola in 1916, in Lichtenberg and in Namaqualand, South Africa, in 1927. The point here was that serious diamonds were being unearthed, not just in South Africa and not just under the control of the Rhodes-established syndicate. Even before the Depression began, diamonds didn't seem so rare anymore, and prices had begun to tumble. To prop up the market and prevent a deluge of diamonds, Sir Ernest began taking control of all the mines in Africa.

Backed by Solly Joel, the Barnato nephew who controlled the huge Barnato stake in De Beers, Sir Ernest would become chairman of De Beers in 1929, the year my father first visited London. Sir Ernest was already a legend, and he would become even more of one in the months and years ahead when the Depression nearly destroyed the world diamond market. It would be fifteen years, before the Depression passed and World War II was over, until the diamond business became a colossus again. Although Dad didn't try to see Ernest Oppenheimer on his first trip to London, he surely surveyed his domain, walking up and down Sir Ernest's "royal mile" on Charterhouse Street.

Not long after my father returned to New York from his European idyll, Wall Street laid its famous egg. Despite the images of brokers hurling themselves out of skyscrapers and endless bread lines snaking past Delmonico's, the October

Crash and the attendant Depression had little effect on his growing business. It was the small investors who bore the brunt of the damage and the working classes who were put out of work. But the Big Money was as big as it ever was, and just as in those Fred Astaire–Ginger Rogers musicals, everyone in Harry Winston's world seemed to live in art deco apartments, fly down to Rio, sail to Europe on the *Normandie*, dance the Continental, and bathe in diamonds. For the super-rich, like Barbara Hutton and Doris Duke, the two leading heiresses of the period, the thirties were nothing but the late twenties.

Typical of the people my father dealt with in the early thirties was Jesse Lauriston Livermore, one of the greatest wizards of Wall Street. Known as the "Boy Plunger," Livermore was famous for having the genius to sell short before the Crash and emerge from 1929 with a $100 million fortune. Much of this he seemed to have spent on diamonds bought from my father for his remarkable stable of gold-digger mistresses. Although Harry Winston still wasn't yet in retail, he did take care of a very few private clients, like Livermore, who bought nearly as much as many grand jewelry stores. Like my father, Livermore maintained a suite in the Sherry-Netherland, a great place for making connections.

The Boy Plunger began his stock-trading career at fifteen, having run away from his father's Massachusetts farm with his mother's blessing. His mother was prescient, for Livermore, immortalized in the thirties bestseller *Reminiscences of a Stock Operator*, became the most legendary short seller in history. Aside from his many mistresses and extravagant nights in brothels, where he would buy jewels for all the hostesses, Jesse had one wife for fourteen years, a former Ziegfeld girl.

In 1932 they divorced, and the next year Jesse married another beauty, whose main distinction was that all four of her previous husbands had committed suicide. In 1940 Jesse made it five, shooting himself in the head in the Sherry cloakroom.

Another enduring Wall Street legend and Harry Winston devotee was "Colonel" Ned Green, another sex-and-diamond addict, who was the multimillionaire son of Hetty Green, the "Witch of Wall Street." Hetty was the Aunt Scrooge of American high finance, by far the richest woman in America in the Gilded Age, after the Civil War. The heiress to a Quaker whaling fortune in New Bedford, Massachusetts, Hetty made her first personal millions by investing her inheritance in Civil War bonds, then went on to one huge score after another on Wall Street, where it was said she ate only oatmeal she heated on an office radiator. Hetty wasn't only tight with herself. When son Ned broke his leg as a boy, she didn't want to spend money on doctors or hospitals and tried to minister to him at home. Ned got gangrene and lost the leg. He had to wear a cork prosthesis all his life, which may have explained his self-loathing and reliance on legions of prostitutes.

When Hetty died in 1916, peg leg Ned became one of the most eligible men on the planet. One of the extravagant gifts that made him famous as a high roller was a Harry Winston–created diamond-studded chastity belt Ned bought for his most unfaithful mistress. Working through Ned Green's famed retail jeweler Harry Fischer in the St. Regis Hotel, my father also fabricated Ned's collection of diamond-studded chamber pots.

Surrounded by such decadent consumers as Livermore and Green with their retinues of diamond-dripping showgirls, my father must have viewed Edna, who devotedly waited. . . and waited . . . and waited . . . as a breath of the freshest, purest air. Here is a letter I found from her to him, which gives a sense of her patience and devotion: "Harry, dearest, I understand your hesitation. You are busy with your work and career. For me there is no other. I wait with warm anticipation for when next we meet."

What, I wonder, was my father waiting for? Probably for the Hope Diamond. Here is one of the rare letters he wrote to my mother, or to anyone for that matter: "Dear Edna, The sun is setting and I am enjoying a drink on my terrace. I haven't had a date in four months." That my father would write my mother such a note from the Sherry-Netherland rather than simply pick up the phone indicates a certain formality and distance in the relationship, which had continued for years at this point. It also indicates he hadn't seen her for months. Yet she was obviously smitten with him, and he clearly didn't want to let her go.

My father began spending his winters at Palm Beach, staying at the posh Sand and Sea Club, attending to his wealthy society clientele, preparing for the day when he would realize his dream of a private retail business with his name on the door. In his free time in New York he loved horseback riding on the bridle paths of Central Park. In the summer the unlikely sportsman rented a cabin on Loon Lake in the Adirondacks, where he loved to swim. As recounted to me by my cousin Bobby, Stanley's son whom my father doted on and often brought with him for the summer, Loon Lake was the scene of numerous aquatic courtships.

Both Harry and Edna were back in Europe in the fall of 1932, but it isn't clear if or where they had a chance to rendezvous, as they had on my father's first trip. That excursion may have been largely sightseeing and escaping the pall of Jacob's death. This time my father was there to do business. He had sailed on the brand-new *Europa*, the pride of German superliners and a symbol of how the Fatherland had risen since its defeat in World War I. Harry was attracted to the *Europa*'s Olympic-size saltwater pool as well as to the glamorous black-tie midnight sailings from New York, with a society orchestra at the pier serenading the voyagers.

It was quite a splash and altogether appropriate for my father, who himself had been splashed all over the front pages for his acquisition of the Lucky Baldwin estate, which included a ruby once owned by the king of Burma, which my father sold for over $1 million. This happened, of course, while the rest of the country was lucky to get a free apple on a food line. There was a great picture of my father walking up Fifth Avenue, carrying a ribbon-wrapped box containing the ruby, surrounded by three massive pistol-wielding policemen, en route to Black, Starr & Frost, which bought the treasure from him.

Harry Winston disembarked from the *Europa* in Southampton, en route to London for his first visit to the De Beers cartel, as a would-be equal, not a supplicant. All London seemed dying to meet him this time, and he was feted at a round of glamorous dinner parties. At 17 Charterhouse Street, Sir Ernest Oppenheimer had reorganized De Beers into a series of corporations within corporations that were meant to obscure the fact that it was a monopoly, pure and simple. There was the Diamond Corporation, the big umbrella, under which were the Anglo American Corporation, the Central Selling Organization, and the Diamond Trading Company, all of which demonstrated the Importance of Being Sir Ernest.

My father was received by Sir Ernest's younger brother Otto Oppenheimer, who ran the London operation. Sir Ernest was away in South Africa, with his hands full, though De Beers would never broadcast any sign of weakness.

The reality here was that the Depression was decimating the world diamond market, with prices plunging by over 50 percent from 1930 to 1932, despite Sir Ernest's closing all the diamond mines in South Africa and the beach mines in South West Africa. The Diamond Corporation's production fell from over two million carats in 1930 to fourteen thousand carats in 1933. As for the new mines that were discovered that Sir Ernest did not control, in Sierra Leone, the Congo, and Angola, the Oppenheimer cartel bought up their output so it wouldn't be dumped on the market. In fact, for all its outer grandeur, the Diamond Corporation spent so much and made so little in the early thirties (by the mid-thirties it had a twenty-year backlog in inventory) that it was secretly, perilously close to bankruptcy. Only the discovery of new military and industrial uses for diamonds would save the industry until the post–World War II boom reanimated the cartel. My father surely sensed this vulnerability, which fueled his own fantasies of becoming ruler of this fragile universe.

But first things first. My father had to get a "sight" from De Beers, hence his visit to Charterhouse. A "sight" was the allocation of diamonds by De Beers to its clients, which were basically rough (unpolished) diamond dealers. It was a shoebox full of gems, usually costing around $50,000 in Depression dollars, which added up greatly, given that hardly anyone was buying. Theoretically the sight holder could come to London every eight weeks or so. Until Harry Winston arrived at Charterhouse, the diamond people De Beers dealt with all were based in Hatton Gardens, Antwerp, Amsterdam, and Paris.

My father wanted to be the first American to get a sight. Not that it mattered if he actually came to look at the goods, because buyers had zero choice in the matter. They could take what De Beers, as the London cartel was simply known, offered to them, or leave it, and leave the business as well. That's what unequal bargaining power can do. Only on stones greater than fourteen carats was there any possibility of a dialogue, and then only via a De Beers–controlled broker from Hatton Gardens, who theoretically represented the sight holder but never would go against the house.

For this purpose my father met the Prins family, who were shareholders in the firm I. Hennig & Co., brokers for De Beers' Diamond Trading Company, which controlled the sight allocations. The Prins family were old friends with the Oppenheimer family, which in turn sat on the Hennig board. The Hennig firm's clients thus got an inside track on the best diamonds, for which Hennig would negotiate the deals and get a 1 percent commission on negotiations that were anything but arm's length. Even in its current straits, De Beers was considered to be God, with infinite wisdom and infinite fairness and, most important, the keys to diamond heaven. Nothing was concluded on Harry Winston's first call to Charterhouse, but the key connections were forged and the impression made by one little giant to another that HW was the man to see in New York.

The dark times for the rest of the world were all sunshine and flowers for Harry Winston. But then Edna Fleischman threw a monkey wrench into my father's best-laid plans not to make plans, at least where matrimony was concerned.

Soon after my father returned from his triumphant second tour of Europe, in the fall of 1932 he learned that Edna, who was turning thirty, had gotten engaged. She had set a huge wedding at the Waldorf Astoria for 150 guests for February 16, 1933. She was planning to honeymoon in England. Hatton Gardens was not on her itinerary.

The lucky man was a fellow named Ben Kaufman, a wool goods agent. Kaufman worked for the J. Stein Company, purveyors of English tweeds and worsted. Like Harry Winston, his trade drew him to England, which ruled the world of wool, just as it did the world of diamonds. Snapshots of Ben showed a rather short, athletic man seated on the bumper of a luxury motor car, in a highly proprietary posture. He seemed like Mr. Play It Safe, and he was offering Edna the ultimate safety of marriage. He had been courting her for months, if not years. Edna tried to use Ben to force Harry off the dime, but it hadn't worked. Edna, near thirty, was verging on spinsterhood and could no longer play the waiting game. She even wrote to Harry about her new plans, but he didn't change his, and so she accepted Ben's proposal.

My father went to Palm Beach, as usual, in December 1932, to spend a winter that promised to be a bittersweet one. He had just that year closed his Premier Diamond Company and segued into Harry Winston, which would become the twentieth century's most famous jewelry mark. He handed out his new business cards, HARRY WINSTON—JEWELRY, up and down Worth Avenue, at every charity gala. He worked the town, worked it hard.

My father was in Florida with his stalwarts Henry Baker and Al Greenspan. He would swim and play tennis in the mornings, do business in the afternoons, socialize at night, topping it off con brio with a round of gambling at Bradley's, Palm Beach's number one speakeasy casino. For all the distractions, Harry Winston was mooning like a wounded stag. He had gained the world, but he had lost Edna. After one too many bibulous nights, Al Greenspan had had enough. "I'm packing you off on the next train to New York," Al declared to the despondent Harry. "You're going up there to make the biggest deal of your life!"

CHAPTER FIVE

Romancing the Stones

I had no idea growing up what a cliffhanger, a romantic game of chess, my parents' courtship actually was. Egged on by his pals in Palm Beach, Harry forsook the balm and glitter of the tropics for the arctic bleakness of February 1933. Alighting from the Havana Special at Pennsylvania Station, he made for his suite at the Sherry, where he prepared himself for the sale of his life, the sale of himself. He called and called Edna's home, but she was not there. Finally, he found her. Where had she been, he pressed her nervously. Actually, right near his office, she told him, at the British Consulate to get her honeymoon visa to England. England, home of De Beers, the cradle of diamonds, was Harry Winston territory. How could Edna, *his* Edna, experience it any other way? I must see you, he insisted. She demurred, and demurred, and demurred. But eventually she gave in.

Harry arrived with a huge bouquet of roses. I'm surprised he didn't bring a ring of his own, his finest jewel, as his "closer," and maybe he did. I just don't know. At first nothing worked. I'm as good as married, Edna told him. They spoke for hours. I'm sure Harry told Edna of the wonderful life he had in store for her, the diamonds, the travel, the success, the kings and princes and maharajas to come. She would be getting in on the ground floor of one of the great success stories in American history and would be riding the plush and gilded elevator to the top of the tower. He needed her to build that tower. He had come a long way, from the lower East Side to the Sherry, all by himself, but he was grief-stricken at the thought of losing her.

Harry flattered, he cajoled, he seduced. He would be the business, the drive, the locomotive: she would be the culture, the love, the home. The home may have been the trump card. All my father's entreaties could do was to reduce my mother to bewildered tears. She reminded my father of her many years alone, alone with her father, waiting for Harry, waiting in vain. She spoke of the depths of her loneliness. And then she brought up what Ben Kaufman was going to give her that she doubted Harry, busy, powerful, absent Harry, could ever take the time for: a family. I know, my father sighed, and he crossed the Rubicon and promised my mother, yes, indeed, we will have a family.

I have no idea how my mother broke the horrible news to Ben Kaufman, but on the morning after my father's grandstand play for her, Harry and Edna were wed in a rabbi's chambers at a local temple. My father's best man was Henry Baker, who must have hightailed it up from Palm Beach in anticipation of Harry's long-shot success, while my mother's maid of honor was her friend Viola, who used to drive her to Harry's office and wait downstairs while my father showed my mother "his etchings." Dr. Fleischman was surely there. There must have been some truncated celebration, as I found in my mother's secret treasures the confectionary bride and groom from the wedding cake, along with my mother's desiccated bridal bouquet. She wore the dress she had bought for her next week's wedding to Ben Kaufman.

After the reception, my father's chauffeur drove the newlyweds to my father's suite at the Sherry. As she innocently told the tale, my mother was in bed, under the covers. Harry emerged in his Sulka dressing gown and slid himself beneath the sheets. He kissed his new wife tenderly. By this stage of his life Harry was a complete insomniac. His last, triumphant words of that enchanted evening were anything but romantic. "I'll sleep tonight," Harry Winston declared to his bride.

Decades later I was able to locate Ben Kaufman himself in Palm Springs, California, where he was living a plush retirement. "I got married," he told me, somewhat dryly. The son of the love of his young life was probably the last person he ever expected, or wanted, to hear from. One of his sons, I learned, was one of the top matrimonial lawyers in Beverly Hills. With great trepidation, I asked Mr. Kaufman how he felt about his precipitous reversal of marital fortune. "Your father," he told me, "was an egomaniac." There was nothing more to be said.

The egomaniac was also a workaholic. There was no way he was going to do a victory lap around the world by taking his new wife on the kind of European honeymoon Ben Kaufman had planned for her. Harry Winston had a new company, with his own name on it, that was the most jealous mistress any man ever had. His own diamond-centered Anglophilia would soon propel his move into the new British Empire Building on the corner of Fifth Avenue and Fiftieth

Streets, the Hollywood and Vine of the luxury retail world. The British Empire Building was one of the lower-rise buildings of the art deco masterpiece that was Rockefeller Center. This was as good as it got in New York, and if you just stayed in this part of Gotham, you'd never believe the city, and the world, were mired in a terrible depression.

Just like the film studios that gave us the glamorous Astaire-Rogers musicals, my father would soon give the world a similarly escapist fantasy in the dazzling piece of crystal that was the Jonker Diamond, one of the greatest rough diamonds ever found. The Jonker was also my father's fantasy come true. When he met my mother on that train to Atlantic City, no great stone, one of legendary proportion, perfection and value, had been discovered for decades. Yet in the Depression, within a few years of each other, two great stones, the Jonker first, and then the Vargas, would be unearthed, and Harry Winston would, against all odds, acquire both of them. In the process, Harry would don his P. T. Barnum ringmaster's top hat and put on a three-ring circus of publicity that hooked the world on the fantasy that significant diamonds provided.

It was found on January 15, 1934, after the most torrential rains of a brutal South African summer, in the heretofore unproductive diamond mine of a Dutch adventurer named Jacobus Jonker. A day-labor digger named Johannes Makani spotted a large stone in the muck. When he cleaned off the stone, his eyes bulged out of their sockets. He likely threw his hat in the air and shouted to the heavens the prospector's cry of ecstasy, "My God, I have found it!" The stone was about the size of an egg, which, for a diamond, was gargantuan. And because a diamond is the most concentrated precious substance on earth, that little egg, if it turned out to be a clear and perfect as it looked, could be worth a fortune.

Jacobus Jonker fell to his knees and thanked a God whom he had begun to doubt. Jacobus's wife trusted neither God nor man. She wrapped the stone in one of her stockings, tied it around her neck, and refused to fall asleep. She insisted her husband and son stand guard around her with loaded revolvers and bolted doors. The next day, Jacobus Jonker, armed to the teeth, traveled the fifty-kilometer journey by car to Johannesburg and presented the stone to the Diamond Corporation, the formal name of De Beers, who had leased him his land and had a kind of right of first refusal on anything he found. Jacobus received a check for £63,000, which was equivalent to about $5 million in 2023 money. Eureka indeed.

As it turned out, the Jonker, as the new stone was named, was the fourth-largest rough stone of high, or "gem," quality ever found. It weighed 726 carats. Two of its three rivals had also been found nearby in South Africa. Number one was the Cullinan, discovered in 1905 three miles away at the famed Premier Mine, which weighed in at a whopping 3,000 carats and was now in the British Crown Jewels. The Excelsior, also South African, weighed 971 carats, was found in 1893, and was cut into twenty one regal stones, three of which were sold to Tiffany.

The third of the stones bigger than the Jonker was perhaps the most famous of all, the Great Mogul, weighing in at 787 carats. It was discovered in the legendary fields of Golconda, in India, in 1650. The stone was lost in the fall of the Mogul Dynasty in the next century but was written about breathlessly by the great French gemologist-adventurer Jean-Baptiste

Tavernier. Harry Winston had read Tavernier, and he saw in
the Jonker similar fables, plus the machine of modern publicity to promulgate the legends he planned to spin.

The Jonker was front-page news around the world, news
that had my father champing at the bit to own it. Legendary
stones only showed up once in twenty, thirty, fifty years.
Sometimes it was centuries between great stones. I'm sure
Harry was consumed with ambition, if not envy, when he
saw the front-page photos of Sir Ernest Oppenheimer taking
the stone from Jacobus Jonker. Oppenheimer looked star-
tlingly like Adolf Hitler, who was also getting into the papers
quite a bit in those days. He had pudgy cheeks, a toothbrush
moustache, slicked-back jet black hair. Then again, for all his
acquired Anglicisms, Ernest Oppenheimer was a real German,
through and through. By contrast, Jacobus Jonker looked like
a peer in the House of Lords. Counting out the pound notes
in an elegant three-piece suit, Jacobus wore his new money so
well he made it look old.

In these hard times of failure, the media was looking for a
success story, and here it was. The serial of Jacobus Jonker's
new wealth played out daily in papers around the world. He,
in effect, had found buried treasure, every person's dream. In
the process, the world learned a great deal about the arcane
subject of great diamonds, which again, played right into my
father's hands.

It must not be forgotten that, for all my father's successes
with the likes of Colonel Green and Jesse Livermore, the diamond business itself was very much depressed. Aside from
the odd impervious millionaire, there was little demand for
jewels in this time of apples. De Beers had shut down its great
mines, including the flagship Premier, where the Cullinan was

found, in order to avoid flooding a nonexistent market. When the Jonker became front-page news, another huge, but flawed, stone known as the Pohl, from the name of its prospector, was found just a few days later, not far from where the Jonker was found. This triggered a diamond rush that never panned out.

The public fed on the Jonker family saga. It wasn't all fairy tales, particularly when the taxman entered the picture. Refusing most of the Jonkers' efforts to claim as deductions the expenses of many years of digging that had gone for naught, the South African government ended up confiscating about half of the Jonker windfall. He still had plenty, and with it, he bought a farm, cattle, a limousine. But after a few years, after all the excitement had died down, Jonker ended up squandering most of his wealth. And, it came to light, he had cheated his digger, Johannes Makani. The poor boy had been promised a farm of his own, but the proffered largesse on the part of Jabcobus Jonker never came to pass, and Makani was totally forgotten. Such was the fate of Black diamond miners in South Africa. Like many great stones, rumors that the Jonker was cursed began to emerge. Fuel for such speculation came with the sudden death in February of Ernest Oppenheimer's wife, Lady O, who succumbed to a heart attack. A year later their son died in a swimming accident, after which Ernest converted to Anglicanism, though many say he was already virtually there.

Undeterred by the threat of a curse, in March 1934, Harry and Edna booked passage to England on the Cunard liner *Berengaria*. Edna was belatedly getting her English honeymoon, but the gratification and excitement of chasing the greatest jewel in the world was surely worth the delay. The Jonker itself had been shipped to England in late February, following the death of Lady O. It was sent by parcel post, rather than by an armed flotilla, as one might have expected.

There was precedent for this. At the turn of the century, when the Cullinan was sent to England to be cleaved and polished, the Transvaal government, which had purchased the gem from De Beers, sent it, with great fanfare, on a ship with a small army of detectives. The Cullinan was deposited in the ship captain's special safe, and the world press took endless note. But it was all a bait and switch. The Cullinan the world was watching was a fake. The real gem was sent by ordinary mail, for the total outlay of a few shillings, and a fortune in free publicity when the hoax was revealed.

It was by no means clear that Sir Ernest would sell the Jonker to Harry Winston, and for what astronomical price, and whether my father could possibly afford it. Still, he and Edna settled in to a suite at Claridge's and prepared to do whatever it took. Running interference for him was his friend and broker George Prins, of Hennig & Co.

The Jonker was the first large rough stone to be handled by the newly created Central Selling Organization, or CSO, which had replaced the former diamond sales syndicate consortium of the assorted interests, like the Barnatos and the Dunkelsbuhlers. The CSO needed a big deal, if only for its own morale. Organization members were basically a bunch of miners, bankers, and accountants, and they must have felt it in their bones that they had a big winner here, one that should be exploited to the hilt.

George Prins quickly arranged a viewing of the Jonker for my father at 17 Charterhouse Street. Dad went straight to a viewing room, with as much daylight as late winter London could afford. I don't think he actually met with Sir Ernest's brother Sir Louis, who now ran the London operation. A lower executive, accompanied by a phalanx of attendants, did the showing, pulling the drawstring of a beige rough canvas sack and sliding out the Jonker onto the white reflecting pad all jewelers used to examine gems. Harry gasped. It was as good as he dreamed it would be.

Harry didn't want to show his hand, so he did everything in his power to curb his enthusiasm. He adopted his father Jacob's favorite pose of arrogant skepticism, his left hand cocked firmly on his hip, his right hand tucked studiously and intently under his chin. No one in the room moved. George Prins, whom I met many years later, told me how none of those in attendance, for all their collective decades of experience, had ever seen anything like this, and Hennig had been in business since 1892. Very slowly, Harry moved to the viewing table and picked up the stone. The glints of light that emanated from it were molten sparks, but the rock itself was cold as ice. He looked at it through his loupe and then put the stone back on the pad.

The moment was Churchillian, a highly appropriate adjective for the Englishness of the scene. Winston Churchill was once asked to pass judgment on a newborn baby who happened to be supremely uncomely. Churchill, never at a loss for words, paused a long moment. How could the great diplomat be diplomatic here? "Oh," Churchill said, "it's a boy, isn't it?" Recalling the incident, which my father must have read about, he took a page from history. "Oh," this other Winston said, "it's a diamond, isn't it?"

Here was a lump of water white crystallized carbon, a big egg, and worth, in my father's calculation, $500,000, in 1934 dollars, which were hard to find in those hard times. It would be the equivalent of at least $11 million in 2023, but today, when paintings, and not just by Rembrandt, sell for hundreds of millions, something that perfect and that rare would probably go for vastly more. The Jonker was one of the biggest of big rocks, but in metric reality its 726 carats were all of two and a half ounces, not even a party's worth of the finest caviar. That much caviar today would cost $1,250. The concentrated value of the diamond is mind-boggling. Nothing else better proved the aphorism that the best things come in small packages.

I am sure my father wanted to immediately put the Jonker in a paper envelope and seal it with sealing wax. The trade phrase for this is *en cachet*, which meant he would have first call on the stone. But that wasn't possible here. A big problem for my father was that for this little treasure there was some huge competition. I'm not sure if Tiffany or Cartier were interested, but other top jewelers undoubtedly had avaricious eyes on this rock of ages. And the competition wasn't confined to the trade. Big diamond collectors from all over the world were in the game, too, including the British royal family. The Royal Silver Jubilee was in 1935, and throughout Britain it was thought that the Jonker might make the perfect gift for King George V and Queen Mary.

The actual sale of the Jonker didn't take place for an entire year after my father first came to England. Before my father made his princely bid of $500,000 for the Jonker, he spent two long months in London "studying" the stone. He didn't go to Charterhouse Street every day to meditate on the Jonker, but he spent much time consulting experts on how best to cut the stone. After all, this was the investment of a lifetime, an investment my business-minded father would have to earn out. There were many decisions to make in this regard, whether to keep the Jonker as one giant stone or to cleave it into many precious jewels. If it were one stone, how many Rockefellers were there to whom Harry Winston could sell it? Financially, the sum of many parts may have proved greater than the whole, though publicity-wise, bigger was better. But first Harry had to get it, and De Beers was asking for a cool million, or double what my father was offering.

Harry took several boat trips across the English Channel to consult with the great rough diamond cutting firms of Antwerp and Amsterdam as to what they might do. The greatest of the lot was Royal Asscher, the Amsterdam concern that had cut the Cullinan diamond for King Edward VII. The Jonker was the ultimate rough diamond, a field my father first learned about in the late 1920s from a New York diamond dealer of Syrian Jewish descent named Shama. Shama sold my father rough diamonds from Sierra Leone known as "crystals," which looked like two Egyptian mini pyramids stuck together, base to base. Shama would cut these into square or emerald, Asscher-cut, diamonds. Shama's cutting produced a 70 percent yield of polished stone from rough, whereas most rough diamonds yielded 30 to 40 percent. The result was a huge profit for my father and deep affection for Shama. Harry would then begin making some of his first jewelry, sliding the Asscher-cut crystals into what was known as a "channel" setting, with two white gold metal rails on either side of the cut gem. This allowed the jewel, not the setting, to shine, which would eventually become the hallmark of Harry Winston.

Dad's unmatched persistence paid off. On May 15, 1935, the front page of the *New York Times* proudly heralded the purchase of the Jonker by "Harry Winston of New York" for the royal sum of $730,000. My father and De Beers seem to have split the difference between his bid and their ask. De Beers sweetened the deal by throwing in the huge but flawed Pohl diamond. Harry insured the Jonker not with Lloyd's of London but with an American company, St. Paul Fire and Marine, for a cool million dollars.

The *Times* suggested that Harry was planning to cut the Jonker big, for as one jewel it would be the "next to greatest in existence." Despite the Depression, or perhaps to spite it, these were *King Kong*, Empire State Building times, in which everyone was thinking very, very big. *Time* magazine also wrote up the sale, to "a Manhattan dealer named Harry Winston," implying that in the country outside Gotham my father was not yet a household name.

Taking his cue from Ernest Oppenheimer, Harry Winston mailed his million-dollar baby to New York for sixty-five cents postage, and reaped a fortune in free front-page publicity over the stunt. Harry made a point that the Jonker "traveled American," on board the United States Lines' *President Roosevelt*. More capital was made over the fact that the maximum insurance the British General Post Office would offer was $100; an extra element of suspense was added as to whether the ship would sink and its treasure be lost. I'm not sure whether St. Paul picked up the coverage, but I doubt my father, for all his Houdini-worship, was taking any chances.

The Jonker arrived, safe and sound, in New York on June 9, 1935. Harry prepared a special press preview to give a scoop to the ten or so top American papers. The Jonker was brought into my father's new Rockefeller Center office in its mailing box and placed on a velvet pad. Harry, whose hands always moved like leaves in the wind, nervously tore the box open.

Eventually, he got the Jonker out of its mummy-like wrappings and rolled the diamond onto the velvet. With a tremor in his voice, he proclaimed, "Ladies and gentlemen, I give you Yonkers." It was a nervous error, mistakenly referring to the working-class suburb of New York. Still, he had every reason to believe in himself. Here he was, the King of Diamonds, with the diamond of kings. And he was all of thirty-nine.

By June 21 the Jonker was on display at the American Museum of Natural History in one of the most heavily promoted and attended exhibitions at the Central Park West institution since *T. rex* drew its crowds. The museum show was my father's joint venture with another great showman, Roy Chapman Andrews, the director of the museum. He had started out there as a janitor in the taxidermy department and went on to worldwide fame as the explorer-paleontologist who discovered the Gobi Desert dinosaur eggs. Chapman knew how to stage an event, and he arranged a small army of guards with cocked revolvers to escort the Jonker to its state-of-the-art bulletproof and impregnable glass viewing case. He then had them repeat their armed walk over and over until the army of seventy-five newsreel cameras got the most convincing take.

Once inside the museum, F. Trubee Davidson, the old-guard president of the museum, made a great ceremony of cutting the strings and breaking the seal of the package that contained the Jonker, which had been rewrapped after the viewing at my father's office. Davidson pried up the lid of the sturdy wooden box, tossed aside cotton wool and tissue paper, and unwrapped the gem. All the dignitaries crowded around gasping, and, as the *New York Herald Tribune* reported, Captain Peter Medvedeff, one of the guards, who said he fought the

Bolsheviks when he was in the Russian army, clutched his revolver and stepped forward to do his duty in case anyone tried to grab the rock and run. More than five thousand people lined up to see the Jonker during its week at the museum.

The museum display was another instant milestone for Harry Winston, the first time a great diamond had been exhibited in an American museum. He was the first American to own a great stone, shipped to America on an American vessel. Plus Harry had decided he was going to have it cut, not in Amsterdam or Antwerp, but here, in America, in New York, another first, foreshadowing a soon-to-be time when patriotism would take on new and vital meaning. Harry wanted this publicity for his jewels, his company, but never for himself. My father, who could mix up Jonker and Yonkers, simply felt awkward in front of the press.

So he stayed away from the museum and only issued comments from the elegant obscurity of his Rockefeller Center offices. "The Jonker stone is much finer, its fire much purer than the Cullinan," he was quoted by the *Sun*. Harry insisted his diamond was better, and, by implication, so was America.

One question lost in all the hoopla was how my father was going to pay for this grandest of acquisitions. Of course he had great lines of credit, and the banks loved him, but this was the Depression, and there wasn't exactly a huge market for diamonds, much less the greatest stone on earth. It could take years, or maybe even decades, to sell the Jonker, and Harry Winston could run up a backbreaking, perhaps bankrupting, debt in the meanwhile. The Jonker could easily become Harry's Folly.

Without a looming Jonker purchaser, Harry may have felt a bit of a panic. He staged the ultimate publicity photo of the era, with America's beloved movie icon Shirley Temple holding the jewel. But what the publicity generated in desire, it failed to accomplish in demand. With no Croesus stepping forward to buy the stone, Dad pivoted with Lazare Kaplan, an Antwerp diamond cutter who had come to New York on vacation in 1914 just as World War I broke out and never went home again. He was considered the top man in his field in New York.

Kaplan and Harry studied the diamond for months and months, before a decision was made to cut it into twelve separate gems, the largest of which would be "only" 170 carats, far less than half the weight of what the first take on what the cut stone would weigh. Twelve perfect would be far easier to sell than one, or so my father thought. A huge amount of new publicity came with the suspense of whether Kaplan would destroy the stone when cleaving it, a terrible event in diamond cutting that the insurance company excluded from its coverage.

Cleaving, which is the most dramatic way to cut a diamond, as opposed to the snail's-pace alternative of sawing, was the route my father, drama addict that he was, naturally chose to go. The disaster-loving world, riveted to the process, got an education in diamond cutting.

Cleaving required making a pilot groove at just the right angle, with the edge of another rough, as only diamonds can cut diamonds. If the angle is off by even a tiny fraction, or if the stone contains an unseeable pocket of hidden stress, the gem will explode as if hit by a sledge hammer.

Kaplan took forever, leaving the public on edge. He was about to cut it once, and at the last second noticed a microscopic bend in a slight surface crack, known as a gletz. After months and months, Kaplan finally hit the nail on the head, and the Jonker cleaved perfectly. The actual polishing and faceting of the stone, which took another year, was done in my father's own tiny workshop off Fifth Avenue, by two experts with the picturesque and animalistic names of Beaverknight and Wolfish, who never entered the public consciousness the way Lazare Kaplan did.

Although John D. Rockefeller was rumored to have bought some of the "Baby Jonkers" soon after the finishing process was complete, the "Big Jonker," known as Jonker I, remained in inventory for fourteen endless years, until my father finally sold it to King Farouk in 1949, after they met at the casino in Monte Carlo. That the king then stiffed my father on the deal is another sad story. But even though my father sold the jewel for the equivalent of $8 million in 2023 dollars, the cost of carrying the stone for so many years, interest, insurance, and so forth has been calculated at $16 million. So, one might ask, what price publicity?

Even though my father had run up his debt by taking on the Jonker, he continued to live like the king that he was, debt and Depression be damned. The night he closed the deal for the Jonker with De Beers, for example, he took Edna out to celebrate at the Colony, which was perhaps the most luxurious restaurant in Manhattan in the post-Prohibition thirties. My mother probably pushed my father into going. "This is the beginning of the great heights of your career," I can almost hear her prodding him. "You can't just stay home."

The Colony, on 61st Street and Madison, was only two blocks away from the Winston suite at the Sherry. Nonetheless, I'm sure my mother wore some of his finest jewels for the occasion. Likewise, I'm sure my father was resplendent in his tuxedo. "Getting dressed for dinner in the twenties and thirties meant nothing less than black tie," my father often told me, in one of his sartorial lectures to his little barbarian who didn't know a dressing gown from a smoking jacket from a bathrobe. Harry and Edna took the two blocks to the Colony in his chauffeured Packard just to play it safe, because there were hungry people in the streets, and angry ones too.

The Colony had strong roots in Prohibition. It had started as a speakeasy, and the floors above it housed a speakeasy version of a hospital, where the upper echelons of Park Avenue society, the clientele of my father, went to get abortions, dry out, go on crash diets, or have their faces lifted. During the Roaring Twenties, there was also a casino upstairs. The elevator was a moving wine cellar.

The Colony, society's darling, featured separate men's and ladies' smoking lounges and also a kennel for the dogs of the patrons, which made the Colony as "European" as a New York restaurant could be. The main bar area was decorated with gay Riviera-ish blue-and-white-striped wallpaper, and the bar itself was covered with a canopy. The dining area was white tie and real jewels formal, all red velvet and crystal chandeliers, with three tiers of banquettes on opposing walls (top tier was bottom drawer), so that everyone could see the procession of the high and mighty as they ran this gauntlet and took their tables.

My father was effusively greeted by Ernest, Park Avenue's favorite maître d'. He had his habitual Dubonnet and gin at the bar, then settled into his prime banquette, lower tier, a power table where he could meet current and potential clients. I'm sure that night he probably couldn't take two bites or two sips before having to greet another tycoon or dowager.

Mrs. Astor's Old New York of the ballrooms, and now gossip columnist Walter Winchell's New New York, all came to the Colony. It was both a celebration with his wife and a publicity coup for Harry Winston, jeweler.

Jacob surely was rolling in his grave at the extravagance of the Colony. They had caviar and blini, and Harry ordered fillet of sole, while my mother enjoyed a tableside-prepared steak tartare. For dessert, which Harry eschewed, Edna would have Baked Alaska. Afterward, my father and mother may have motored over to the Stork Club for a nightcap, or maybe El Morocco. When you're famous, and your fame feeds your business, staying up late is part of the job. Besides, my mother loved going out and cutting a rug. My father, on the other hand, just didn't have the moves: my mother told me he danced like a trained bear.

The strongest evidence of my father's alleged clairvoyance came in 1938, in one of the most amazing and improbable coincidences in the history of great gems. One and a half years after the discovery of the Jonker in South Africa, another gigantic, perfect diamond was unearthed near the town of Coromandel, Brazil, in the state of Minas Gerais, several hundred miles north of Rio. Diamonds had first been discovered here in 1730, and until 1870 it was the source of most of the world's diamonds. Then came South Africa, but Brazil could still yield treasures, and this was one of them. It weighed 726 carats, almost precisely the exact weight of the Jonker. Lying on its side, it looked like the map of Brazil. But once it had been cut it would look like the inside of Fort Knox. Of course, my connected father heard about it before almost anyone else, and, of course, he had to have it. Two identical super stones in four short years. Harry had hit the daily double of diamonds. He would be a "rock star" long before the term existed.

In its diamond heyday Minas Gerais had been known as Terra Magica. The place where the first alluvial stones were found was a gold mining town of Tejuco, which was promptly renamed Diamantina. The men who found the first small, shiny stones were gold prospectors called *garimpeiros* who found something else entirely. A new diamond rush began, as quick-buck men from all over the world sailed to Rio and went off into these magic mountains to stake their claims. The Indian diamond fields had been exhausted around this time. The Brazil strike couldn't have happened at a more opportune moment, supplying diamonds to the crowned heads of Europe until the next century saw their fall from power. After that, the spectacular gems mined at Terra Magica made their way onto the open market.

The modern-day *garimpeiros* who found the Brazilian rock, Joaquim Venancio Tiago and Manoel Miguel Domingues, did far better for themselves than poor Johannes Makani, who found the Jonker. But then again, Makani was a poor Black serf in South Africa, while Tiago and Domingues were soldiers of fortune. Guarding their treasure with guns and machetes, they made their way to the elegant capital of Minas Gerais, Belo Horizonte, which had grown baroquely rich with gold and diamond money. There they sold the diamond to a local broker for $56,000 (close to $750,000 in 2023). Of course the lucky miners may have wanted to shoot themselves when, a short time later, their broker resold the diamond for $235,000 ($4 million) to a rich local merchant named Oswaldo Dante Dos Reis.

My father, well aware of Brazil as a supplier but not expecting a stone of this magnitude to be found there, already had agents in Brazil, as well as in Venezuela, where diamonds had been discovered in 1890. His man in Brazil, Leon Monte, cabled him when he learned of the find, and my father took my mother on still another "honeymoon." Harry and Edna boarded one of the fabled Pan Am Clippers and, emulating Fred and Ginger in the 1933 film that put the beach city on the map of vacation fantasies, they "flew down to Rio" and checked in to the Copacabana Palace, with a splendid view of Sugarloaf Mountain.

Harry planned to wine and dine Dos Reis and take the stone off his hands. He was prepared to pay the same $500,000 he had initially offered De Beers for the Jonker. But this was Brazil, where De Beers was out of the picture, so Harry expected a much easier time of it. But he was shocked to learn that the stone, named the President Vargas in honor of Brazil's strongman president, was not even in the country. Dos Reis had sold it, without even giving Monte a chance to bid for it, for an undisclosed sum to a diamond syndicate, financed by the Union Bank of Amsterdam. The President Vargas was en route to Amsterdam, so Harry and Edna, in their own version of a Hitchcock thriller that could have been entitled "North by Northeast," embarked for Holland.

My father used to describe himself as "air minded." He believed in flying. These were the early days of commercial aviation, and I don't think Pan Am even had a route between Brazil and Europe. Accordingly, he and Edna boarded the fastest ship they could find for London, and on to Holland.

As with the Jonker, it took over a year for my father to work out a deal with the flying Dutchmen. He ultimately paid around $700,000 for the President Vargas, and, in a reprise of his Jonker showmanship, he insured the stone for its paid value, but had it shipped from London by sea mail, for the grand total of seventy cents. The Vargas arrived in New York on July 16, 1940, to a battery of newsreel photographers and armed guards. Instead of the Museum of Natural History, Harry let the public share his joy by displaying the Vargas at the Brazilian Pavilion at the futuristic World's Fair being held in Flushing Meadows. Thirty armed guards surrounded the stone.

Again, as with the Jonker, Harry Winston decided to cut the big stone up, this time into eleven cut diamonds, compared to the Jonker's twelve. The Vargas One, the superstone of the group, an emerald cut weighing forty-eight carats, was sold to a high-leverage, low-profile gem collector, Fort Worth oil and cattle baroness Mrs. Robert Windfohr, in 1944. Harry only had to carry the Vargas for four years.

It's amazing that, given the depression and the size of the loans he carried, my father not only was able to make a living but also became very wealthy in the 1930s. The answer, I believe, was his determination to purchase the largest, most rare diamonds in the world and sell them to the wealthiest people in the world. He understood instinctively that doing rarified business was good business. But my father also kept his hand in the "rough trade," the wholesale trade, and in truth, this was the bulk of his business. With his friend Shama's inspiration, the old estate jewelry that had been the cash cow of the Premier Diamond Company had been supplanted by the rough trade that became the bedrock of Harry Winston's business.

My father's biggest rough customer was one of the smoothest operators of all time. This was Harry's "man in Hollywood," Paul Flato, who became "jeweler to the stars" long before Harry Winston—and I—assumed the mantle. I'm still not sure why my father himself never opened a store in Los Angeles; that was something I had to do. I think it was a question of logistics. My father hated those endless cross-country train rides of his youth.

Now he could travel first class on the 20th Century Limited to Chicago and then the Super Chief onward to California, but the journey, however lush, still took a good four days, and my father was a very impatient man who was always on the phone or sending cables or striding into a boardroom. To be out of action for that long would have driven him crazy. Plus he was "air minded," and in the thirties planes were bumpy, slow, unreliable, and, frankly, scary.

So Harry left California and its stars to Paul Flato. Flato, who was close to my father's age, was his total opposite. Flato was a cowboy. Born in the family ranching hamlet of Flatonia, Texas, Flato discovered a love for jewelry as a child watching the Romany people who camped out on his family's land making their junk jewelry. He was transfixed. Flato, itching to get off the ranch, went to New York and enrolled in business courses at Columbia. When his father ran into financial trouble, Flato dropped out and went to work in the diamond district, where his Texas drawl, his Southern charm, and his disarming wit stood out among the serious Talmudic types who dominated the trade.

A natural salesman, by 1928 he had his own salon upstairs at One East 57th Street, very much in the orbit of Harry Winston. He attracted a stellar clientele, including Florence Gould, a gold digger who struck it rich and married the son of railroad tycoon Jay Gould; opera diva Lily Pons; cosmetics queen Elizabeth Arden. But Flato's true specialty was movie stars, who were entranced by the romantic, fanciful floral designs made by his workshop of "society" designers, who included Josephine Forrestal, wife of James Forrestal, Roosevelt's Secretary of the Navy, and the Italian aristocrat the Duke di Verdura, who had previously worked for Coco Chanel.

By 1938 Flato had opened a second branch, which would become his main store, right on Sunset Boulevard in Los Angeles, across from the star-studded Trocadero nightclub. Flato provided all of Katharine Hepburn's jewelry for the film *Holiday*, as he did for Greta Garbo in *Two-Faced Woman*. Often, when the stars were as antifashion as Hepburn and Garbo were, the jewelry was returned, but other stars that were Flato-ized, like Merle Oberon, Joan Crawford, and Rita Hayworth, had to own everything they wore. Both Oberon and Crawford would go on to marry industrial tycoons and, in Hayworth's case, the Aga Khan, all of whom could, and did, keep their star brides in serious gems. For the mass public to see all their idols on screen dripping in Flato jewelry, or written up by gossip doyennes Hedda Hopper and Louella Parsons, was more great publicity for Harry, who was known to the world as Flato's supplier.

While what Harry was selling were in-your-face big rocks, what Flato sold were his witty designs: a "corset" bracelet, with garters in rubies and diamonds, inspired by Mae West; a gold digger bracelet featuring an eighteen-carat-gold pick-axe; a compact with an angel on a chamber pot, for Gloria Vanderbilt. I doubt my father, who took diamonds dead seriously, was all that amused. Nor did Harry see much humor in Flato's financial shenanigans, in which he would obtain jewels on consignment from fellow jewelers and then sell them, without reimbursing the lenders. By the early forties, Flato was forced to close his two stores when he was sent to prison for sixteen months. Later, fleeing more grand larceny charges, he relocated to Mexico City, where he was the toast of society for decades and opened a luxurious salon in the Zona Rosa. He died in Texas at ninety-eight in 1999.

While my father may have been loath to cross the country, he had no such reservations about crossing the Atlantic. It may have been because my mother loved Europe so much; it may have also been that, for all the dislocations of World War I, there was still a lot of money over there, old and often titled money that had been buying jewelry for centuries and wanted nothing but the very top diamonds, with which my father had now become synonymous. Yes, there were Cartier and Van Cleef and Garrard and Bulgari and many more, great and venerable European names. But my gutsy father, having successfully taken on the Tiffanys and Black, Starrs of his own turf, had no fear about playing to win in any arena, however foreign and intimidating. So brilliantly did he establish his beachhead on the Continent that with the outbreak of World War II, millions and millions of dollars' worth of diamonds were sent to him by Jews fleeing Europe, addressed with nothing more than "Harry Winston, New York City."

From the quest for the Jonker in 1934 until 1939, Harry and Edna sailed to Europe at least eight times, usually for a month or more on every visit. During this time Harry would usually visit De Beers in London and then call on the rich, famous, and acquisitive in Paris, Deauville, and the Cote d'Azur. They usually took the *Normandie*, though they also sailed on the *Queen Mary* and the *Aquitania*. How glamorous it must have been, like a floating version of the Waldorf, the Colony, and the Stork Club, all in one gleaming hull. In London it was

Claridge's, Paris the Ritz, Cannes the Carlton, all the stuff of a Noel Coward drawing-room play, albeit incongruously starring Harry and Edna, strangers at the party who somehow, because they *had* what everyone else *wanted*, managed to fit in.

That their floating idyll could be shattered by the rise of Adolf Hitler seemed as foreign a concept to my parents as it did to the clueless British prime minister Neville Chamberlain. My mother's letters to her father focus on the luxury and name-dropping dazzle of it all, without any reference to the unmitigated horror that was about to come. For example, on August 19, 1938, Edna wrote the good doctor, "Last night we had dinner at Count Sarges and we met Prince Faud, the brother of King Farouk. I sat next to Count Villermancy, the oldest aristocratic family in France. Our host was entertaining Simon Marks (of London's Marks and Spencer). Everyone was mad for my pink diamond." On September 14, 1938, she wrote, "Harry doesn't feel there'll be war. Charlie Simon will keep us up on the news." Simon, a new friend, came from a prominent Franco-Jewish family. He was less sanguine than my parents and actually emigrated to New York soon after my mother's note.

Back in Europe in July 1938, dancing on the very edge of the abyss, Mother wrote the doctor about her and Harry's adventures in France. "Blustein is here. He is very rich, owning a department store in London, like Macy's. He wants to buy a 35 carat diamond for $150,000. We are going to Cannes to hire a yacht for a month. Read *Wake Up and Live* by Dorothea Brande." *Wake Up* was the ultimate self-help book of its day, selling millions of copies worldwide, extolling the power of positive thinking. Ironically, the bestselling Brande was married to a man who would be denounced for his fascist affiliations.

Wake up, Mom, is all I can think when I read her missives.

She soon had the rudest awakening imaginable. After cruising the Mediterranean coast from Monte Carlo to St. Tropez to Marseilles, doubtlessly with few newspapers to distract them from their pleasure, Harry and Edna visited Vichy, soon to be the home of the collaborationist government. Even this didn't register with my mother. To her father on August 29 she wrote, "Vichy is the center of France. Things are going on as usual. Please write me care of La La Adouth, 18 Rue Lafayette, Paris." Adouth, a wily and wise Turkish Jew who was shorter than my father and twice as wide, was Harry's retail representative in Paris. He was supposed to be a great salesman, the pride of the Levant. Harry's wholesale agent in Paris, for rough stones, was Jean Rosenthal, whose religion was the only thing he and La La had in common. Rosenthal, from an old diamond firm on the Place Vendôme across from the Ritz, was tall and regal, and he wined and dined my parents at La Tour d'Argent and other similarly soigné venues when they returned to Paris.

Wherever they went, it must have seemed in retrospect like the Last Supper. Three days after my mother's Pollyanna letter from Vichy, on September 1, 1939, Harry and Edna, along with the rest of the world, were rocked by the news of the German invasion of Poland. The Nazi blitzkrieg had begun. Harry sprang into action. He had no choice. With many of his great jewels, including his gem of gems, the 144-carat Jonker I, on consignment to prospective buyers in France, he stood to lose much of his new fortune. With Poland gone, how far behind was France, which was desired by the Germans as the prize of Europe?

My father may have been naive about politics, but he understood greed the way Freud knew sex. The Germans coveted jewels as much as they hated Jews, and surely the two emotions were deeply connected. Harry had to get his diamonds back. It wasn't a question of his money or his life. In this case, his money—embodied in the diamonds—*was* his life. Accordingly, he hired a driver at the most extortionate rate and drove all over France to collect his jewels, west to Deauville, south to Bordeaux, east to Vichy, south to Cannes, back north to Paris. My mother may have been more terrified of their driver than she was of Hitler. He drove like a madman, a Juan Fangio (the Argentine grand prix racing champion) of the preautoroute, winding, tree-lined, very dangerous *route nationales*. They did the whole of France in a week.

Then they returned to Paris, to collect what Adouth and Rosenthal had been holding for them. Rosenthal, who specialized in colored stones—emeralds, rubies, sapphires, pearls—was soon to become a hero of the Resistance. He gave the collection back to my father, who begged him to leave and join him in business in New York.

"I can't," he told my father. "After all, I am French."

"Yes," Harry replied. "But you are also Jewish."

Rosenthal would not be moved. The tall jeweler hugged the tiny one, and they said goodbye.

With war brewing, Lloyd's of London, Harry's main insurance carrier, abruptly canceled his policy. If anything was force majeure, which would let an insurer off the hook, Hitler was it. Leaving the jewelry in a European vault was out of the question. Harry knew he had to have his treasure with him. But a continent on the edge of apocalypse was no place to travel with a fortune in diamonds. So my father put some of the stones in his shoes and used adhesive tape to stick garlands of the rocks inside his trouser legs. Fortunately my mother was quite voluptuous. Her ample brassiere was called into service to secrete a fortune in gems, while what wouldn't fit into the D cups were hidden under a wig my mother bought on the Rue Saint-Honoré. Dressed to the nines, they had their wild driver beat the hastiest path from Paris to the docks of Le Havre.

On September 3, 1939, the day Britain declared war on Germany, the British ocean liner *Athenia was sunk* by a German U-boat. Many passengers, mostly women and children, were saved, but 118 people, including twenty-eight Americans, lost their lives in those dark and deadly waters. The Federal Maritime Commission, based in New York, saw the situation as extremely grave and mobilized fifty ships to evacuate Americans from Europe. Luckily my parents were able to book passage on one of the first of these, the *Washington*, for a departure of September 12. They boarded the relatively newly christened (1933) luxury liner laden with hidden diamonds.

This was anything but a festive cruise, more like *The Voyage of the Damned*. All the portholes and glass windows were blacked out. In preparation for the distinct possibility of "women and children first," my parents were separated. Edna was to sleep in her stateroom, while Harry, and all the other men, were issued bedrolls and ordered to sleep either on deck, or in the empty first-class swimming pool. Edna was extremely fearful. She described how she didn't want to separate from my father. She held on to him passionately. "Dearest, will we make it?" she asked.

He told her not to worry. "Besides, if we go down, we'll be together," he said, offering scant consolation. Then he added, "At least we don't have any children to worry about." My mother must have winced.

My father was quartered in the bottom of the pool with two hundred other men. Rope ladders of the kind seen in circus acts hung down the sides. On deck was a huge hand-cranked klaxon to warn of impending attacks. The *Washington* sailed from Le Havre under cover of night. The officers pried my parents apart and sent Harry to the pool. Just after midnight the siren alert went off, and all the ship's internal lights that were not essential were extinguished. My mother was of course terrified. Assuming the alarm to be an air raid or U-boat attack, she didn't want to die all alone. Thus she groped her way in the darkness, wearing her bejeweled bra and wig, to the swimming pool. Somehow she climbed down a rope ladder and found my father. She crawled into his bedroll with him and held him for dear life. The siren must have sounded for hours. It only ended when dawn broke. The other men must have been amused to awake and find a woman in a bathrobe in their midst. Little did they suspect she was also wearing over $2 million (more than $42 million in 2023) in jewels.

Once the ordeal of escaping the French coast was over, it was smooth sailing for the remainder of the voyage. The *Washington* arrived in New York harbor on September 18. The city never looked so good to the Winstons. But Harry Winston's wartime adventures were only just beginning. And the biggest adventure of his life, becoming a father, my father, was only two years away. These worst of times were also the best of times.

CHAPTER SIX

War Baby

"What a terrible time to bring a child into the world, especially a Jewish child." Those were hardly the words of shimmering pride my mother's doctor father might normally have exclaimed at the birth of his first grandchild. However, the date of my entrance into the world on January 10, 1941, was so close to the other date in 1941, which President Roosevelt declared would "live in infamy," that my grandfather's bleak pronouncement was justified.

Despite their hairbreadth escape from Europe, despite Hitler's relentless blitzkriegs, despite the Nazis' psychotic mission to exterminate worldwide Jewry, Harry and Edna Winston were hell-bent on having a family. I gather that my mother was probably a lot more hell-bent than my father, given that she was in her thirties and after my father's endless evasive courtship and their five years of globetrotting she was ready to settle down, establish a household, and have children.

I was conceived in high style, in April 1940, in Cuba, which, back then, was the playground of the Western Hemisphere. Havana was glamorous and a little dangerous, with its gambling casinos and deluxe bordellos. Batista had just come to power, Hemingway had come to fish, and Errol Flynn had come to party. Everyone came to party. Havana was just an overnight boat ride from Miami, but it was as close to the sophistication and decadence of Europe as Americans could get during the war.

My parents stayed at the Hotel Nacional, which was the "Mafia Ritz," because it was also the favorite of the likes of Lucky Luciano and Meyer Lansky, who made the city the pre-Vegas Vegas. They drank mojitos at Hemingway's haunt La Floridita, and if Edna got Harry lubricated enough, she probably tried to teach him the cha-cha and the mambo at legendary nightclubs like the Tropicana and the Sans Souci. By day they recuperated on the white sands of Playa Varadero, and somewhere along this tropical way, the gleam in Harry's eye bore fruit.

My first name came from my mother's movie idol, Ronald Colman, the urbane British star of *The Prisoner of Zenda* and *Lost Horizon.* He would later win an Oscar for *A Double Life.* My middle name, Harivman, was as far from Ronald Colman as Minsk was from Mayfair. But Harry kept the faith, his own faith, even if he never practiced it. Maybe it was pride, or maybe it was the insecurity of not being a college man, that kept him in the Jewish fold.

When I was born, I weighed all of six pounds. My poor mother turned the same shade of peridot green that she was when my father first met her on the train to Atlantic City. She had contracted jaundice and had given it to me. I was as yellow as a banana and as wrinkled as a walnut. My being his newest Jonker wasn't quite enough to keep my father at the hospital. One look at me, and he fled to the bar of the Colony and got colossally drunk. After spending a week in the hospital with my mother, I was bundled in swaddling blankets and taken in our Packard to the new country estate in Scarsdale, immodestly named Stonwin, an inversion of our last name, with an emphasis on the "stone."

The property dated back to Revolutionary days, having belonged to a British officer. There were rumors that its last owner had been a member of the P. T. Barnum circus clan, and that my father had traded a diamond for it. There were thirty-five acres and a thirty-room Colonial Revival house with a portico entrance and two half-mile sweeping driveways. There were woods and farmland and barns and stables and a clay tennis court and a pool. It was all very country squire. This was before Scarsdale had become synonymous with Jewish rustic upward mobility, a Semitic Greenwich. In the early forties it was just as exclusive as Greenwich. My mother used to describe Stonwin's location as "in the farming section of Scarsdale," a section that the newly opened Hutchinson River Parkway would within a decade turn into very fancy suburbia.

My earliest days were suffused with this gentility, starting with my English nurse, Miss Pinder. The theme of my room was classical blue and white, echoing the Athenaeum Club on London's Park Lane. I slept in a bassinet wreathed in crinoline and white gauze. The floor was a blue linoleum, with a seraph-lettered "Ronnie" in white at the entry door. Within a few weeks the jaundice subsided, and the wrinkles ironed out. My father could finally bear to look at me. "You suddenly became handsome," he later told me.

While I remained at Stonwin, my father was driven in the Packard to Manhattan and his new headquarters during the week. These were located in a town house, across the street from St. Patrick's Cathedral, just off Fifth Avenue. By now he was arguably the most famous living jeweler in the world. As the war escalated, he was inundated with parcels of rough and polished diamonds sent by Jews from all over the falling countries of Europe, in an attempt to keep their treasures away from the plundering Nazis. Harry created a special storeroom for the safekeeping of these jewels not knowing, in 1941, the horrid fate that would befall so many of their owners. The Wannsee Conference, in which Hitler and company created the blueprints for "the final solution," did not take place until 1942.

Harry was basking in the flattery of being famous. His spectacular clientele, which included the grandest ladies in America, as well as titans of business, such as men like Jules Bache, Walter Chrysler, and John D. Rockefeller Jr. These were the first names I remember hearing as a child, and, because they were embedded in the folklore of capitalism, they were impossible to forget. While Rockefeller senior handed out dimes to caddies and was famous for being cheap, his son made his name in philanthropy, having built the Cathedral of St. John the Divine, Rockefeller University, and the Museum of Modern Art, not to mention Rockefeller Center, where my father had just left his offices to move into the townhouse. Imagine my mother's elation, then, to have Junior as a guest in her very own home.

Despite his philanthropy, Rockefeller, Jr. was still a tough customer. On their first meeting, he announced, "Just because my name is Rockefeller doesn't mean I'm not interested in value."

My father assured Junior, "Don't concern yourself, Mister Rockefeller. I'll take care of you." And he did, supplying him with one breathtaking diamond after another for his wife, Abby Aldrich, the queen of the eastern establishment. Abby was the main force behind the creation of Colonial Williamsburg, and she loved jewels with the passion of an English royal, not a Yankee revolutionary.

How did my mother feel about someone like Abby Aldrich Rockefeller? She never said.

My mother wasn't the envious type. Besides, what more could she want? But she did want respect. One day Junior came to see Harry, whose receptionist Miss Shaw announced the big, great man. The little great man, my father, whose office was on the second floor, descended the regal, Medici-like suspended marble staircase to greet the tycoon. "Very pleased to see you, Mister R," he said.

"The pleasure is mine, Mister W."

Just as they were heading up the grand staircase, my mother stepped out of the small private elevator next to the landing. "Harry," she said quietly, but he didn't seem to hear her and started up the stairs. "Harry!" she said again, this time a little more forcefully. Harry and Junior kept climbing. Finally, Edna put her hands on her hips and shouted. "Hey, Harry! Remember me? I'm the woman you *slept with* last night!" My father and Junior, turned and came back down the stairs, and my mother was formerly introduced to Rockefeller. Once respect had been paid to my mother, Harry and Junior made their way up the grand staircase and got down to business.

As I got a little older, my parents began bringing me into the city, and I became a part of my father's daily ritual of all work, no lunch, and no play, at least until the last tycoon had gone home with a new treasure. Then Harry would repair to our duplex facing the gothic spires of St. Patrick's, have a few drinks, and then join me for some "Ronnie time." I'd be playing on the floor, and my father would kneel before me in his bespoke three-piece suit (he liked vests, probably because he could pocket more jewels). Then he'd take a folded envelope called a "parcel," which was peculiar to the stone business, out of his breast pocket and shake out one or two spectacular gems. He'd hold them before me and tell me what made them so valuable. These were my first tutorials in the family business. For all I knew, they could have been marbles, but my father sincerely believed that a Winston, even a baby Winston, would sense quality when he saw it.

The gay New York of the previous decade was drastically transformed by Pearl Harbor. There was rampant fear that New York would be next. The city was continually reminded of its possible grim fate by the radio dispatches of Edward R. Murrow, who was reporting on the devastation of the Blitz in London. The bright lights of Broadway went dark to shroud the city from German bombers, and squadrons of planes flew above the city, spewing out black smoke to hide the city below. The great liners that had taken my parents to Europe now sat in drydock at the Westside piers, until they were all refitted, like the *Queen Mary* and the *Queen Elizabeth*, as troop transport vessels. The most elegant of all, the *Normandie*, went up in smoke in a terrible fire in 1942, reputedly set by the Lucky Luciano–directed Mafia, as proof to the authorities that the mob controlled the waterfront.

Whether it was true or not, smoke and darkness were the leitmotifs of my early years. My very first memories, aside from my family and my father's gems, were of the blackout shades put up in my room, which were meant to keep Manhattan dark.

To dispel the gloom, my parents kept me at Stonwin, where they planted a victory garden behind the greenhouse. When I say "they," I mean the nine gardeners they employed, men who had somehow missed the draft but were now conscripted into the Winston corps to rake and hoe four acres of rough lawn into a fruitful Eden of tomatoes, peas, squash, and beans. We even had a chicken coop, and I loved watching the sweet little chicks the color of forsythia, huddled around the incubator, which looked like a flying saucer to me. My parents created for me a cosmos garden, next to my sandbox, where I would bend their high blooms and watch the butterflies sipping their nectar. It couldn't have been more idyllic, particularly during the Holocaust. It was proof of the lengths my parents went to, in an attempt to create a perfect world for their perfect child.

Of course my parents couldn't hide all the imperfections. One day I saw my father and uncle hacking a large snake to death with golf clubs. *Whack! Whack! Whack!* Clearly, no serpents were allowed in the Winston Garden of Eden. Another time, when I was around three or four and was playing with an elaborate Lionel train set on the floor with my father, I accidentally jabbed him near an eye with the pointed end of a track connector. He reacted by slapping me. This frightened me as much as watching him club that snake, and my mother, who was nearby, sat in stunned silence. Striking a child simply wasn't in the book of Jewish parenting. Spare the rod and spoil the child was the idea. "I'm a jeweler, and I need my eyes. Don't you ever do that again!" he scolded me. I broke down crying, but he didn't hug me and say, "Oh, Ronnie dear, everything's okay." He meant it, because his eyes were his business, and his business took precedence over all else. I never played with my train tracks in front of him again. I was more than chastened. I was terrified.

Intimidation was something of the coin of the realm at Harry Winston. As I grew a little older, I started spending more and more time at the town house, and I started noticing things. It became apparent to me that my father was a great man and a purveyor of great things, and this required gravity and seriousness. My father put in endless hours at the store, which he called the "salon." He would have never used the former appellation, which smacked of his father Jacob's plebeian trials and tribulations.

One reason John D. Rockefeller, Junior, may have felt so comfortable with my father is that the same famous architect who had designed the Winston town house had also done Rockefeller's Westchester estate, Kykuit, which was not far from Stonwin. This prototypical celebrity designer was Ogden Codman Jr., who was the coauthor with Edith Wharton of *The Decoration of Houses* and who himself had left America to live in a chateau in the Loire Valley. What all these men seemed to have in common, aside from lots of money, was Francophilia.

The entrance portals of the town house, which could have easily blended into a side street of the Sixteenth Arrondissement, were massive dark wrought-iron affairs that whispered more "keep out" than "come in." These heavenly gates would one day become a symbol of Harry Winston, and they were at once forbidding, foreboding, and exclusive, which is precisely what my father wanted.

It didn't get any homier once you were inside. The massive marble staircase that dominated the ground floor had widely spaced bronze balusters, so there was nothing to hold on to—at least for a little boy. I was so afraid of the stairs that

I would only use them if my mother was there to hold my hand. I came to realize that my father actually wanted people to feel a little off balance, a little intimidated, as they climbed up toward his offices.

Speaking of his offices, in front of them was a large Flemish tapestry of a biblical scene, which hung over a Gothic cathedral pew. Both were imported from France. This is where he would have the diamond dealers sit and wait before granting them an audience. Because these dealers were almost always Hasidic Jews, this not-so-subtle reminder of the old-world Christianity that had persecuted them may have rattled these men enough to give my father a slight bargaining edge.

For all my father's love of French decor, there was no substitute for having a British secretary with a posh accent. Harry's Cerberus was a very proper English refugee named Miss Jones. Her endless war stories of having been pulled half-dead from smoldering post-Blitz rubble terrified the office and brought home the reality of the global conflict. Otherwise, the Harry Winston premises were blissfully insulated from all hardship, in fact, all reality.

My father's office itself was a monument to intimidating grandeur. Three towering windows looked out onto St. Patrick's ecclesiastical majesty. My father had a priceless French Louis XIV desk in front of the middle window. He would sit there for ten or more hours at a stretch, getting up only to receive the Rockefellers of the world. His posture was always the same, his right hand tucked under his chin in laconic contemplation, evocative of Rodin's *The Thinker*. He had kept this pose from his youth, as evidenced in that 1911 photo of him in Jacob's Los Angeles store. There were two buzzers under the desk. One was hooked to an elaborate

Pinkerton alarm system, which would summon the guards and the police. The other would summon staff, who would bring in the black velvet trays of jewels kept in the main vault on the second floor.

Between the other windows were vitrines displaying cast glass models of the rough and cut diamonds of the Jonker and the Vargas. My mother was always dressed to the nines in the mode of a female executive, at a time when those were rare. I was rarely in his offices, as my father preferred not to mix parenting with business. But sometimes my mother would bring me in. "How's my little fella today?" Harry would ask and then send me and my mother on our way. "Little fella." I suppose I was the only person in the building who was smaller than he was.

Harry didn't have much time or patience for anything other than work. When I was three, he sold the two riding horses, Lady and Kiddie, he kept in our barn. I liked the horses and liked feeding them apples and sugar cubes. I was sad when he got rid of them. Later on, I asked why he had let them go. "You never showed much interest," he told me. Aside from sitting on the fine English saddle, how much more interest could I have shown at three?

My father was always in search of great salesmen who could help him spread the gospel of diamonds. Harry Winston's two supersalesman of the early forties were both big men, if not college men. Because there was only so much Harry Winston to go around, and usually only to the buyers who graced the cover of *Time*, my father needed disciples who could do justice to his jewelry. One was Charlie Steiger, a bear of a man with a bald pate and a stentorian voice that got louder after his invariable three-martini, or Rob Roy, lunch. He called my father chief, which amused me because it made me think of him as Sitting Bull or Crazy Horse, which was as far from the case as anything could be.

The other supersalesman was Dick Vena, who was tall and thin with slicked-back hair. He was Italian and courtly and a quiet counterweight to the ebullient Charlie. In short, Dick was the spitting image of a refined Mafia don, which wasn't a bad type to have around the office. Charlie, the guy's guy, usually sold to the men, the Di Maggio or Babe Ruth sportsmen or the high-rolling Wall Streeters or the hard-drinking Madison Avenue admen, who wanted baubles for their wives and mistresses. Dick, on the other hand, was a ladies' man, a great favorite of the Park Avenue grande dame and dowager set.

Both Charlie and Dick worked in the main salesroom on the first floor, which was known as the salon, but since my father loved the word, you could never have too many salons at Harry Winston. It was a grand room with extremely high ceilings and six or so Louis XIV desks with black velvet pads on which the gems would be displayed. The salon was painted in varying shades of gray, which were meant to allow the jewels to stand out. The effect was all quiet good taste, so quiet it would seem totally boring today. But the forties were a gray era, nothing roaring, nothing swinging. With a world war going on, any kind of flash seemed highly inappropriate.

For all the deprivation, the rationing, the tragedy, New York during the war was still a very lively place. Eat, drink, and buy diamonds, for tomorrow we die, summed up the mentality that made my father's business boom, even during these straitened times. World War II saw New York finally assume the mantle of the most important city in the world. London was under siege, Paris had fallen, Rome was history. Much of Europe's aristocracy had fled to Manhattan and regrouped at the Stork Club and El Morocco, joining American café society, which partied harder than ever, as if there would be no tomorrow, which often seemed the case.

In many cases, money was mobility, and New York was the urban manifestation of social Darwinism, the survival of the richest. Plus, New Yorkers, at least at the top, were making wartime fortunes on shipbuilding, munitions, and clothing. No smart capitalist ever got poor during a war. And few of those with the big money could live without jewelry, hence the wartime success of Harry Winston. By 1940 my father was De Beers's largest sight holder in America, which meant he got the biggest supply of diamonds in the country from their London syndicate. During the war, without the offshore competition of the great European houses, Harry Winston was the preeminent jeweler in the world.

But if you think my father was fiddling while the world was burning, trading in baubles with self-absorbed, vain heiresses like Barbara Hutton and Doris Duke, living in a velvet-lined vacuum while the Nazis were pulling gold out of Jewish teeth, you'd be wrong. Harry Winston would never brag about this, because the whole enterprise was top secret, but my father was indispensable to the war effort. He was not only a key provider to the Allies of industrial diamonds essential to weapons manufacturing and precision tooling, but he was also something of a high-level secret agent in keeping the Nazis from gaining control of Brazil itself, and with Brazil, South America.

My father supplied Ingrid Bergman with the jewels she wore in the 1946 Alfred Hitchcock romantic thriller, *Notorious*.

The film's producer, David O. Selznick, who made *Gone with the Wind*, was a Winston client. Many people felt my father was a dead ringer for Claude Rains, who played the film's villain, the Nazi agent in Brazil whom American agent Cary Grant blackmails Bergman into going to Rio to seduce and spy on. Grant naturally falls in love with her, and his intense jealousy gives the movie its erotic charge. In the plot, Rains was smuggling uranium to the Nazis. But you could easily substitute diamonds as the MacGuffin, the Hitchcock term for the thing everybody is after. In reality, the thing Hitler was after in Brazil, far more than uranium, was diamonds. The whole film itself was inspired by my father's wartime work to block Brazil from becoming the Nazi's diamond source. He had taken the Vargas diamond. Now he had to take on the dictator Vargas himself.

To understand the gravity of the threat of Germans in Brazil, it is first important to understand the threat of Germans here at home. Ironically, my father would be forced to deal with German espionage on both fronts. The Germans had been one of the dominant ethnic groups in New York, as well as America. The greatest of all New York families, the Astors, were of German stock. The double pride of the Yankees, Babe Ruth and Lou Gehrig, were both of German blood, as was President Herbert Hoover (né Huber), not to mention all the great German-Jewish families, the Kuhns, Loebs, Schiffs, Guggenheims, that dominated Wall Street and looked down on poor Russian peasants like Jacob Weinstein.

My mother's first language was German, and she remained partial to the German butchers and bakers and other old-world craftsmen of Yorkville, New York's thriving "Little Berlin" on East 86th Street. Lüchow's, a classic Oktoberfest *biergarten* with walls hung with stuffed wild boars, on East 14th Street next to Tammany Hall, was where the most important political deals in the city were brokered.

Sending a son for graduate work to Heidelberg or Tübingen was every bit as prestigious as Oxford and Cambridge. I am sure I would have been groomed for such a continental education had World War I not made Germany something of a pariah. During that war, my mother told me, if you were heard speaking German in public, people would literally spit at you. Now with Hitler giving Germans the blackest reputation of any nation in history, Yorkville had become the home of the German American Bund, the most notorious pro-Nazi organization in America. Street battles were commonplace. Nonetheless, some traditions died hard, such as getting our meat from Hoexter's Meat Market, where the booming German voice on the phone—"*Da butcha!*"—rang in my childhood ears. Also ringing in my ears were the beatings given to me by the German nanny hired by my mother, until she discovered her Gestapo style of discipline and fired her.

A lot of New York's Germans had left the city after World War I and moved to Brazil, which had a huge and highly influential German population of eight hundred thousand, mostly in its southern provinces near the Argentine border, where the towns could have passed for Bavarian and the beer, or *chopp* in Portuguese, was as good as in Munich. There were also three hundred thousand Japanese, mostly coffee growers, around São Paolo, and two million Italians. Brazil was a happy hunting ground for the Axis powers, and one of the things the Axis was hunting for were diamonds. What Hitler was looking for was not another Vargas super gem to give to Eva Braun; what he wanted and desperately needed were industrial diamonds, whose durability was essential to mass-produce the precision parts for his weapons of destruction. Between the two world wars, the battlefield had grown very high tech, and diamonds were a key part of the technological advance, not just in weaponry but also in communications technologies like radar.

American intelligence, before it became something of an oxymoron in our times, determined that Hitler's supply of industrial diamonds was rapidly dwindling and desperately needed replenishing. It therefore became crucial to block the flow of diamonds to Germany. Cutting off Hitler's diamonds was tantamount to castrating the dictator. But because De Beers basically had a monopoly on all the world's diamonds, where else could Hitler get his stones but somehow through the Oppenheimer cartel, which was Jewish in origin and British in location?

America had its own enormous needs for industrial diamonds, and even Roosevelt had a terrible time in getting the Oppenheimers to open their London vaults to transfer part of their stockpile to the States, or at least Canada, where they would be safe in case of a German conquest of England. The Oppenheimers didn't trust anyone, including Roosevelt. They were less afraid of Hitler somehow releasing the diamonds and flooding the market and depressing the prices that the Oppenheimers tried to obsessively control.

The Germans could, and did, try to smuggle diamonds from De Beers' African mines, and there was indeed a pipeline through Tangiers. But it was by no means a big enough pipeline. South America, on the other hand, was the one source of diamonds in the world that was not controlled by De Beers, and so Hitler and company made a play to make this tropical paradise their personal mineral warehouse.

For all my mother's personal naïveté regarding the charms of Vichy France on my parents' final grand tour before all hell broke loose, my father was on to the Führer, and therefore on to Brazil, early in the game. After all, hadn't Harry Winston bought the prized Vargas stone? In the mid-1930s he saw how rich Brazil's potential was, both in the possibility of discovering more Vargases to sell to more Rockefellers, in addition to mining the less glamorous industrial stones. There was also quartz for time pieces and chromium for alloy steel, asbestos for insulation, and rubber for tires. None of these mineral riches were available in the United States, yet Harry knew they would be vital to the war effort, before the war even started.

So in 1939 Harry dispatched a young man named Daniel Frey to become his man in Rio. Daniel was related to Harry through his sister-in-law Bessie. Daniel was a bookworm, a Phi Beta Kappa graduate of City College, who felt stifled by the daily grind in the back rooms of Harry Winston. It was one thing to be a "face man" selling to the Junior Rockefeller and Barbara Hutton and quite another to be a Dickensian clerk doing bookkeeping and managing inventory. Imagine Daniel's surprise when he was moved out of the backroom and sent down to Rio.

My father didn't want to go back to Brazil himself. Despite the elegance of the Copacabana Palace Hotel where he and my mother stayed, the country was very much third world. There was little refrigeration; the Cariocas tenderized their meat by sandwiching their steaks between two halves of a papaya, and letting the enzymes turn flank steak into tournedos. It was tasty but savage, and my father had had enough roughing it as a boy to last the rest of his lifetime. Plus, flying down to Rio sounded glamorous, but the flights were long and sometimes dangerous. No, Harry left Rio to Daniel. He'd do his part on the phone.

Daniel never quite became Cary Grant, and he didn't romance Ingrid Bergman, but with his quiet manner and the endorsement of the Harry Winston imprimatur, he was welcomed into Brazilian society, and what he saw chilled his blood: "You better get things moving. There are a lot of diamonds, and the Germans and the Japanese are all over the place ready to sop up these supply lines."

Harry and Daniel were on the phone together virtually every day. Daniel and Harry's man in Rio, a local bigwig dealer named Leon Monte (né Leon Greenberg), began buying all the Brazilian diamonds they could at Monte's Avenida office, which was in downtown Rio, near the ornate Opera House, a duplicate of the one in Paris. The office stayed open until very late at night, and Daniel, wearing his Fifth Avenue suits, would entertain rugged prospector types from all the mining regions of Brazil. Coromondel produced the large stones, Belo Horizonte the industrials and the *carborandos*, the Mato Grosso the pink and green round diamonds. *Carborandos* were found only in Brazil. They look like brownish hailstones and are the hardest kind of diamonds, which are already the hardest known material. They never fractured, and as such, were in the highest demand for diamond tools and rock drills.

The sellers arrived with small rough canvas sacks tied with ribbons, and they would spill their treasures onto Monte's white pads. Using special tweezers, Monte would push the rough stones into separate piles, each according to a category: industrial, sawable, cleavage, makeable, and other terms of the trade. The stones in each pile, gathered in a kind of sugar scooper, would be weighed in a compensating balance scale.

It was all very old-world, the same in Rio as in Antwerp back in the Middle Ages. Then the haggling would begin, as it had for centuries. The sellers would never take their eyes off their treasures until the negotiations were completed. Once a deal was struck, both sides, regardless of religion, would say, "Mazel," or good luck, in Yiddish. Payment was almost invariably in cash.

Naturally, the Germans wanted these same stones and were more than willing to match Harry Winston's prices. The Abwehr, or German intelligence agency, funneled money to their commercial attaché in Brazil, who made the funds available in large bundles of Brazilian cruzeiro notes. Such was the power of the stones to warm Hitler's evil heart. But here was little Harry standing in the way of the bloody dictator. These Germans were not above using inducements such as torture and murder if they would help them outbid my father. Their strategy was to make Brazilian suppliers offers they could not refuse. The whole scene in Brazil was spy versus spy and very tense indeed. Daniel Frey, Leon Monte, and even my father, were all in perpetual danger because of their efforts to thwart the Führer and the Fatherland from getting Brazil's diamonds.

But Hitler wasn't the only dictator in the picture. Getúlio Vargas, the namesake of Harry Winston's big rock, while nominally the president of Brazil, was very much a Führer wannabe. A native of the heavily German southern province of Rio Grande do Sul, Vargas, who grew up in a family of gauchos, made his way first through the military, then the law, then into politics. Vargas was a provincial rabble-rouser who stirred the masses by attacking the entrenched privilege of the dominant São Paolo elite, whose power came from coffee.

I remembered as a little boy hearing Carmen Miranda sing "There's a Lot of Coffee in Brazil." But there were also a lot of diamonds and minerals and everything else in this underdeveloped land of plenty.

Vargas represented Brazil's industrial future, and he was so flattered when my father named the gem after him that, in 1939, he entertained Harry in the presidential palace in Rio.

At that meeting, my father turned on the charm, assuring Vargas how famous the eponymous stone was going to make him. Harry compared the Vargas to the Jonker and told the president about the global publicity storm he had whipped up for that rock. He talked of the "romance" of the stone, of the "human interest" in the poor digger who first discovered it and how that interest would give Brazilians hope, and in turn give hope to Brazil in resuming its rightful place in the diamond universe. Since 1870, when diamonds were discovered in Kimberley, South Africa, Brazil had been demoted as the diamond mining capital of the world. Harry promised to bring that crown back to Rio. What was particularly attractive here was that Brazil was outside the orbit, and control, of the Oppenheimers. Brazil could be Harry's own sphere of influence. Harry told Vargas that Brazil's diamonds had been "neglected." He was convinced, he told the strongman, that Brazil had the quantity and quality of stones to compete with South Africa. All Brazil needed was the right public relations, which had been nonexistent, which was to say that all Brazil needed was Harry Winston.

My father's biggest problem in dealing with the dictator was that the surly Vargas was beyond charm, though not beyond greed. He had become a deep admirer of Hitler and Mussolini, employing their fascist tactics in extirpating the entrenched power of the Paulista old guard. The most visible political movement in Brazil in the thirties was integralism, whose foot soldiers were a green-shirted, anti-Semitic paramilitary organization directly funded by the Berlin-Rome axis.

The Integralistas espoused "Christian virtues" and attacked Jews and Marxists as the combined Antichrist. Under the guise of safeguarding the nation from a Brazilian communist manifesto known as the Cohen Plan, Vargas assumed dictatorial powers in 1937. Vargas and Hitler exchanged birthday telegrams, and Germany became the second-largest market for Brazilian coffee, after America, and the largest for Brazilian cotton. But when push came to shove, Vargas could never quite join the Axis. Money talked, and Harry Winston money mattered.

America wanted Brazil as much as Hitler did. Roosevelt dispatched Junior Rockefeller's son Nelson, who later became the governor of New York and who bought diamonds from Harry for his wife Happy, to head a commission to bring Latin American nations into the Yankee fold. Roosevelt's goodwill ambassador was none other than the embodiment of goodwill himself, Walt Disney. Disney actually made an animated film *Saludos Amigos*, which featured a cartoon character named Ze Carioca, or Rio Joe. The most memorable scene in the film is when Joe teaches Donald Duck the intricate steps of the samba, which soon became the dance craze at El Morocco.

Although my father's initial attraction to Brazil was economic, the rise of Nazism and the attraction of Vargas to Hitler converted my father into a patriot. By 1940 he'd heard enough horror stories about displaced Jews to be stirred into action.

He knew he was one person who could make a difference, and so he stepped up to the challenge.

Aside from buying up all the industrial diamonds before Hitler could get them, Harry also came up with an ingenious scheme to make gold available to Vargas through the English, whose financial institutions acted as correspondent banks for the very soft Brazilian currency. Harry Winston would provide the dollars to London to buy gold, which would then be available to back the Brazilian cruzeiro. Harry could then draw down money in Rio to buy diamonds, and because of the gold backing, Vargas would give preference to the Winston buyers. Even though Hitler and Vargas shared the same totalitarian ideology, Hitler could simply not match the economic strategies, like my father's gold gambit, that America could offer. Still, throughout the war, Hitler remained in the Brazilian picture, and German smuggling and black-market deals remained rampant.

While Harry Winston was getting involved with the Boys from Brazil, he had his own brush with espionage right in his own backyard. When he first acquired Stonwin in 1940, in preparation for my arrival, my mother insisted on German help. My mother was a Pollyanna insofar as the war was concerned. She was seduced by the charms of Vichy, and she *was* German, or at least she was a product of the Austro-Hungarian German-speaking empire. All the clichés about Germans—being efficient, clean, industrious—spoke to Edna, plus she spoke the language.

She hired a German gardner, who brought in his Italian assistant. This, my father would joke later, was our horticultural contribution to the Axis. But the joke would be on Harry. The German, named Franck, was an excellent gardener and

became quite close to my father. He was also a horse whis-
perer of sorts, having calmed Lady, who had nearly thrown
my father and was bucking so wildly that Harry was unable
to dismount. My father was puzzled as to why this normally
docile animal got so spooked. Franck showed him why. Lady
had a golf ball–size wound on her head, right below her eyes.
She'd been hit by an errant ball driven from the adjacent
Quaker Ridge Golf Club. Franck was able to calm her enough
for my father to dismount. He then attended to her wound.
From then on, Franck would act as my father's groom. Harry,
who was small enough to be a jockey, would be hoisted up
onto his mount each morning by Franck and ride the perime-
ter of Stonwin. Franck always stayed close by when my father
was riding, just in case he was needed.

Franck was, in fact, good at everything. My mother wondered, however, why he was spending so much time in our
basement. He explained to her that he was stoking the coal for
a temperamental hot water boiler. "See how well the Germans
fix things," my mother said proudly to Harry.

Early one Saturday morning in May 1941, Harry went to
the pool for one of his polar bear crack-of-dawn swims. That
was the Russian in him. I remember him standing in the shal-
low end beating himself on the chest, like Tarzan, or more like
a Kremlinite contemplating a winter plunge into the Moscow
River. The water came from our artesian well. Its temperature
was a teeth-chattering fifty-five degrees. This swimming ritual was the most physically animated I ever saw my father,
much more than selling to the Rockefellers. He would whoop
and holler and plunge himself into the pool. He would swim
two laps, and when he got out, his body would be beet red
from the cold.

After every Saturday swim, my father went to the pool cabana to change into his Saturday outfit of white duck trousers, canary yellow polo shirt, and brown tasseled loafers, always with elevators and always worn without socks. His next stop would be to sit and have breakfast on the veranda in his Venetian-style wicker chair and listen to the radio, Toscanini, Ellington, a Gene Autry serial, anything except more bad news from Europe. My mother, who was not a morning person, rarely joined him. Instead, his company was a caged canary whose hue was exactly that of his polo shirt. (If Harry Winston, King of Canary Diamonds, couldn't get that color right, no one could.)

But the world's bad news was hard to avoid, and Harry's ears pricked up when he heard the potting shed radio emit the disastrous announcement that the current program was being interrupted with news that the mighty HMS *Hood*, the pride of the British fleet, had just been sunk by the even mightier *Bismarck*, Hitler's floating Armageddon, in the Denmark Straits near Iceland. Of 1,419 crew members, only three survived.

But what Harry heard next was even more chilling. *"Deutschland! Deutschland! Ja, Ja! Ourah! Ourah!"* It was the elated voice of his trusted Franck, spontaneously cheering. Almost by reflex, Harry stepped out of the cabana and saw Franck step out of the potting shed, having belatedly realized that his moment of unbridled ecstasy may have been overheard. A shaken Harry uttered a terse, knowing hello, and a chastened Franck silently nodded back.

But now Harry was suspicious, and so he called the FBI. They arranged to meet him later that day in his office. He shared what he'd overheard with two officers. A few days later, they returned with the bad news: Franck wasn't just a casual German nationalist. He was a full-fledged Nazi spy.

Franck had been planted in the German employment agency by the Abwehr, the Nazi intelligence network, with the express intention of learning the secrets of Harry Winston's industrial diamond purchasing network. The FBI told my father that Franck knew he spoke to Daniel Frey in Rio almost every evening. His mission was to report to the Abwehr the quantities of diamonds the Winston organization hoped to buy and from whom, so the Germans could get there first.

Because the phone lines to Rio were primitive, my father had to shout into the telephone from the knotty-pine-paneled library that he used as his country office. The conversation was punctuated by endless "I can't hear you"s, "Can you repeat what you said?" and "Is that correct?" I remember later similar problems he had in telephone conversations with the maharajas in India. He was talking so loudly, I didn't think he needed a phone to be heard across the world. In any event, Franck was in the cellar, picking up every word.

The FBI identified Franck as a danger to national security. The information he gathered was passed on to his handlers in Yorkville and from there to Mexico City and then on to Berlin. My father was shocked. He didn't call my mother, who was with me at Stonwin the day of the FBI report. But he knew that Franck knew that he knew, and the FBI told my father they would give Franck twenty-four hours to leave the country or be tried for espionage. This was before Pearl Harbor and before America entered the war and explains why Franck was treated so lightly. Another few months, and similar German spies who were caught were executed. The FBI actually apologized to my father for depriving him of such a good caretaker.

They knew that good help was hard to find, especially during wartime.

My father knew that anything could happen in twenty-four hours. He jumped into action, dispatching Paul Haase, his chief of security, to Stonwin to patrol the grounds with an off-duty Scarsdale police officer to assist him. As I grew older, I remember Paul as an intimidating G-man type, big, with a broad nose and a white moustache, and always packing a .38 revolver in a well-worn shoulder holster. He spoke in a low voice at all times, as if a perp was right around the corner.

Only after Paul and his cop aide were at Stonwin did Harry call Edna to tell her that her Franck was a spy. "Don't go outside, and don't take Ronnie out in the baby carriage until I get there," he warned her, assuring her that Paul was guarding the house. Then the chauffeur, John Simpson, who lived with his wife in the chauffeur's cottage, made tracks in the Packard from Manhattan back to Scarsdale. John was short and bald and paunchy, but he was a real Irish American patriot type, a George M. Cohan Yankee Doodle Dandy. If he had known Franck was a traitor he probably would have killed him.

John got my father back to Stonwin in record time and cleared us out of the house even faster. Back in Manhattan, Harry called Dan Frey in Rio to put him and his suppliers on alert. He ordered Dan to get a bodyguard. "Be careful. Be very careful," Harry cautioned. As it turned out, the FBI was worried too. Two of their men were shadowing Paul Haase and his hired cop, for safety's sake. Meanwhile, Franck was arrested and deported. And we holed up, on 51st Street for the next few weeks.

As it turned out, my father unmasking Franck was key in cracking a huge German spy ring in Yorkville. The Americans' chief spycatcher was an FBI double agent named William Sebold. A German-born engineer who worked in aircraft factories and industrial plants in North and South America after World War I, Sebold was "recruited" by the Abwehr via grisly death threats against his family to work in New York under the alias Harry Sawyer, to spy on the likes of Harry Winston. His code name was TRAMP, and he had plush offices on 42nd Street, set up as a high-end consulting engineer. But before he took on this assignment, he went to the American Consulate in Cologne and offered to become a double agent. It was 1941, and the FBI embraced him with open arms.

Sebold's main contact in New York was a German spy named Fritz Duquesne, code name DUNN, who was so paranoid about bugs in Sebold's office (he was right to be) that he insisted the two agents meet at the Automat. Together they set up a shortwave radio station on Long Island that became the main channel of communication between New York's German spies and the Abwehr. Through Sebold, the FBI intercepted hundreds of messages to and from Europe and Brazil, surely including some involving my father.

The Franck crisis prompted the FBI to make their move. In an *Untouchables*-style series of dramatic raids, in June 1941, thirty-three German agents were arrested. Nineteen pled guilty immediately. The other fourteen went to trial that fall. Unfortunately for them, the final arguments were made just at the time of Pearl Harbor. On December 13, they were all found guilty, and the "Yorkville 33," otherwise known as the Duquesne spy ring, were sentenced to a total of over three hundred years in prison. The ringleader, Duquesne, died in prison in 1956.

This remains the largest espionage case ending in convictions in American history. The mastermind, Sebold, went into an early version of the Witness Protection Program and was never heard from again. For himself, Harry Winston took no kudos. That kind of publicity, while a great suspense tale for Hitchcock, would have been bad for a business in which fantasy and flawlessness, not fear and jeopardy, were the coins of the realm.

What turned out to be my father's greatest tragedy of World War II was a direct legacy of World War I. His brother Charles, the big, powerful "enforcer" of the family, had proudly served overseas in the Great War, where he had been gassed by the Germans. The agent was chlorine gas, a forerunner of the Zyklon B that was used in the concentration camps. The Germans released the poison when the wind was favorable, and being heavier than air, it flowed in noxious green waves into the Allied trenches, choking the troops.

With his scarred lungs (the family had a terrible history of respiratory ailments) and excess weight, Charles wheezed and sauntered through the days. But he was tough, a fighter, who never complained. He and his brother Stanley and their lighting fixtures business, located on 53rd Street only two blocks away from the Harry Winston palazzo, were doing so well that they opened a second store in Queens, when Queens was a family-friendly leafy suburb, where Charles was raising his four children. But Charles was sicker than he ever let on. One day, he came to our town house and took the elevator up to the fifth floor, lay down on his brother's antique bed, and died. Harry was devastated.

One token of his love for his brother was to convince Charles's son Richard to join Harry Winston. This was not easy. Richard, an Amherst graduate, was a great scholar-athlete who was the star pitcher on the varsity baseball team. The

Yankees came courting and, wowed by his arsenal of pitches, offered Richard a contract. He beat out Whitey Ford, the legendary pitcher, for a berth on the legendary team, which my father was obsessed with. But Harry wanted another Winston on his team. He told Richard this: "Assuming your arm holds up, you'll earn $5,000 a year for ten years. Then what? I can give you a career for life with much better earnings and a lot more security." That was Harry's pitch, and it worked. In those days, before television and before endorsements, even the likes of Yankee Clipper Joe DiMaggio didn't get rich. But Harry Winston salesmen did. Richard left the baseball diamond for Harry Winston diamonds, and he became a successful salesman.

In 1943 the global political tide would finally turn. The Allies began winning the world war, and Harry Winston had done his part in helping them win the diamond war. Never one to bet on a loser, Getúlio Vargas expelled the Abwehr from Brazil. Hitler, forced to rely on African smugglers for his industrial diamonds, came up short, and the German war machine eventually starved to death. My father, always an optimist, must have been feeling especially confident. In the summer of '43 my mother was pregnant once again. Her own father, the great doctor, had been a doomsayer on the occasion of my birth, pointing out what a terrible time it was to bring a Jewish child into the world. But my parents obviously believed that the times were changing, and for the better. I was going to get a brother, a pal, a sidekick. He arrived in January 1944.

CHAPTER SEVEN

Courting Jewels

One of the most visually dramatic moments in American history occurred in July 1945 when I was four years old: the lights came back on in New York City. They had been turned off ever since I had been born, to conceal the metropolis from the Luftwaffe bombers that, thank heavens, never arrived. By summer of 1945 Hitler had committed suicide, and the Japanese had surrendered, and the city went wild. The war was over; the celebration that would become the baby boom began in a brilliant burst of electric joy. Because my family's own baby boom had just exploded with the arrival of my brother Bruce, we were spending most of our time out at the baby-friendly Scarsdale estate, and I might have missed the initial flipping of the switch that turned the legendary "bright lights of Broadway" back on. But eventually I did see Manhattan in its full illuminated glory from the top floor of our town house. My life, which had been lived behind black-out shades, was now exposed to the light.

This festival of lights seemed to have a symbolic effect on the spectacle that was Harry Winston. Even though he had been selling diamonds to the aristocracy throughout the war, not to mention his industrial trade for the Allied cause, Harry Winston's game was one of showmanship and flash, which he had to suppress during the war years.

It was time to put on the dog.

In 1943 Harry got lucky again. A 155-carat alluvial stone was discovered in Venezuela's Gran Sabana region of grasslands and streams, along the border with Brazil. My father leaped at it, buying it for $63,000, which is over $1 million in 2023 and which was an eye-popping fortune during the time of postwar austerity. He named the treasure, with great patriotic fanfare, El Libertador, after Simón Bolívar, the George Washington of Venezuela. He cut the stone into a flawless forty-carat showpiece and three smaller stones, all emerald-cut.

Following his pattern of taking years to recoup his investments, Harry waited until 1947 before he sold the big gem to *Denver Post* heiress May Bonfils Stanton, whose all-Carrara marble mansion Belmar was an exact replica of the Petit Trianon, the home of Marie Antoinette. Stanton slept in Marie Antoinette's actual bed. Just to show she wasn't all let-them-eat-cake, Ms. Stanton also played Chopin's piano. Ms. Stanton, who would become one of my father's highest-profile clients, was not only the Queen of the Rockies but also the Queen of Rocks, and she gave Harry Winston the kind of publicity most businesses could only dream of. Then, in 1949, my father made headlines again when he sold the Jonker to the postwar king of conspicuous consumption, Farouk of Egypt.

He also bought a diamond mine in Venezuela, believing there had to be more great gems in "them thar hills." The idea of being completely vertically integrated, from shaft to showcase, had enormous allure for Harry. He would be going Ernest Oppenheimer one, actually two, better, by selling, both at wholesale and retail, from the fruits of his own mining labors.

Oppenheimer had problems of his own. His mines were closed, his London offices had been bombed and nearly destroyed, the Roosevelt administration was besieging him for his refusal to part with his industrial diamonds, and there were loud whispers of collaboration with the Nazis. Through the bravery of London's firefighters who hosed down De Beers's red-hot safes for three days to cool them, the syndicate's vast cache of stones was saved from the ashes of the Charterhouse buildings. But the colossus was paralyzed. Sir Ernest himself was sitting out the war in Johannesburg. For all Harry knew, he could be sitting a long while, and Harry Winston, who could not sit for a minute, saw Venezuela as a great opportunity.

I'm not sure Harry ever went down to survey his domain in Gran Sabana, and therein lay the problem. There was absolutely nothing glamorous about the mining operation, which was highly primitive. A work crew armed with little more than picks and shovels would dig into the bank of a river until they hit gravel, which was scooped up and placed into a device known as a Denver jig, which sounds like a kind of barn dance and is just about as old-fashioned. The jig, which is the size of an old Volkswagen Beetle, sprayed water on the gravel to wash off the river soil, then strained and shook the gravel before pouring it over greased plates. Finally the gravel would be washed away, and any diamonds in the mix would stick to the grease.

This was a far cry from Fifth Avenue and the white-gloved matrons who shopped there. Alluvial mining was dirty and brutal, and stealing was considered part of the game. The miners got a little, the bosses got a lot, and Harry got nothing. "I was buying my own diamonds three miles downstream from my own mine," my father lamented. "The miners were a pack of thieves." Nor did my father get bragging rights to a vast, dramatic pit like Kimberley. That might have at least provided a publicity angle. In short, and literally, Venezuela did not pan out. It was no country for absentee landlords. By the late 1940s my father abandoned his South American operations.

But by then he was well on to another continent. By 1945 Harry decided to stake his fame and fortune on India, the land of the fabled Golconda diamond fields. His one true goal was to purchase every famous large and historical diamond in the world, most of which were Indian in origin. To maintain his stature as the ultimate diamond mogul, he would buy out the Indian Moguls themselves.

My father couldn't have picked a better time to be in India. The maharajas were, quite, literally, on the rocks. The country, in thrall to the ascetic Gandhi and on the eve of a blood-drenched forced partition between Hindus and Muslims in 1947, was in a state of disarray.

In the early fifteenth century, the Moguls, a Muslim people, swept out of their central Asian home in what is now Uzbekistan and conquered first the Punjab, then Delhi, and eventually Uttar Pradesh, creating an empire that stretched from the Himalayas to the Ganges River. The empire was one of the most opulent dynasties in history. The Moguls were lured to India not only by its fabled treasures of precious stones but also by the equally fabled lush full-bosomed beauty of the Hindu maidens. The sensual symbiosis of sex and gems was in play, and no one loved jewels and women more than the Mogul emperors.

Their very names connote the most lavish imperialism the world had ever seen: Akbar, Jahangir, Aurangzeb, and, of course, Shah Jahan, who built the ultimate testament to opulence and love, the Taj Mahal. In India, perhaps more than anywhere else, diamonds were a symbol of power.

Sir Thomas Roe, the English adventurer and statesman who was Viceroy of King James I from 1615 to 1618, said it best when he described his drinking buddy Jahangir in full regalia as "wearing the treasury of the world." No other potentates had ever had access to such gem wealth as existed in India. Most of the greatest diamonds, coming from the Golconda mines in southern India in the state of Hyderabad, were kept in the royal treasuries for four hundred years, but by the 1940s, many of India's five hundred or so maharajas or nizams or princes, or whatever (the subcontinent was loaded with kingdoms) found themselves in need of funds to fuel their lavish spending habits. There were palaces, armies of servants, sumptuous wedding banquets, elablorate tiger hunting parties, private railway cars and planes, trips to London and Paris and Venice, Eton and Oxford educations; all these expenses strained the royal exchequers.

The British had used these princes as the pawns in their imperial game for three centuries, beginning with the East India Company's grant of a monopoly on trade in 1600. The British were after spices, rather than diamonds, for the Golconda fields were virtually played out by the time of their arrival. But by the end of World War II, the British crown was tottering, and its hold on India gone. As a going-away present, the last viceroy, Lord Mountbatten, arranged for the final two generations of princes to retain their titles and their privy purses, the latter being a money-for-nothing kind of poll tax levied on their subjects. But the natives were restless, and these princes would no longer be able to live in the style to which they had become accustomed. So they turned to Harry Winston to sell their jewels and buy some time.

What I would later call my father's Indian Period, or, in chess terms, the King's Indian Defense, began in 1945. Our Scarsdale estate became the Taj Mahal of Westchester, and the fabled silk route to the Indies now took a detour up the Hutchinson River Parkway. I don't think there was a major maharaja who did not find his way to Stonwin. Even today, the closets there contain bolts of sari cloth of priceless gold and silver brocade fabric, which had been offered as gifts to my mother. She would take these fabrics to Paris to her personal couturier, Mainbocher, to craft into stunning bare shouldered, strapless gowns to wear with her burgeoning Indian jewel collection.

The first maharaja I met was His Royal Highness Yashwant Rao, the very, very grand maharaja of Indore. Known to his intimates as "Junior," he frequently visited us at Stonwin. He had his own estate in Greenwich, Connecticut, not far from Scarsdale. I could tell the maharaja was special, even at my tender age. Tall and rapier thin, the Oxford-educated rajah dressed only in the finest Savile Row tweed suits. He sent us crates of the finest mangoes in the world. The sweet smell of the tropics wafting from those crates was one of my Proustian memories, along with the curry powder from the Pierre Grille, a lavish Indian restaurant in the basement of the hotel, catering to the many maharajas who made the Pierre their New York home.

The pride of the Indore jewel collection were two beautiful pear-shaped forty-seven-carat Golconda diamonds, actually purchased in Paris from Napoleon's jeweler Chaumet. With partition looming, Junior decided to sell Harry his treasures. In 1946 Dad bought the Indore Pears from Junior, in addition to the Porter Rhodes, a fifty-six-carat South African diamond from Cecil Rhodes's Kimberley Mine, which Junior had acquired in Paris in 1937.

Aside from Junior, my father was able to do deals with other great maharajas. They weren't exactly easy to meet, so Harry worked through their ADCs, or aides-de-camp. Junior's ADC was a man named Colonel Harry Nedu, a descendant of an ancient Kashmiri family that owned a grand hotel near one of Srinigar's Alpine lakes. The colonel had no need to work, but he enjoyed the challenges of buying and selling and travelling with the maharaja. Harry Nedu often stayed with us in Scarsdale. I'll never forget his elegant poplin suits, his slicked-back, jet black hair, his military brush moustache, and, most indelibly, the way he smelled. Harry's patchouli cologne evoked Kashmir's fabled Shalimar Gardens. It hung in the air for days after the aide-de-camp decamped from Stonwin.

Sometimes in the summer, Junior would bring his young son Richard to swim in our pool. I was six and Richard was two, and we would grow up to become dear friends. He would later be a magical host to me in India. I remember once when Harry Winston, Harry Nedu, and the maharaja were so distracted in their discussions of diamonds that the true jewel in the crown got away and teetered on the edge of the deep end of the pool. When they saw Richard about to fall in, I never saw three grown men move so quickly to catch the baby, who could not swim.

My early childhood wasn't all maharajas. The most excit-
ing person I would meet was my baby brother Bruce, who
arrived in the world three years and three days after me on
January 13, 1944. Bruce's birth had been far more arduous
than his conception. My father later told me that he had been
a blue baby for not having received sufficient oxygen. I can't
recall the fragility, only a round-faced, reddish-brown ring-
leted cherub with intense, hypnotic blue eyes. Now that Bruce
had arrived, my mother slept in his room, leaving me to my
own devices. I learned to draw my own bubble bath and run
the radio, setting it to the stations that played America's great
bands. Then I would slide into those voluptuous bubbles and
groove to the swing of Benny Goodman and Artie Shaw.

Despite his new family and great success, Harry Winston
never forsook his family of origin. His brother and sister were
still living proof that the bad old days were not that far behind.
Oddly enough, the only time the three Weinstein siblings,
who were all now Winstons, would spend time together as a
family was at Christmas. I never heard of Hanukkah. Mother
told me that she enjoyed going to Christmas Midnight Mass
across the street at St. Patrick's. She said the mass gave her
a sense of peace, and she loved the music. I had absolutely
no idea of my own ethnoreligious heritage until, some years
later, when I asked my mother a psychological question as to
why I felt so driven to excel at school and in sports. "Because
you're Jewish," she said.

I must have had some idea, without knowing what that
idea was, because soon after Santa's arrival came that of the
whole *mishpochah*, Yiddish for extended family. For all Harry's
lordly clientele and English suits and Edna's patrician man-
ners and midnight masses, my parents often included a few

Yiddish phrases in their dialogue. I thought they were doing
it to keep secrets from me, but the biggest secret was my own
Jewish heritage. The first holiday arrival was Uncle Stanley,
in his Cadillac Eldorado. Stanley sold chandeliers, and lots of
them.

While my father could be serious and grave, Stanley was
the joker in the family. Once, after a trip to Moscow, I brought
him the gift of a traditional astrakhan hat. I had no idea what
his head size was, so when he tried it on, it slid down his head
and covered his eyes. He smiled at me and quipped, "Don't
worry, Ronnie. I have another head at home."

After Stanley, Aunt Dora would arrive, driven out to Stonwin
by my father's live-in chauffeur. Dora always wore a brown
velvet dress and shoes with large square heels that propped
her up so she was nearly Harry's height. One Christmas, she
gave me a copy of *The Little Prince*, St. Exupéry's paean to childhood and fantasy. As I leafed through the pages, Dora knelt on
the floor beside me with her dyed red hair in a top-knot bun.
She stroked my cheek and murmured, "My little prince."

With her duties to Jacob Weinstein as surrogate wife and
to my father as surrogate mother, Dora had missed her youth
entirely. She'd probably never had a boyfriend, had never
been engaged. She was, my father told me years later, afraid
of men. For a time after Jacob died, she lived with Charles in
Great Neck. But eventually Charles's wife, Gertrude, threw
Dora out because she gave too many baths to their infant
Johnny. Dora moved to the Barbizon Hotel for Women on
Lexington Avenue in the East 60s, where she had a single room
and shared a bathroom down the hall with the much younger
college girls, some of whom came to Manhattan hoping to
snag a man who would shop for them at Harry Winston.

Dora could have had anything she wanted from Harry Winston; my father was well aware she had sacrificed her youth for him, but Dora had the simplest of tastes. She lived at the Barbizon for the remaining forty-five years of her life. She worked for the Educational Testing Service, the company that created the SATs. And she was thrilled when I aced them and got into Harvard.

For our Christmas feast, we would repair to our baronial dining room, with a long Georgian mahogany table and painted Chinese wallpaper, with scenes of birds and butterflies. Harry would have his third Dubonnet and gin by now, Stanley his Scotch on the rocks, and Dora her one dry sherry, which would last the entire meal. Mother would nurse a glass of wine. The Christmas turkey would arrive. It had been perfectly carved in layers by our Belgian chef and served by our English butler, Newlings, who was very tall and as proper as a Coldstream Guard.

Our Christmas dinner seemed to go on for eternity. I coaxed my baby brother under the table, whose dark recesses provided a vast jungle for our imaginations. Bruce giggled in delight. He was such a good-natured baby. At these "family" dinners, my father did not include his late brother Charlie's widow or children, even though he would put all the boys to work for him. I think Gertrude got on his nerves. Not that Dora didn't, but she was "blood," and Gertrude wasn't. At the end of the endless meal, Dora would fold her napkin and say, "Edna, dear, it's almost nine. It's late. I might get raped. I should take the car and go back to the city." My mother looked at her tiny sister-in-law and, waiting two beats for comic emphasis, riposted, "Dora, do you have an appointment?" It was a cruel joke, but Dora, who took everything quite literally, missed the wit entirely.

My mother could be funny, but she took some aspects of herself very seriously, specifically her vanity. Until Bruce was born, she used to love going to Florida and spending days sunbathing. She used to speak of her "Egyptian bones" and her need for solar beautification. This was all fine for my father, for many of his richest clients would be wintering in Florida, certainly during the war. In Miami we would stay at the grand Roney Plaza, where Walter Winchell filed all his winter dispatches, and on Collins Avenue in front of us, thousands of troops in summer khakis and black neckties drilled and marched off to war. I somehow thought the hotel was named for me, such was my princely sense of entitlement.

One childhood year my mother got a nose job. These were the pioneering days of plastic surgery, when the Broadway star Fanny Brice shocked the nation by "cutting off her nose to spite her race," as Dorothy Parker quipped. My mother's beauty apparently could not be enhanced by the sun alone, so she went under the knife. Maybe she wanted the retroussé nose of the women in the *Social Register* set my father catered to. Harry, who was so proud of his wife's beauty but exasperated at the time she devoted to it, loved Edna just the way she was. But Edna didn't love the Edna of the Lower East Side. I'll never forget catching my mother cutting her "old" face out of all the photographs taken of her in Florida, Europe, Cuba, Mexico. She was equally vain about her age. Once, when I was older, she caught me looking at her passport at an immigration checkpoint, and she whacked me hard. She felt violated, betrayed. But so did I. And I whacked her right back.

CHAPTER EIGHT

Big Rocks

In 1946, Harry Winston embarked on his biggest buying spree, acquiring six of the world's greatest diamonds. Two of them, the Indore Pears and the Porter Rhodes, came from Harry's friend and neighbor, Junior the maharaja. Another was the Idol's Eye, a heavenly seventy-carat diamond that had been mined in Golconda around 1600, had been set in a Roman statue in Libya and was owned in succession by a Persian prince, a Spanish count, a London collector, and, in 1946, my father.

Unlike most of his other big rocks, Harry held the Idol's Eye for less than a year, selling it to the May Bonfils Stanton of Denver for $675,000, which naturally got him a new round of front-page headlines in those lean postwar times. Another jewel in Harry's 1946 crown was the ninety-carat Briolette of India, which was reputed to be the oldest diamond of record in the world, more venerable than the Koh-i-Noor. Somehow Cartier had acquired it and sold it to the head of the American branch of Lazard Frères, upon whose widow my father pounced. She soon succumbed to my father's inducements to sell it to him. Dad would hold the Briolette for nearly a decade until Mrs I. W. Killam, the Canadian tallow heiress, fell under its—and my father's—spell.

Helping Harry cast his spell was Igor "Gigi" Cassini, the Italo-Russian aristocrat who wrote the influential Cholly Knickerbocker society gossip column for the Hearst newspapers, including the *New York Journal-American*. This was the dawn of the age of Madison Avenue and the rise of the art, or science, or voodoo of "public relations." Whenever Dad bought or sold a great stone, Gigi Cassini would get the scoop, and the buzz would spread from El Morocco to the Stork Club and onward around the world.

My father put Gigi to work for him, because there was no one in New York better connected. Not only did Gigi marry the daughter of oil billionaire Charles Wrightsman (she later committed suicide), but his brother Oleg, one of the few straight fashion designers in a gay business, married Gene Tierney, would become the love of Grace Kelly's life, and was Jackie Kennedy's official White House couturier. I'm sure Gigi was well compensated, and the issue of journalistic ethics didn't seem to apply to gossip columns until the sixties, when Gigi's ties to Porfirio Rubirosa and the Dominican Republic got him canned by Hearst. By then Harry Winston had become a global household name.

Harry not only sold to the leaders of big business; he was big business himself, with gross revenues estimated at over $20 million a year at the end of the 1940s. He was the "little big man" of the American jewelry business, the only jeweler in the country who did it all, at every level. Even though Harry derived most of his publicity from his big rocks and his big shots, he loved, and traded in, rocks big and small. He was the only jeweler in the country who dealt in wholesale and retail, in industrial diamonds, in rough diamonds, in colored stones like rubies, sapphires, and emeralds. He had a huge diamond-cutting operation and a preeminent design studio. He also sold to chains of jewelers all over the country, including the big catalog houses. That thirty-dollar engagement ring that was bought from Montgomery Ward may have been wholesaled to the store by my father. The only thing he didn't do was mine the diamonds himself. He had tried in Venezuela and had failed. But my father wasn't used to failure, and who was to say he wouldn't try the Rhodes-Barnato mining route again? He was a colossus, and colossi didn't give up.

And therein lay the rub with the only player in the diamond world more powerful than Harry Winston: De Beers. The syndicate, as the South African cartel was known and feared, controlled 95 percent of worldwide diamond production. Despite its problems with Hitler's bombs and Roosevelt's antitrust lawyers and dwindling wartime demand, the war's end had spelled an enormous resurgence in the diamond business that redounded in fortunes to the "two Harrys," Winston and Oppenheimer, the latter who had taken over the daily reins of what was still the family business. But to De Beers, there could be only one Harry. The diamond world was too small to accommodate them both. De Beers had watched with certain rage at my father's Venezuelan gambit while they were powerlessly ducking the Blitz in London. They knew there were lots of diamonds in the world that they didn't control, and Harry W. was clearly a wildly ambitious and wildly brilliant competitor.

In the forties a maverick Canadian geologist named Dr. John Williamson had discovered in Tanganyika, now Tanzania, a kimberlite pipe like that of the Kimberley mine, the first outside of South Africa. De Beers of course tried to buy him out, but Williamson refused. He now was running the mine himself, with a labor force of thousands. De Beers hoped to starve him out, but what would happen if he teamed up with a deep-pocketed capitalist like Harry Winston? De Beers's main insurance that such a mésalliance would not occur was that Harry W. relied too heavily on Harry O. for his own diamond supplies. He spent millions at the De Beers "sights" in London, now in high gear once more. Harry Winston couldn't get out of hand because he didn't dare risk being cut off. The wrath of De Beers was too severe.

Nonetheless, De Beers never really embraced my father as their most important ally and customer. In its cloistered, reconstructed boardroom on Charterhouse Street, it was surely annoyed by the talents of this Lower East Side upstart who had somehow vaulted over all the other stone merchants, the men whom my father himself looked down on and disparaged as "dealers." Sometimes Harry W. would refer to the black-suited, gray bearded, frock-coated Hasidim who were his clients for the De Beers rough stones he bought and sold for profit as "the candlelight brothers," referring to their archaic shtetl ways. Harry W. looked down on the Hasids, and Harry O., the new Anglican, looked down on Harry W. as if he *were* a Hasid. All that arrogance marked a deep jealousy and fear.

After the Crash of 1929, there had been a huge depression in the diamond market, tracking that of the world itself, which had deeply shaken De Beers. To try to better control the market that De Beers monopolized, Harry Oppenheimer in 1938 had taken one of his rare trips to the United States to secretly visit the advertising colossus N. W. Ayer in Philadelphia. Ayer

186

139 Monroe Street tenement, one of Harry Winston's childhood homes, circa 1905.
Courtesy Municipal Archives, City of New York.

Harry, Dora, and Jacob in the Winston Store, opening day, Los Angeles, July 1911.

Harry Winston, age 18, 1914.

First Harry Winston retail office, 40th Street at 5th Avenue, New York City, 1922.

Edna and Harry Winston working on advertising in the 51st Street office, New York City, 1943.

Harry and Edna Winston with Edna's father, Dr. Henry Fleischman, 1945.

Edna Winston, 1955. Photo by Cecil Beaton, reprinted with permission, Cecil Beaton Archive @ Condé Nast.

Edna Winston, 1955. Photo by Cecil Beaton, Cecil Beaton Archive @ Condé Nast.

Edna Winston at the Red Cross Ball, Monte Carlo, August 1955.

Ronald and Harry with fish, Palm Beach, Florida, 1957.

Edna Winston donates the Hope Diamond to the Smithsonian Institution, 1958.

Ronald Winston, 1959.

Ronald Winston with Mary, Bridget, and Harry Oppenheimer, Durban, South Africa, 1963.

Ronald Winston with African Miners and the Lesotho diamond, 1965.

Ronald Winston, 1965.

Harry Winston with his siblings, Dora and Stanley, 1976. Photo by Alfred Eisenstaedt, courtesy of Ronald Winston.

Harry Winston with the Star of Independence diamond, 1976.

Harry Winston, 1976. Photo by Alfred Eisenstaedt, courtesy of Ronald Winston.

Harry Winston's 80th Birthday Party, March 1, 1976. Courtesy of Jessica Burstein.

Harry and Ronald Winston, Mt. Kisco, New York, 1976. Photo by Edward Kelley.

Harry Winston louping a diamond necklace, circa 1980.

Ronald Winston and Princess Yasmin Aga Khan. Photograph by Henry Wolf, *Town & Country*, September 1981.

was the oldest ad agency in the country and had created some of the greatest campaigns in American business: Morton Salt's "When It Rains It Pours." "I'd Walk a Mile for a Camel." Harry Oppenheimer wanted to buy some of that magic for his magic stones, to stimulate the flagging demand.

Ayer took on the account. Oppenheimer's goal was to get Americans to start buying more expensive engagement rings, as these made up three quarters of De Beers's American sales. This bread-and-butter business was getting cheaper and cheesier, with the average price of a ring having declined during the Depression to a mere eighty dollars.

Harry O. wanted to see Americans step up and make a grander gesture. To that end, Ayer began doing a subliminal seduction campaign by putting diamonds in Hollywood movies, in one of the earliest exercises of product placement. My father did the exact same thing by lending Ingrid Bergman her jewels for *Notorious*. There followed a series of tasteful ads in high-toned magazines like the *New Yorker* juxtaposing diamonds with famous paintings by Picasso, Dalí, and others, the idea being another subliminal seduction suggesting that diamonds were works of art.

After the war, De Beers didn't need any sublimation to stoke desire. The whole world was getting married. The trick now was getting the suitors to pony up for better rings. In 1947 De Beers turned to Ayer's best copywriter, Frances Gerety, to give them a tagline to end all taglines. The initial pitch was to spark competitive envy, but Gerety wanted something more subtle, kinder, more elegant. She lay her head on her desk and prayed, "O, Lord, give me a line." And the good Lord came back with "A diamond is forever," which Gerety scribbled down on a scrap of paper before she went home for the night.

De Beers embraced the slogan, which spurred a huge increase in the volume and prices of engagement rings. Frances Gerety, having inspired a nation of young lovers, never received a diamond and never married.

De Beers's "forever" campaign benefited no one more than Harry Winston, whom, it was estimated, sold at wholesale a quarter of all diamond engagement rings in America. But for all his financial successes, my father remained obsessed with his big rocks and his Grail quest to acquire all the greatest diamonds. His biggest score of all came in 1949 when he scored the most famous gem in the world, the Hope Diamond. The Hope's owner, the flamboyant and eccentric Washington, D.C., heiress and socialite Evalyn Walsh McLean, died of pneumonia at age sixty in 1947. She had decreed in her will that the Hope, unique for its deep hypnotic, midnight blue color, not be worn or even shown for twenty years after her death. It was her way of assuring the diamond, famous for its many curses, didn't cause any more trouble. But where there was a will, there was a way, at least where my father was concerned. The Hope was the ultimate score and somehow, my father was able to court Mc Lean's executor, Thurman Arnold, Franklin Roosevelt's chief trustbuster and one of the premier Washington fixer lawyers. Harry convinced Arnold that it was in everyone's best interest to sell the Hope now. To sweeten the deal and break the will, Harry paid over $1 million for the iconic gem.

Both Evalyn and the Hope were the stuff a publicist's dreams were made of. Evalyn had been the daughter of an Irish immigrant miner who struck gold in Colorado and moved his family back to Washington to buy their way into international society. Evalyn was sent to a finishing school in

Paris and returned with a penchant for outrageous coiffures so complex that Evalyn couldn't wash her hair for fear of her maids' inability to reconstruct the hairdos. Her father asked his spoiled baby what it would take to get her to fix her hair like normal women. "Jewelry!" was her one-word answer that set Evalyn on the road to Golconda, by way of Cartier. She found a second powerful luxury enabler in 1906 when she married Ned McLean, heir to the *Washington Post* fortune.

Evalyn, who bought the Hope in 1911, actually pawned it in 1932 to give $100,000 to an ex–FBI agent turned master con man named Gaston Means, who promised to use it for ransom to get Charles Lindbergh's kidnapped baby back. When the baby was found dead, Evalyn helped lead authorities to Means, who was sent to prison for twenty years. Evalyn then went back to the Simpson Pawn Shop in Washington to retrieve the Hope. Like Edna with the smuggled European jewels on the eve of war, Evalyn stuck the Hope in her brassiere and walked home alone. She decided to forgo her security detail because she had had enough of detectives at that point.

The Lindbergh sting wasn't the only manifestation of the notorious Hope curse. Soon after she bought the diamond, Evalyn's first son was killed in an automobile accident; her husband was tarred in the Teapot Dome scandal with his dear friend President Harding and later died in a mental hospital; and in 1946 Evalyn's daughter died of a sleeping pill overdose, just before Evalyn's own untimely death. Such tragedies burnished the legend of the Hope curse. Mined at Golconda, the Hope first became famous as the Tavernier Blue, when the French merchant-adventurer Jean-Baptiste Tavernier purchased the 112-carat stone from a maharaja in 1660. Tavernier, who was the Harry Winston of his times, sold the diamond to the Sun King, Louis XIV, in 1668. The court jeweler cut it in half, into a pear shape of sixty-seven carats, whereupon the stone became known as the French Blue. It became the favorite gem of Marie Antoinette. When she was beheaded, revolutionary thieves stole the diamond and took it to London, where it disappeared for twenty years, until the statute of limitations for the crime of theft expired in England.

The next owner of record was London banker and diamond collector Henry Philip Hope. One of the Hope heirs, who inherited the gem, married an American actress named May Yohé. The curse hit both of them hard. Mister Hope went bankrupt, even after selling the Hope in 1911, and May, who left him for the dissolute son of New York Mayor William Strong, died in a Boston rooming house while working at a sixteen-dollar-a-week scrubwoman job during the Depression. The stone then crossed the Atlantic several times before Cartier sold it to Evalyn, who loved and wore it. She loved to clip it, along with her other Indian treasure, the Star of the East, on her Labrador's collar in order to shock her guests as the frisky dog ran wild around the McLean estate with a fortune on its throat.

Like that Labrador, Harry Winston got not only the Hope but also the hundred-carat Star of the East, which once decorated the turban of the Ottoman sultan, in his deal with the McLean estate, in addition to seventy-two other glittering items. My own first awareness of the monumental transaction came while listening to the radio in Florida in the winter of 1949. My mother had taken Bruce and me with her on one of her beauty cures and to escape the New York cold to the Alhambra fantasy that was the Boca Raton Resort. "The famed jeweler Harry Winston has just purchased the Hope Diamond from the Evalyn Walsh McLean estate," the newscaster intoned. "The estate, which includes many other famous jewels as well, was reportedly bought for the sum of $1 million."

My eight-year-old mind could not have understood fame in and of itself. I had no idea who Mrs. McLean was and what an estate was. But I knew what a million dollars was: the treasure that marked what everyone in America fantasized of becoming, a millionaire. So my father had to be a millionaire to spend a million dollars, and he must be famous, whatever that was, to be on the radio. I felt my own frisson of family pride. My mother, who had overheard the broadcast with me, beamed. Her huge smile seemed to say, "That's your little dad."

But now I felt a new element of insecurity. Not only was my father wealthy, he was famous as well. I developed a deep and abiding sense of worthlessness, yet at the same time a great self-confidence. If Dad could do it, so could I. Maybe. In my second grade at Rye Country Day School, near our estate, I was elected class president. After a few days, however, I announced to the class that I had to resign. There must be someone more worthy, I berated myself. After the Hope deal was done, my father joined us in Boca Raton and regaled my mother with the endless intricacies of the transaction. "Tell me, Dad," I pressed. "What is the Hope Diamond?"

Harry, who embraced any opportunity to sing the song of stones, filled my head until bedtime with the legends of the Hope. He also tried to explain to me about its color. "Some very special diamonds have a color other than white," he told me. "The Hope is blue, midnight blue." I thought to myself and tried to conjure up a full moon gliding against a blue-black clear winter night sky. This act of imagination thus began what would be for me, as it had been for my father, a long affair with great colored diamonds, an affair that for Harry Winston almost became a case of fatal attraction.

But now, with the acquisition of the McLean treasure chest, my father was able to execute the greatest publicity coup of his career. At the end of the tumultuous decade, in November 1949, Harry commandeered the Forum of Rockefeller Center and upstaged its giant Christmas tree by presenting his "Court of Jewels" a drop-dead display of ten of Harry Winston's Greatest Hits. The new Hope was there, along with Evalyn's Star of the East. Dad's favorite golden oldie, the Jonker I, which he still hadn't sold, was shown, along with Junior's Indore Pears and the Dudley necklace, plus the Idol's Eye. Outside of Golconda, he also showcased the 337-carat Catherine the Great Sapphire as well as the Spanish Inquisition Necklace of Colombian emeralds, plus, to give the public hope, the Mabel Boll, a sixty-carat emerald-cut stunner owned by the former cigarette girl who married big enough to become known as the Diamond Queen of Broadway during the Roaring Twenties. Mabel, who was fearless, nearly beat Amelia Earhart to be the first woman to fly across the Atlantic.

Harry's show at Rockefeller Center, which featured gurgling fountains and palatial decor, plus demonstrations by gem cutters and polishers, was a fusion of Walt Disney and Cecil B DeMille. Dad had no patience with the subtlety of De Beers. He gave the public what it wanted, flash and filigree, and they lined up for blocks to pay the fifty-cent admission charge (a quarter for kids like me). Harry Winston's answer to

England's Crown Jewels really was his own self-coronation as the King of Diamonds.

Harry Winston was too driven to rest on his laurels. In the aftermath of his Court of Jewels triumph, for several years in the early 1950s, he and my mother began traveling to Portugal, usually for two months at a time, in the beginning of summer. They stayed in a hotel called the Palácio Estoril, right on the Atlantic, an hour from Lisbon. It wasn't the French Riviera, which was my parents' go-to destination before the war. Why were they there? Portugal was a time warp, the poorest country in Western Europe, which seemed apparent from the junky toys, stuffed dolls and animals, and religious effigies that Mother brought back for Bruce and me. Portugal, as I would later learn, was Europe's own banana republic, complete with its own dictator, a former mild-mannered academic economist turned military-backed strongman named António Salazar.

But Portugal had something Harry Winston wanted, in the biggest way. It had an African colony, Angola, that, after South Africa and the Belgian Congo, was the largest source of rough diamonds on the continent with an annual output of 750,000 carats. Dad made his name and fame on his Big Rocks, but he made his fortune on the small ones. At this point, he didn't want to be dependent on De Beers. Harry Winston didn't want to be dependent on anyone. He wanted his own source.

Harry Winston had proven to the world that he could get the great stones, but he had tried to own and source a mine in Venezuela in the forties and had failed. Now in the 1950s, with De Beers still distracted, Harry Winston decided to try once more to beat the cartel, this time in its own backyard. His audacious goal was to cut a deal with the dictator to acquire his own De Beers–like monopoly on the Portuguese colony's diamond output. By his calculations, controlling the rough could yield him upward of $7 million to $10 million a year in additional annual profits. In the 1950s that was serious money, upward of $100 million in 2023.

Even with that fiscal incentive, Dad was not about to rough it by visiting Angola, a wild and beautiful country on the West Coast of Africa, whose biggest export was coffee, followed by diamonds. There was a large and prosperous Jewish population in the capital of Luanda, the descendants of Sephardim who had escaped the Iberian peninsula during the Spanish Inquisition. He saw himself hiring some of them, if his plan worked out.

Until then, he relied on the multilingual Greek American diplomat, Ted Xanthaky, to help him make the deal. A close ally of Truman's old-school secretary of state Dean Acheson, Ted was stationed in the embassy in Lisbon, a key post because of Portuguese neutrality during World War II. There he had won the trust of António Salazar and was Dad's main man in pleading his case to become the strongman's diamond supplier. Harry Winston's main bargaining point was simple: he would pay Salazar more for the Angolan diamonds than anyone else, including De Beers.

But after three long years, meeting everyone who was anyone in Portugal, Dad threw in the towel, as he had in Venezuela.

Secretly on behalf of De Beers, the British Foreign Office threatened Portugal that if it didn't keep Harry Winston out of Portugal and its colonial business, the British Empire would boycott Lisbon's cork, olive oil, and port, which the Englishmen, as well as the Anglo wannabe Oppenheimers, consumed in great volumes. When I was much older and working with Dad, I asked him why, as a man who could never be called a quitter, even in the face of treacherous British diplomacy, he gave up this brilliant opportunity to free himself from De Beers. "I didn't have you, and I had a business to run," he replied dryly. Decades later, when Harry Winston had me, and when Dad and Salazar were both gone, I took courage and made my own play for Angola in the war zone of Jonas Savimbi. As it turned out, Angola was indeed the treasure trove Harry Winston had believed it to be.

CHAPTER NINE

The Exhibitionists

Harry Winston may have spent the better part of the 1950s in his diamond wars with the London-Johannesburg cartel. But the decade signified much, much more for my family than just my little Captain Ahab of a father pursuing the great white whale of diamonds that was De Beers. While, on the supply side, war may have been hell, where demand was concerned, nothing in the history of retail luxury could have been more glamorous than Dad's conquest of the market of the high and mighty.

The decade started with Harry reeling in the biggest fish in the sea of spending, King Farouk of Egypt, without doubt the highest rolling ruler of the century. A billionaire by today's exchange rates, Farouk had driven the hated imperial British out of Egypt after World War II. However, Farouk had the public relations misfortune of being morbidly obese. The true cause was a genetic glandular disorder, but the British tabloid press, which despised the king for his lack of respect for *their* king, blamed it all on his decadent excess. The result was that Farouk probably got the worst newspaper coverage of any monarch since the American colonies went after George III.

My father, on the other hand, liked King Farouk. He and my mother were enormously impressed by him. Harry first met Farouk on the French Riviera in the summer of 1951, when Farouk, thirty-one, had taken his new queen, Narriman, seventeen, for a three-month European honeymoon. What a royal couple the Egyptians were, and what a royal entrance they made, alighting from their yacht, the *Fakhr el Bihar* ("Pride of the Seas") dressed in matching blue blazers, red ties, and white peaked yachting caps, joining a sixty-strong entourage in a fleet of seven black Cadillacs, and descending on all the great hotels, restaurants, and luxury stores from Paris to Rome in an orgy of spending that made the world forget the postwar poverty, ravages, and rationing.

My parents, who also tended to live as if the war was a distant memory, frequented the same grand tour–*grand bouffe* circuit as the Farouks. The Winstons were a rather striking couple themselves, my mother in Harry's jewels and her Indian saris, my father in his tuxes, his white stuffed shirts, his gleaming elevator shoes, and, on top of it all, his aura and mystique as the man with all the baubles. They were an adorable pair, this tiny Tom Thumb and his Thumbelina from New York who had the verve and audacity to descend into this playground of royalty and wealth.

No prospective customer was a bigger and better quarry than King Farouk.

I was ten at this time, and Bruce was seven. After being shipped off for part of the summer to luxurious camps for privileged youths in the Adirondacks, we spent the remainder of the season with nannies at Stonwin, which was our own private summer camp. It killed my mother with guilt to leave us, but she was torn between her maternal preoccupations and her duties to Harry and his business. The King of Diamonds couldn't wheel and deal without his queen, whose charm and grace were essential to the entire Harry Winston experience. Although my dad loved to swim and loved the sun, he could have had his sand and sea right in the Hamptons with me and Bruce. However, I understood early on that a holiday was not what he was after.

My parents liked to stay at the La Réserve de Beaulieu, a haven of peace and beauty between the hot spots of Cannes and Monte Carlo but close enough to the casinos for my father to enjoy his favorite summer pastime, gambling. "Harry is gambling quite chummily with Farouk," my mother bragged to my grandfather in a letter that summer. Among the other company Harry was keeping at the tables were the kings of Hollywood, Jack Warner and Darryl Zanuck, the latter having taken Farouk for a record $150,000 at baccarat one hot night at Cannes' Palm Beach Casino, to the delight of the world press. Excess was what sold papers, and soon Dad and Farouk would give them all the excess they could ever dream of.

My father never won—or lost—on a Farouk scale. No one did. But he played the game. One crack of dawn he came back to La Réserve and woke my mother up. "Edna, I just won a fur coat at the casino," he exulted.

Mom was too sleepy to get excited. "I didn't know they had raffles at the casino," she replied with a yawn.

"No, Edna, dear, I won the equivalent in francs."

"Wonderful," she replied and rolled over to try to get back to sleep.

As Mom told it, that fur coat got shorter and shorter from the ankle-length creation Dad first promised, with each visit to the wheels of fortune. Three weeks later, Dad announced a change of style. "Edna," he said, "the fashion this fall is going to be the bolero." And that was exactly what he bought her, a sleeveless mink vest. Nonetheless, she treasured it forever, if only for the anecdote it afforded.

Had Harry been willing to cross-collateralize business and pleasure, Mom could have had mink wall to wall, for that summer on the Côte was probably the most profitable in my father's career, thanks to his new gambling buddy, the king of Egypt. The two men had things in common besides cards. In 1959 he had made a four-pound tiara for Farah Diba for her beyond-lavish wedding to the Shah of Iran, whose first wife, Fawzia, was Farouk's sister. Thus there was a royal tie, even if it had failed to bind. Furthermore, Farouk was much taken with my mother. The Muslim king had a severe weakness for Levantine Jewesses, and Mom, while far from the Levant, had the right look, enhanced by her Riviera suntan.

The most beautiful and enduring of Farouk's many mistresses was an Alexandrian Jewish princess named Irene Najjar, who went on to marry a Brazilian Guinle, the polo-playing family that owned Rio's Copacabana Palace Hotel. Mom may have reminded Farouk of Irene, or of his most recent flame, Lilian Cohen, the headliner at Cairo's most glamorous nightclub, the Auberge des Pyramides. Lilian, the "royal songbird," had perished the previous summer, when her plane crashed en route to meeting the king in Paris for his pre-Narriman bachelor party.

Whatever the attraction, the Farouks spent a lot of time with the Winstons. "The other night," Mom wrote Grandfather

Winkie, "we had a great honor bestowed upon us. King Farouk, his queen, and his whole entourage had dinner with us. He stayed until five in the morning." As the sun was coming up, with the rest of the royal party on the patio overlooking the Mediterranean, Dad somehow took Farouk aside and began selling him diamonds. He got his opening when Farouk told him how every single day of the long honeymoon, he would wake up Narriman with a different gift: silver, dresses, furs, jewels, watches, even her own private train. *Aha*, Dad must have thought. *What do you get for the woman who has everything?* This gave Harry the brilliant idea of clearing his inventory of its two most expensive items.

First was the Jonker diamond, the stone that made my father world famous but that had been gathering dust in the Winston vault for over twelve years. The second was the Star of the East, the ninety-four-carat Turkish imperial treasure he had bought, with the Hope Diamond, from the Evalyn Walsh MacLean estate.

As a boy I once asked Dad if he was ever sorry to see a great stone go to a new owner. "Ronnie," he told me, "I had to decide long ago whether I was a collector or a merchant. I can't afford to be a collector. I am a seller." Then he grew nostalgic for what might have been. "Maybe if I had kept my piece of those Texas oil fields," he mused, referring to the great strike that got away from him in one of his gambling-like speculations, "I would have been a buyer of what I sell." Harry had fantasies of putting together his own collection, one that would rival any royal treasury. But that was not to be. Instead his lot was to build the collections of his wealthy and notable clientele.

In another dispatch to Winkie, Mom wrote, "The other day we were called over to have cocktails with him [Farouk] and he bought a 70m carat emerald and the Star of the East. I think I told you he bought the Jonker. He can't pay us right away. It comes to over a million dollars, so naturally we are still hanging around."

Farouk's splurge with Harry that summer was surely the biggest retail purchase in the history of selling. This was before private jets and $450 million da Vincis. Nothing cost more than diamonds then, and these were the biggest diamonds for sale in the world. Farouk was buying both of them, plus even more, to sate his "twelve days of Christmas" routine with his new teen queen. The $3 million cache of purchased gems would be valued at $34 million in 2023. Because a king was involved and because my father, his love for publicity notwithstanding, was as discreet as a Wall Street banker where his clients were concerned, the press never got wind of this Big Bang.

It was just as well, for my father would soon be eating humble pie instead of the celebratory caviar. My mother's casual phrase "hanging around" to be paid reflected a situation that was vastly more complicated than it sounded. Although the Jonker was eventually paid for in the coming months, the $1 million for the Star of the East was never received. Barely had he returned to Egypt from his European honeymoon in 1951 than Farouk found himself with a revolution on his hands. By the following summer, he was deposed. The deposer, General Nasser, it was claimed, had confiscated both the Jonker and the Star of the East for the wealth and glory of his new regime.

Farouk wanted to be seen as a man of honor. Before he was exiled to Capri, he secreted the seventy-carat emerald Mom had written about, sealing it in a plain envelope and slipping it into the hand of American Ambassador Jefferson Caffrey, "This belongs to Harry Winston in New York," he said, echoing the countless Jews who, fleeing Hitler, sent their gems to "Harry Winston, New York City." The stone was returned by diplomatic pouch to my dad. The Jonker vanished in the smoke and dust of the Egyptian revolution, as did many great stones during the Russian Revolution. The Star of the East seemed to be gone forever, as did the $1 million my father expected for it. But great jewels have a way of coming back around.

A man of great persistence, Dad took his case for the return of, or payment for, the Star of the East to Nasser's revolutionary legal council. It took three long years, but the council eventually ruled in my father's favor. The Star was his. However, nobody knew where the Star was. Dad was undeterred. Like the great fictional British detective Bulldog Drummond, who always got his man, Harry Winston always got his stone. One of Farouk's aides-de-camp offered him a deal. He claimed that he knew that the Star of the East had been secreted in a Swiss safe-deposit box. If he was right, he wanted a commission of 5 percent. Dad said yes. After several more years of litigation to access the box, there, in all its glory, was the Star of the East. Dad sold it once again in 1969. This time he was paid without the drama of a coup d'etat.

All the drama surrounding of the Star of the East couldn't deter my father from his desire to conquer Europe. America was his, and the Old World, for all its losses, still had money to burn on jewels. It was easy to sell great stones in Europe; he just had to know who the customers were. Because of his ongoing conflict with De Beers, my father knew he needed help finding the big spenders. Enter the truly remarkable character of Manfredo "Fred" Horowitz, who was arguably one of the greatest salesmen who ever lived. Fred was the son of a prosperous Polish Jewish family that had emigrated to the safety of Lugano, Switzerland, and was in the wholesale paper business. A superb skier, sailor, and tennis player, the lanky, Fred was, first and foremost, a bon vivant and ladies' man. In short, he had all the ingredients for a dolce vita existence, except the right job.

Before the war, Fred worked for his parents, which he hated. Then he joined a shipping company, which he also hated. Finally, he answered a cryptic want ad for a "person of trust," which led him to the top jeweler in Geneva. The first year there, Fred increased the store's sales by 100 percent. He had found his métier, but he found his bliss when he met Harry. In 1951, the year of the Farouk sales, Harry was looking to set up an office in Switzerland, which was then the center of Europe and a haven for wealth unscathed by the war. Zurich was the richest city, but Zurich was German, and Mom had forsaken her roots and had become a Francophile. Furthermore, Dad somehow divined that Geneva had softer light than Zurich, better for viewing gems. So Geneva it was, and in Geneva all roads led to Fred.

Not that Fred was around town that much. He spent most of his winters skiing in St. Moritz and après-skiing at the bar and lobby of the Palace Hotel, where the richest people in Europe came to play. Fred's best childhood friend from Lugano was the Baron Hans Heinrich Thyssen-Bornemisza, whose father was a shipping and coal magnate on par with the Krupps of Germany. His was one of the great industrial fortunes of the continent. He also owned an unrivaled art collection. Fred would not only introduce the Baron to his final wife, a former Miss Spain and former girlfriend of Fred's who would move the baronial collection to Madrid, but he also introduced his first ex-wife to Muck Flick, another of the great industrial heirs of the postwar "German miracle."

Flick married the former Mrs. Horowitz, who stayed friendly and grateful to Fred, hence cementing his network by conjugal ties that were even thicker than those forged on the slopes or the clay courts of the Palace. Fred was also a great confidant of Madame Claude, the Paris-based premier sexual matchmaker of the postwar haut monde. Through her, he was always surrounded with a retinue of stunning, and willing, models and ambitious playgirls.

Fred was a master in the art of connections and, hence, the art of the deal. He knew the best girls and the best restaurants, threw the best parties, and even had the most lively yacht in Cannes, which he christened the *Diamond D*. Fred, he of the infinite Rolodex, would sell jewels to his rich and titled sporting buddies for both their wives and their mistresses, both of whom Fred had probably introduced them to. If you needed to buy jewelry, you would go to Fred, because not only did you get a Harry Winston diamond, but you also got the time of your life.

I first met the great Manfredo when I was a very impressionable sixteen and he was in his dashing thirties. My parents had now begun taking Bruce and me to Europe with them in the summer. Dad and Fred were having lunch at La Réserve, planning what would be Fred's great contribution to the art and science of selling jewels: the exhibition. It may seem obvious now, but back then, the exhibition was a radically new concept. Before the war, great jewels were sold exclusively at deluxe emporia like Garrard and Cartier and Tiffany in world-class cities like London, Paris, or New York. The client would enter a very controlled and sedate environment and view an array of nearly priceless objects with the utmost solemnity. Fred, as was his wont, knew how to make the whole process fun, by turning it into a party, a special event, held in the ballrooms of Europe's most exclusive hotels. In summer, Fred's venues of choice were the Carlton in Cannes and the Hotel de Paris in Monte Carlo; in winter, it was the Palace in St. Moritz.

Fred held court at the entrance to each ballroom, the dashing gatekeeper. Dad would stand at the periphery of the room, the éminence grise of the world of jewels, a Delphic oracle whose opinion was sought by all. He was treated like royalty *by* royalty.

As I got a bit older, Dad would bring me to these exhibitions, making an exhibit of me, his brilliant son. I'm not sure what made me more uncomfortable, being shown off like the Hope diamond or all the ostentatiousness that came with the shows. "Really big sheeew," as Ed Sullivan would announce on his television variety show, and Dad's shows were even bigger, where value was concerned, than Ed's. For all the titles and dowries, it was still a circus. I didn't really appreciate these red and green and blue and white lumps of rock. To me they were all just gumdrops, minus the flavor. How the men and, especially, the women, could get so orgasmic about them was a mystery to teenaged me.

I did, however, appreciate the magnificence of Fred Horowitz. His bushy eyebrows framed his intense, kind eyes. His reassuring, slightly professorial German accent said, "Trust me." Everything would be more than all right, if you were with Fred. He knew that aligning himself with the iconic Harry Winston would bring him great success. If you buy and wear Harry Winston jewels, your life will be beautiful. Early on, Fred would take me on walks and regale me with tales of his lifetime of adventures, from steerage to peerage. On occasion, however, he would do bizarre cloak-and-dagger stuff, like suddenly secreting us both behind one of the stone portals of the La Réserve de Beaulieu as a red Ferrari was approaching. "Shhh!" he'd whisper, pressing his index finger to his pursed lips. "That's the prince. We don't want him to see us here."

Fred never told me who the prince was or why he shouldn't see us. Maybe Fred didn't know. Maybe it was intrigue for the sake of intrigue. Whatever, Fred seemed to have a dossier on every potential client on the continent, what his or her tastes were, what his or her kinks were, and he proceeded accordingly. He reminded me a lot of Sherlock Holmes. All the concierges in all the hotels were on his payroll. He had spies at all the yacht harbors and at all the airports, in addition to spotters who took down the license plate numbers of all the expensive cars, so that Fred could track who they belonged to and where they lived.

Both Fred and Harry were in accord that potential clients were most vulnerable, particularly to top-dollar jewelry, when they were on vacation. Fred was great at playing to women's lust for diamonds and to men's lust for women, all to the great benefit of my father. His dinner parties at the chicest restaurants of the Côte, places like Tetou or La Bonne Auberge, were summer's most coveted invitations. Among his greatest early clients were Agnelli of Italy, Krupp of Germany, and his virtual in-laws, the Thyssens and the Flicks, but the list of names and titles was endless.

My youthful immersion into this intense summer paradise was so far removed from my studious winters at Riverdale Country School in the Bronx. For the first few years, the glitter and glory of the Riviera were totally lost on me, as was the whole point of my father's luxury business. I just didn't understand the concept of conspicuous consumption. Being seen in Winston jewelry traipsing around Monte Carlo and its HDP, as the Hotel de Paris was affectionately referred to, meant you were at the top of the A-list. The moneyed crowd came in May for the Grand Prix, then went to the Film Festival in nearby Cannes and partied until the season culminated in Prince Rainier's Red Cross charity ball in August, where Winston jewels were virtually de rigueur. The locomotive for all this flashy aspiration were not the Thyssens or the Agnellis but the newly rich feasting on the spoils and endless opportunities rising from the ashes in postwar Europe. Ferraris for the men, jewels for the women, were the obligatory status symbols, and the jewels cost much, much more than the Ferraris.

While Fred Horowitz largely specialized in selling to the men, who in actuality did most of the choosing and nearly all of the paying, Dad was great at dealing with the distaff side of the business, especially when the prospective customers were women of independent means. Dad seemed to have a clairvoyant's ability to plumb feminine minds. One of his greatest clients was Dorothy Killam, Canada's preeminent female philanthropist. Her husband Izaak Walton Killam was a press lord and paper baron, the partner of England's Lord Beaverbrook. When he died in 1955, his widow, Dorothy, a St. Louis–born swimming champion, went on a binge of charitable giving and diamond buying.

On one of my early trips to the French Riviera, I came down with a terrible case of food poisoning and was confined to my room at La Réserve for several days. One night during my quarantine, Dad brought in Mrs. Killam to cheer me up.

Having given many millions to found children's hospitals and special schools, the childless Mrs. Killam surely had pressed Dad to let her see to my well-being. As they approached my sick bed, Mrs. Killam leaned over me to touch my head to see if I had a fever. I didn't see kindness. I saw a witch, with a cadaverous face and a gray, sallow complexion. The diamonds Dad had sold her did nothing to enliven her or make her beautiful.

The next morning, I chided Dad for bringing this witch to my room. "Poor dear," he said with a sigh. "She was concerned about you. She's no raving beauty, but she's so kind." I was very cruel to have reacted with such intolerance and ingratitude, but perhaps I just resented all these flashy rich people who were stealing my parents away from me, and I took it out on poor Mrs. Killam, who looked ghastly because she turned out to be dying of cancer. In any event, this may have been the genesis of my vow never to follow my father into his business. I had a teenage desire to change the world, if not save it, or at least to blow things up, having created numerous big bangs in my own chemistry lab at Stonwin.

Another thing Dad did that did nothing to endear him to me was to try to send Bruce and me to Le Rosey, the most exclusive boarding school in the world. This "school of kings," as the press called it, had two campuses, the summer one in Rolle, on the shores of Lake Geneva, close to Dad's new European headquarters, and the winter one in Gstaad, the famed ski resort. What other school had a lake campus and a ski campus? The Aga Khan had gone here, as did the Shah, future King Juan Carlos of Spain, Prince Rainier of Monaco, and King Farouk's son Fuad, not to mention generations of Rothschilds, Metternichs, Borgheses, Hohenlohes—in short, every family that was either a current or potential Harry Winston client. I got the sense that this was a major career move for my father and had nothing to do with his children's educations or happiness. Again, and always, business came first.

Not that Bruce and I had any choice in the matter. Dad, ever self-flagellating that he was anything but a college man and was totally lacking in what the French call *formation* and the English "upbringing," felt his sons were very much in need of polish of the sort they would never get at home. "In today's world," Harry decreed, "you need French, contacts, and social grace." What he meant by "today's world" was *his* world, the world that he sold to. He wanted to buy us class by sending us to class. Thus, in 1956 we were dragooned into the summer course at Le Rosey to prepare us for full-time enrollment the coming fall. It was a big year for Europe, the year Grace Kelly married Prince Rainier, a royal romance that, given the endless breathless press coverage, made royalists and Europhiles out of the lowliest, most insular Americans. There was nothing like it until Prince Charles married Diana Spencer.

Not happy with my summer lot, I tried to find amusement in the old-school traditions, the medieval buildings, the Franco-Swiss pomposity. Bruce couldn't take it. He promptly came down with a persistent fever that landed him in the school infirmary for most of the summer session. It was a fever of unknown origin, psychosomatic to be sure, as there were no strains of Alpine mosquitoes that transmitted malaria, the one illness that matched Bruce's symptoms. Mother wanted to pull Bruce out, but Dad wouldn't have it.

I hated the other kids, many the progeny of the biggest arrivistes on the planet. I had never encountered such a lack of motivation. The name of the game at Riverdale was "Can you top this?" while at Le Rosey, it was "Easy way out." The most my summer classmates would be dreaming of was a Ferrari at graduation and a sinecure in Daddy's factory.

That I could fall into the same dolce far niente fate of the idle rich was horrifying to me. "Get me out of here, Dad," I pleaded. "You must learn French and make friends around the world," he insisted, and I swore I would. The French part was easy, after six years of studying it, and having two girl-friends in Paris. The contacts came in due course. At sum-mer's end, Dad let Bruce and me go back to Riverdale. Mom was delighted that she would have her babies home again.

Freed from this high-status reformatory, I finally began enjoying the Riviera when I was initiated into a group of con-temporaries that called itself La Bande. My sponsor for this very exclusive circle of friends was a highly sophisticated boy named Michael Pochna, who was a few years older and far wiser in the ways of the world. Michael was a Le Rosey grad who was on his way to Harvard; thus, no one could accuse him of being unmotivated. Michael's drive came from his lawyer father, John, whose client was Aristotle Onassis. John and my father met when Dad was selling a 426-carat rough diamond to Onassis, promising he would have it cut to the Greek magnate's specifications.

There were about fifteen very seen-it-all kids in La Bande. We hung out at a place called the Beach Hotel in Monte Carlo. The pool scene boggled my adolescent mind: sleek bronze Euroteen goddesses, the quintessence of jeunesse dorée, wearing tiny bikinis that flaunted their violin-case figures the way Mrs. Killam flaunted the assets she pur-chased from my father. What a contrast to the Scarsdale beach bunnies in their clunky one-piece Jantzens that filled with water after each swim and had to be emptied with a squeeze of liquid from the crotch. Everything was all grace and charm here. We'd lunch on pâté and rosé on the terrace of a restaurant called La Vigie, where Michael would explain to me that the couples that I assumed were fathers and daughters were actually roués and their young mistresses. How shocked I was! How far I was from the beach clubs in Mamaroneck!

La Bande members held parties at their families' Riviera summer homes. The Pochna estate, the Villa Iris, sat on a ledge overlooking the deep harbor of Villefranche. Michael had a very artsy stepmother, Jean, who sang and played guitar in the Sylvie Vartan "ye-ye" style of the times. My personal highlight at the Pochna fetes was my very hot blind date Estelle Von Shenkel, whose father was a Swedish diplomat at the Paris embassy. Estelle may have been only a year older than me, but I was as intimidated as if she were Mrs. Robinson.

After dinner, the guests would repair to the Pochna pool, which had an underground bar with portholes for spying on the aquatic hijinks. Estelle put on her bikini and began cavorting with a visiting Yale underclassman. Their swim was followed by a walk into the pine forest surrounding the villa. An hour later, she emerged from the woods. I was beside myself with insecure rage. "Halloo," she taunted in her Anita Ekbergian accent, then grabbed an open bottle of Scotch and jammed it into my gaping mouth. "Here," she said. "Have some fun." That was my first—and last—taste of whiskey, for this lifetime.

I didn't really have a role model where affairs of the heart were concerned. My father may have been a bon vivant in his bachelor days at the Sherry-Netherland, but after twenty years of marriage my father had zero interest in racy women, even though he had in his possession a treasury of the world's greatest aphrodisiacs. Dad never traded on his jewels as tools of seduction. Maybe because he had such a complex about his size, he may have thought that he couldn't make time, even with the Hope Diamond. Not that my Mother wasn't gorgeous or stylish enough. Never once can I recall Dad ever kissing her with any real passion.

They weren't Bogie and Bacall. But in business, they were a team, the artist and his muse, and business, not sex, was the thing that counted to Dad. I looked at them as the Nick and Nora Charles of diamonds. I remember how in New York Dad would come home late from work and perch himself on the side of the tub where Mother was luxuriating in a bubble bath, recounting to her the wheels and deals of his busy day. It was clear that he would be lost without her. Even on a rare non-business date night, they would go to dinner at the Colony, then hold hands for the drive back home, where they would fall asleep in their separate adjoining bedrooms. I know my father loved my mother, and she said she knew it, too, but I never heard him say the words in my entire life.

At the end of our European summers, we would come back to reality in New York. As a boy, I hated the formal, gloomy 51st Street office; it generated the same trepidation as having to go back to school. The main salon, with its five antique desks, had no natural light, other than the glittering gems, which must have been what Harry wanted. Nothing about it called out to me to join my father's business, which was his. Great wish. Meeting one of his greatest clients, the Shah of Iran, when I was in my teens in the early 1950s, was presented as perhaps the biggest moment of my young life. It was intended to be a siren call to my destiny in diamonds. However, it had the opposite effect and was more like an air raid siren, a warning of danger dead ahead.

As we rode down Fifth Avenue from our apartment to the salon, Dad laid down the rules of my presentation to royalty. The Shah was bringing his bride Soraya to New York, and he wanted to say how much he loved her with an epic gift from Harry Winston. "I want you to be a perfect gentleman and not say a word unless I ask you a question. If the Shah speaks to you, you have to address him as 'Your Majesty.'" I tried to nod confidently. *What if I said, "Your Highness,"* I thought to myself. *Would the great Harry Winston be disgraced? Would he lose the Shah's patronage? Would little Ronnie be barred from the salon?*

The building was all lit up when we arrived. Dad's employees were dressed in black suits like CIA operatives and were lined up on the steps. I had never seen my father so excited. There was literally a spring in his step as he bounded up the grand marble staircase to his own imperial office, where he was greeted by his then right-hand man, Ed Carnevale, whose task today was to bring the pieces from the vault. The obsequious Ed, or Eddie as Dad called him, would hover over Harry's left shoulder like a homing pigeon about to take flight. Ed was totally authentic and utterly loyal.

"Is Sabet coming?" my father asked Ed. "Yes, Mister Winston," Ed replied. "He'll be coming before the Shah." That's what advance men did—they came in advance. Sabet was the king of royal advance men. He had been my father's connection in Tehran, where Sabet had made a fortune as the Coca-Cola bottler and the owner of several Detroit auto franchises. Iran was newly rich itself, awash in oil, and it loved all things American. Those were the days. Sabet was to the Shah something on the order of what Ed Carnevale was to Dad, although far more creative and cunning. The Shah confided in him all his desires. In this case what the Shah wanted was a necklace befitting his new consort, Soraya, like Farouk's Narriman, a teen queen. Soraya was all of nineteen, a Russo-Persian beauty who had been on the cover of *Life* and was considered to be one of the great beauties of the world. When I found out she was coming, too, the teenager in me got excited because Soraya was close to my age.

Sabet arrived to meet with Dad. I sat there in deferential silence. He dressed like an English gent, in tweeds, but spoke in tones of the Middle East souk. They devised an elaborate sales strategy for presenting the jewels to the Shah, worked out in incredibly small details, like a royal protocol. Then there was a din outside, and Dad rushed over to his big window overlooking St. Patrick's and the street below. There was a caravan of cars, the centerpiece of which was a big black Cadillac limousine with huge tail fins. I had never seen my father move so quickly, as he fairly sprinted down the staircase to greet the Shah.

I stayed in the office and stood waiting at attention for the Shah and his queen. The Shah was dressed in a dark suit, as opposed to the military garb he always wore in magazine pictures. He was regal, erect and proud, if a bit stiff. Soraya was a knockout, with huge lips and eyes that reminded me of Sophia Loren, the new superstar from Italy. Those big eyes turned down deferentially as she began examining the jewels that Ed brought in. Harry Winston sold, but he never pushed. "This, your Majesty, is my newest design," he said, displaying a garden of emeralds swooped down with diamond festoons. "Eddie," he quietly motioned to Carnevale, "hold these up to Her Majesty." Dad studied the effect, cradling his cheek against his left palm. The Shah looked and looked, then said something in Farsi, and Soraya tried it on. Pressing the necklace to her lush young bosom, she gave the faintest suggestion of a smile, the only emotion I had seen all morning. The Shah nodded his approval.

"What do you think, Ronnie?" my father turned to me, the first acknowledgment of my presence.

This was my big moment. I was on the spot. "Beautiful, Daddy," I shot out. "For a queen."

Dad laughed, though the Shah was impassive. "I want him to observe and learn, Your Majesty," Dad said, as if apologizing. Nonetheless, a deal was struck, and I was bursting with pride that I hadn't fouled things up and may have even contributed to the transaction in some small way. For all my inherent confusions, I couldn't help but be impressed by the way my father had performed his magic. As the world's leading expert, he didn't have to say very much. Less was more. Like Fred Astaire dancing, Harry Winston made selling diamonds look easy.

On other sales occasions, Dad might apply different techniques, always, however, playing to what he termed "the vanity of women." Ezra and Cecile Zilkha, who lived in our new Fifth Avenue apartment building, were Jewish and were as tiny as Mom and Dad, so there was lots of common ground there. On the other hand, Ezra was an Iraqi Jew whose family could be traced back to Nebuchadnezzar and the Babylonian Captivity. The Zilkhas were the greatest banking family in Iraq until they had to flee when the country began to destabilize after the war. Ezra quickly became one of the great bankers in New York and amassed a major art collection. Dad did his best to turn him into a jewelry collector as well, though Dad always treated him as a friend first and a buyer second.

Once I was in the salon when the charming Cecile was trying on, with Ezra there, a pair of diamond drop earrings, jewels that would, as Dad might say, "make a big statement." But Dad refused to close. "My dear," he said, "you are much too young and beautiful for these. One day . . . but not today. May I suggest these?" And he showed her something small and youthful. She was sold, and, more importantly, so was the eagle-eyed Ezra, who paid the bills. Ezra became a longtime client and referred the cream of Jewish society, or at least the ones who weren't already customers, to Harry Winston.

Much as his clients and would-be clients might like it, Dad couldn't do all the selling himself. In Ali Baba's cave he had a motley crew of salesmen like Ed Carnevale, who made me question just how glamorous this business really was. Maybe Dad was just doing his version of the melting pot. There were those five desks, widely spaced. One was occupied by the one family member in the outfit, my cousin Richard Winston, the almost Yankee star who had traded the big diamond in the Bronx for the small ones on Fifth Avenue. There was Ed Carnevale's brother Don, as loyal as Ed and as small as Dad, both qualities surely endearing him to my father. Don, who specialized in selling to the wives of politicians, spent lots of time in Washington. He had the verve and bonhomie of a lobbyist and almost as much nervous energy as Harry.

Then there was the blustering and boisterous Charlie Steiger, who specialized in the three–Rob Roy lunch. When he returned to his desk, he hardly seemed to need a telephone to call his clients, many of whom were Wall Street high rollers of a similar ilk. Dad, who was an abstemious teetotaler during business hours and who never ate lunch, tolerated Charlie's decadence as long as it was good for business.

Next was Julius Cohen, whom Dad considered a true friend until he left to set up a rival business, taking with him the top secret Harry Winston mailing list. Julius used to come to work in cowboy boots and a ten-gallon hat. "Howdy," he'd say, affecting a Texas accent with a Bronx twist. Fake as it was, Dallas society ate it up and made Julius one of their own.

Last on the roster was Dick Vena, who catered to the Upper East Side Ivy League society crowd. He didn't come close to qualifying as a member, but the Junior League women overlooked his lack of sophistication because of his Marlboro Man rugged good looks.

Off the floor and in a category of his own was Dad's front man, the Russian Count Adelburg, whose father in the Romanoff days had been the czar's governor general of St. Petersburg. Nearly six feet five and straight out of central casting as an aristocrat, "VaVa," as he was known to his blue-blooded fellow émigrés, filled my father's need to have a big man fronting for him. This went back to the 1920s, when Dad had found the august Judge Garby to run interference for him with the bankers who couldn't believe little Harry was the man of substance. Dad understood that style equaled substance, so he always had at least one drop-dead aristocrat in his employ. VaVa was totally amusing and was a highlight of any visit to the office. "Send the count up," Dad would order, and I knew I was in for a treat.

Stunningly dressed in a pearl gray double-breasted pin-stripe suit garnished with a pointed white handkerchief and a blue bachelor's button popping from his lapel, the count would enter with his slight limp (romantic war injury) and take a seat across from Dad. Twirling his gray Colonel Blimp moustache, VaVa would proceed to spin a story, which would be enhanced by his slight lisp superimposed upon his cultured Russian accent. This was class to the max, I assumed. "Meeester Veenston," he would commence, "we had the most magnificent weekend at Marjorie's." Marjorie was Marjorie Merriweather Post, the cereal heiress; the venue was her estate, Mar-a-Lago, in Palm Beach.

VaVa described the weekend of Easter egg hunts, charades, Scrabble, swimming, croquet, not to mention the dining and the dancing, and noted how Mrs. Post printed up a schedule of activities, none of which were optional. What the count recounted sounded worse than summer camp, both to me and to my Dad, who was far too twitchy to endure a weekend under this blue blooded drill sergeant, even if he were to have the honor of being invited. "I make a very bad houseguest," Dad admitted to me. A cameo dinner appearance with Mother was all Harry could endure. It was quite enough to live vicariously through VaVa. Aside from the frolics, what most interested Dad was what the guests, most of them his clients, were, or were not, wearing. "Show her the emerald set," Dad would instruct the count after the royal recitation of the morning's private gossip column. "It sounds like she might need something like that."

Dad didn't pay the handsome count all that handsomely, as if he had been a commission salesman like Manfredo Horowitz. The count was above selling; his job was in the far-less-lucrative field of public relations, and his reward was in fringe benefits and a lavish expense account. Sometimes the Count's accounts reflected his need for enhanced compensation. I was there once when Dad's eagle-eyed chief financial officer, Jerry Schultz, discovered a $2,000 overrun on some decorations the count was overseeing. Jerry wanted to call VaVa on the Aubusson carpet. Dad wouldn't hear of it. A nip here, a tuck there, Dad knew, was part of the price of being in business with a fallen aristocrat ill-prepared to face the ignominy of having to sing for his supper.

CHAPTER TEN

Lady Dye

Turning sixty in 1956, Dad began thinking about posterity, not only his own, but that of his clients. The enormous success of his Court of Jewels roadshow had convinced him that America needed its own national jewelry collection, a democratic version of England's Crown Jewels. He was so proud when magazines pointed out that he, Harry Winston, owned the second-largest collection of historic jewels in the world. The queen of England was ahead of him, but she and her forebears had been collecting them for over five hundred years and could claim the de Beers monopoly as a royal subject. Harry, on the other hand, had been at it for only three decades and got to be number two all by himself. Number two, in a lot of ways, was better than number one. To quote the famous Avis ad of the period, "We Try Harder."

To lay the foundation of the gem collection he envisioned, Dad, in 1958, donated the Hope Diamond to the Smithsonian Institution in Washington, along with several other treasures from the Court of Jewels. He had considered the Museum of Natural History in New York, but he ultimately decided to go with "where the government is." His underlying idea was that the First Lady should wear the Hope, or such, on state occasions. He didn't want her to be outshone by the queen of England.

There was the son of an immigrant's patriotic pride at work here. There was also tremendous cunning. The Smithsonian became part of Dad's sales pitch. A lot of his clients, like Mrs. Killam, had no heirs. "What do I need jewelry for?" They might ask. "I'll wear it and then what?" Now Harry created the perfect answer: "You'll wear it and enjoy it during your lifetime, and afterward you can donate it to the Smithsonian, and the world will remember you forever." Adding fuel to Dad's fire was the fact that the Hope had quickly become the most popular exhibit at the Smithsonian, eclipsing even Lindbergh's *Spirit of St. Louis*. Conspicuous consumption was immediately alchemized into philanthropy, all with the wave of the magic wand of Harry Winston.

But the Hope alone wasn't enough of a monument to Dad's self-image. He wanted his shop to be *on* Fifth Avenue, not just off it.

Cartier was on the Avenue, Tiffany was on the Avenue. How, then, could Harry Winston be elsewhere? An opportunity arose in late 1958 when the Steuben Glass building at the corner of 56th and Fifth went up for sale. Steuben was moving to a larger headquarters. The location was made even more perfect by the fact that it was directly across the street from the great beaux arts palace that had housed the Duveen art gallery.

Harry began refurbishing the Steuben Glass building as a temple to himself and proceeded to pour millions of dollars into the gold and travertine makeover. Dad explained once why he chose the travertine by recalling taking me to the Coliseum in Rome on one of our grand tours. "If it lasted two thousand years in Italy, it's good enough for me," Dad said, sounding a little like those epic Texas oilmen of the fifties, who spent like modern Caesars.

Dad hired as his interior designer Stepháne Boudin, the head of Maison Jansen, the leading Paris decorating firm. Boudin had already made a big name for himself in America by decorating the home of Perle Mesta, the famed Washington "hostess with the mostest" who was the inspiration for the hit Ethel Merman musical *Call Me Madam*. Boudin would soon make an even bigger name by being hired by Jackie Kennedy to frenchify the White House.

Meanwhile, ever the whirling deal dervish, in real estate as in diamonds, Harry found a buyer for the 51st Street salon, in a company named Benziger that sold religious objects, apparently lots of them, and liked the notion of being close to St. Patrick's.

By the end of the fifties, my father was on a major roll, and so was I: I became a Harvard man when I matriculated in 1959. Dad had his dream of a college man in the family, and a Harvard man at a time when the ascendance of John F. Kennedy had made Harvard by far the hottest, and hardest, ticket of any American campus. I was thus not only a college man but, now over five feet ten, also a big man, at least relative to Dad, over whom I towered. The only thing missing was any interest in the family business. But to Harry, this was a sales issue, just one more deal he would have to close.

There used to be a feature in the *Saturday Evening Post* called "What's Wrong with This Picture?" where readers had to locate the flaw in an otherwise perfect tableau. And so it was with Harry Winston, whose entire life seemed as flawless as the Hope or the Star of the East.

Enter Nina Dyer, one of the great adventurers of the twentieth century. Nina was an exotic Anglo-Indian beauty of the Merle Oberon school who went from the slums of Liverpool to become a top model in Paris in the postwar fashion renaissance. Like most of the top models of the day, Nina was "discovered" by Fred Horowitz, who cultivated in her a taste for the finer things, not the least of which were the diamonds he sold for Harry Winston. He also introduced her to Baron Heini Thyssen, who fell hard and adorned her with diamonds chosen for him by Fred. The Baron took Nina back to her roots in Colombo, Ceylon (now Sri Lanka), for a romantic wedding in 1954. She was twenty-three, he ten years older.

Nina was obsessed with black pearls, and Fred obliged by selling them a necklace of huge black pearls, with matching earrings, and a black solitaire pearl ring. On their global honeymoon's Caribbean portion, Nina spotted a paradise-like island off Jamaica, which Heini bought for her on the spot. He also bought her a chateau outside Paris, plus a zoo that would feature a flock of exotic parrots, two black panthers (to match her pearls), and a baby leopard. No sooner was the honeymoon over than the marriage ended as well. It had lasted all of ten months. In the divorce proceedings, Heini gave Nina all the weddings gifts, the island, and the chateau, plus a million pounds.

Armed with this settlement, Nina was instantly one of the most eligible women in Europe. She had developed a taste for royalty and began dating Prince Aly Khan, who would soon marry Rita Hayworth. Nina's consolation prize was Aly's half brother Prince Sadruddin Aga Khan, fresh out of Harvard and three years Nina's junior. The prince, who was studious and innocent fell hard under Nina's sophisticated spell. Her exotic background only endeared her to Prince Sadri's father, the Aga Khan, one of the richest men on earth, famous for his annual weighing in, in gold and diamonds gifted to him by his loving subjects (hence the expression "worth his weight in gold"). The Aga Khan liked the idea of his son marrying an Asian, particularly one who was enthusiastic about converting to Islam.

In 1957 the prince and the ex-baroness wed at Sadri's chateau outside Geneva. Nina took the Arabic name Princess Shirin, which meant "sweetness." Fred Horowitz was right on the scene; the Prince's wedding gift to Nina was a six-figure-valued blue diamond. And that was just for starters. In 1958, at the one-year mark of the marriage, the strain of maintaining Nina's happiness, which had been too much for Baron Thyssen, was beginning to weigh on the Muslim prince. The only remedy was jewelry. Catering to Nina's passion for black pearls, to match her now-beloved panthers, Fred Horowitz sold the prince a necklace of black pearls with a clasp of an exceptional canary diamond of a very vivid yellow that would match one of Nina's favorite parrots, plus two sets of rare black pearl earrings. The price befit the rarity: $500,000, far beyond a prince's ransom.

Nina was thrilled, and the marriage got a shot in the arm. Then my father got a shot in the heart. After six months, the royal couple noticed that the pearls and the diamond seemed to be fading. But how could that be? Diamonds—and, by extension, pearls—were forever, weren't they?

A new process had been invented whereby diamonds could be colored by irradiation in a cyclotron, and Dad, a babe in the woods where science was concerned, had fallen under the spell of an august Harvard wizard named Frederick Pough, who could turn dross into gold. The process was supposed to be permanent and untraceable. But it turned out not to be permanent, and science, in its relentless march, had just discovered a way to detect whether a colored diamond was the handiwork of God or of man, even if that man was a deity of science. Nina Dyer, whose name was the ultimate in coincidence for a woman who had dyed herself royal and rich, now set out to, in effect, blackmail the King of Diamonds and thereby add still another royal scalp to her ermine belt.

Harry couldn't have been a better target when the scandal broke just before Christmas 1959. He was basking in the glory of his creation of his own Crown Jewels at the Smithsonian and the erection of his own Versailles of Fifth Avenue, scheduled to open in spring 1960. His rivals on Fifth Avenue were beyond jealous of the pushy upstart who was crashing their pearly gates, their pantheon of luxury. The old-guard merchants feared and scorned the modern Napoleon in their midst the way the way the British had despised the "little Corsican" himself.

Although Dad had refunded the prince's money, all $500,000 of it, after the complaint was made that the stones had faded, Nina Dyer still went to the press, despite Fred trying to persuade her not to.

The tabloid *Daily Mirror* first broke the story as a half-blind item, referring to the prince and princess by name but only to an "American jeweler of excellent reputation." All Manhattan went into a guessing-game frenzy, whipped up further by a succession of eight highly sanctimonious full-page ads in all the papers, day after day, by Tiffany, Cartier, Van Cleef &

Arpels, and five more, each stating the same disclaimer: "We now find it necessary, as internationally known jewelers, to assure our patrons and friends that we are not the jewelry concern in question." If not they, who, the city and the world asked. All fingers pointed to Harry Winston.

But not for long. I had no idea what was happening when I arrived back in New York for my first Christmas home from Harvard and found the Fifth Avenue apartment dark and funereal, with none of the festiveness of the season. My mother greeted me at the door with a finger over her pursed lips. She steered me into the dining room. "Your father's in a very bad way," she said and then told me the bad news. Mom had been spending every minute with Dad and Jill Ciraldo, his in-house public relations woman, trying to figure out how to beat the dreadful rumors and the vicious press. But, for all Jill's calls, for all her considerable charm, she couldn't spin her way out of this one. Each day, things got worse. Dad, who had never met an obstacle he couldn't surmount, had fallen into a deep depression, Mother said.

Mom described how every evening, Dad would take to the bottle, drinking straight Chivas Regal. She described him as reverting to a little boy who's hurt himself, wishing his mother could just kiss him and make the pain go away. One night it had gotten particularly bad, and Mother had to call Uncle Stanley and his beautiful new Italian American wife Lillian to pull Dad out of this downward spiral.

They found him on the couch in the library, overlooking a wintry Central Park. He was lying there in his little elevator shoes, the Chivas bottle on the floor. A bottle of Seconal sleeping pills was clutched in his tiny, fleshy hand. He woke up, but he wouldn't let go of the pills. "I'm ruined," he cried. "They're trying to dig my grave." He lashed out at the scientist Pough, the wizard of irradiation, calling him "the bastard." "He said the process was all natural. He lied!" Dad wailed, pulverizing himself for having trusted the Harvard man. Mother then told me the whole Pough story.

My father had first met Frederick Pough when he was a curator at the Museum of Natural History and Dad was doing his exhibits of the Jonker and the Hope. Pough had a PhD from Harvard and was the author of the Museum's *Field Guide to Rocks and Minerals*, which was a million-copy bestseller. In short, Pough was a star. Pough and Dad found that they shared a passion for colored diamonds. Pough had spent years trying to understand how nature made diamonds of color. He figured out that blue was engendered by small amounts of boron, the element in the cleanser borax; that green came from proximity to uranium; yellow to nitrogen; and so on. Once he had unraveled these mysteries of the universe, Pough set about trying to re-create these conditions in the laboratory.

Other scientists tried to do the same thing, inducing color changes in diamonds by exposing them to radiation, through radium salts and high-intensity X-rays. However, the technology never really worked. The colors were ugly, they didn't last, and the residual radioactivity of the gems was dangerous. It could take six months or more for the radioactivity to wear off.

Pough was not one to be deterred. In the early 1950s he began doing experiments in the cyclotron of the prestigious Brookhaven National Laboratory on Long Island. By bombarding gems this way, Pough was able to create stones of tremendous beauty. Pale yellow diamonds could be turned a vivid canary color or a lizard green. White could change into blue. It was day for night, and truly a eureka moment that Pough shared with Dad, who was awed. Pough assured him that the process was "natural," which probably meant that Pough was claiming to be doing God's work, only faster. Dad trusted him. What was not to trust? Accordingly, Dad gave him several big white rocks to experiment with, and they all came back in living color. The rich women clients of Harry Winston loved colored diamonds, to match their infinite wardrobes. Plus one could charge ten times more for a colored diamond than for a plain one. The commercial possibilities were infinite. Pough left the History Museum to found the Gem Irradiation Laboratories of New York, and started making plans to be to become that rara avis, the rich scientist.

But a funny thing happened to Dad and Fred Pough on their way to the vaults of Chase Manhattan. Another scientist came in to rain on their colored crystal parade. This man, Robert Crowningshield, the director of the laboratory of the nascent Gemological Institute of America, was an advocate of putting gemology on a sound scientific basis rather than resting, as it had for centuries, on what was called "anecdotal connoisseurship." In 1958 Crowningshield published an article asserting that cyclotron-treated diamonds left a tell-tale profile uniquely their own and *not* found in nature. Furthermore, this unnatural color was subject to fading. The Crowningshield thesis and its impact on the diamond industry, which now decreed that any artificially colored diamonds had to be declared as such, became a nightmare for my father.

Fortunately for Harry Winston, he and Pough had not gotten into high gear, or even off the ground, so there wasn't going to be a run on his doors of dowagers and heiresses demanding their money back. There was just Nina Dyer, trying to bring the house down.

Mother recounted to me how she had sat on the couch every night, stroking Dad's head. "Don't leave Ronnie and Bruce without a father," she pleaded, evoking the suicide of her own mother as a horribly negative example. Several times she tried to sneak the pills away from Dad, but he overpowered her.

Stanley resorted to memory rather than force. He sat in a leather armchair across from his brother and reminded him how he and Dad and Charlie, now gone, would fight the bullies who attacked them for being Jews. It was just like that now, just with fancier bullies, Stanley exhorted Dad. "We've seen too much. Don't let them defeat you. Don't give them what they want. I'll help you. We'll solve this."

Dad picked up the Chivas and poured another four fingers of Scotch, emptying the bottle. Misty eyed, he somehow drifted off, somewhere in the netherworld between sleep and stupor. Mother was able to get the barbiturates from him, and she, Stanley, and Lillian managed to carry his 180-pound frame, a lot of weight for such a short man, down to the master bedroom at the end of the long hall. In the morning, Dad awoke and said he had absolutely no recollection of the previous evening. Dad's amnesia notwithstanding, the problem wouldn't go away. "He's asleep on the couch. Go sit by him," Mother urged me.

"Mother, you should have called me," I said, disaster scenarios racing through an eighteen-year-old mind that had never before been exposed to a family crisis.

"Your studies," she justified with her brave face.

"And Bruce?" My brother was still boarding at Riverdale.

"I decided not to tell him. It might make matters worse." I didn't know the term then, but "denial" was a major feature of my mother's existence.

For the first time in the ten years we had lived in the palace in the sky, the apartment seemed to smell musty, like a burial cave. With trepidation, I made my way into the library. Dad was lying there, making noises, something between snoring and moaning. I sat down across from him. Tucked between the armrests of the love seat, he seemed even smaller than he actually was. The commercial titan who was my father now seemed quite helpless and very sad. I felt as if I were sinking through the floor into a quicksand of disaster.

Dad opened his eyes. "Oh, Ronnie," he sighed, staring at me. He began to sob inconsolably. "I was deceived. They said it was a process in nature," he tried to explain what he couldn't really understand, but he sputtered on. "Maybe I deceived myself," he confessed. "I don't know. I might be ruined. Fifty years of hard work, hard, hard work—gone."

"Dad, let me help you," was all I could say. "I'm pretty good at science," I said. But the situation was way beyond science.

"Nina Dyer, that bitch!" Dad raged. I had never heard him call a woman a bitch. He loved women. Without women, there would be no diamond business. "That dirty bitch!" he repeated. "All she wants is money. It's blackmail, son. I'll give her what she wants, but I don't know . . ." After "that bitch," he wailed and railed against "those bastards," the Fifth Avenue Eight, who had done a McCarthy number on him with their sanctimonious "it ain't me" advertisements.

Particularly galling to Dad was Claude Arpels, whom Dad had sponsored in fleeing France and getting into America during the war. The seeds of treachery were always there.

Dad told me how he once caught the newly arrived Arpels standing in the shadows of Dad's salon portals, trying to snag Dad's clients. Dad put his hands over his eyes, as if to try to stroke away the pain. "And all those Judases," he said, again alluding to his rivals who didn't want him on the Avenue. "They want to put you in the ground. Be careful of people in the world. So many want to dig your grave."

I struggled hard to make sense of it all. I could understand Dad's falling under Fred Pough's spell, where the irradiation of diamonds was concerned. Pough, alas, had been blinded by his own light, and my father had made an honest error in putting his own blind faith in the great, and greatly credentialed, man of science.

I went back to Harvard, calling home each day to make sure Dad hadn't done something awful to himself. Fortunately, the tide turned. All his friends and clients rallied behind him. Then Elsa Maxwell, gossip columnist and in-print arbiter of high society, both at home and abroad, came to Dad's aid. Maxwell was as integral a part of the social world as my father. They needed her parties and buzz the way they needed his jewels. Born in Iowa, Maxwell was as self-invented as Winston. In her first column, in 1915, she got everyone's attention by declaring "New York's elite was a collection of pompous mediocrities occupied only with petty feuds and suffocatingly dull receptions." Proving that society was totally masochistic, Maxwell was lionized for it. The nastier she was, the more they ate it up.

Maxwell's party-giving philosophy was, "Serve the dinner backward, do anything, but for goodness sake, do something weird." The weirdness she embraced went back to her Iowa farm girl days. As public relations director of the Waldorf

Astoria, she gave "barnyard parties," which transformed the hotel's ballroom into a farm, complete with horses, cows, and pigs. For her April in Paris balls, she added elephants. New York loved her. And listened to her. Including when Maxwell devoted her entire column in the *New York Journal-American* to affirming Harry Winston's integrity. "Now, I do not believe the jeweler in question is a dishonest man. In fact, I'm gradually finding out things which prove he is not." Once the oracle had spoken, the world she ruled fell into line. Prince Sadruddin Aga Khan soon divorced his princess, who committed suicide in her French chateau in 1965. Nina Dyer was dead at thirty-five. She had taken an overdose of sleeping pills.

In March 1960 Dad triumphantly opened his new Fifth Avenue flagship. Lillian Ross and Brendan Gill of the *New Yorker* did a highly flattering "Talk of the Town" lead that made no reference whatsoever to the Dyer disaster. Instead, Ross and Gill wrote in awe of the grand new digs and the "tens of millions of dollars' worth of precious stones that were being shoveled into trunks for the five-block ride north." They affectionately described Dad as a "pink-cheeked, cherubic looking" hypochondriac worrywart. Here's how they quoted him: "Worrying over the new building has given me a sore throat. All I eat these days is Coricidin. I'm troubled about the new door up there. It's a typical eighteenth century French palace door, a black iron grille trimmed with gold medallions, but is it too ornate? I'm in the dumps. Everything is tearing me away from the jewels."

The writers described my father as never wasting an ounce of precious metal. "After we move, we'll melt the linoleum on the factory floor and get the gold and platinum dust out of it." They made no mention of the weird science of irradiating diamonds or dyeing pearls. It was a time for celebration, not aspersion. They spoke of Dad's fondling of his newest creation, a fifty-eight-carat diamond tiara with fifty-four large pear diamonds, inspired by a crown Dad had bought last summer from the Duchess of Westminster as the "master warming himself by the diamond bonfire." Still, they correctly caught the sense of my father never being satisfied. Talking about the $2 million he spent on the new, glitzy building, he said, "I felt New York needed this sort of showcase. The question is, what did *I* need it for?" Harry was worried that his new palace of diamonds might actually be *too* flashy.

As ever, Mother was right there to calm him down. "It'll tone down, Harry. All it needs is to get rained on."

CHAPTER ELEVEN

Leary in the Sky with Diamonds

In my sophomore year at Harvard, I read Aldous Huxley's book *The Doors of Perception*, whose title was taken from a line by the mystical poet William Blake, from his book *The Marriage of Heaven and Hell*. Jim Morrison must have been reading the same material as well, for a few years later his group The Doors would rock the world. The year 1960 was a time of early rock and the early days of experimenting with psychedelics. I found a fellow traveler in a chubby, witty boy from Philadelphia who lived down the floor in Claverly Hall, our sophomore lodgings, which we called the Clavitorium. His name was Andrew Weil, and he would go on to become the most famous holistic doctor in America. We bonded over our interest in biochemistry, but what really turned us both on was mind expansion. Who cared about grubbing for A's when you could soar completely out of this world? As for Dad's diamonds, I learned how to create my own, in the deep, vast mine of my own mind.

Both Andy and I were certain that the field of psychedelics was going to be the growth industry of the sixties, and we fancied the idea of being present at the explosion of the birth of this brave new universe. We were dying to try the stuff. Resourceful Harvard men, we located a small company with the beguiling but somewhat misleading name Nutritional Biochemical. Andy wrote the company on Harvard stationery requesting information on how to secure a kilo of mescaline sulfate hemihydrate, the scientific basis of Huxley's polymorphic dream state. The drug company, obviously in awe of Harvard, promptly wrote back, dignifying Andy as *Dr. Andrew Weil* and sending him a Drug Investigator's Protocol form, which we filled out, noting in academic-ese that our work was part of an ongoing scientific study of mood and setting on the psychological outcome of drug-induced states. We sent a check for $200.

Lo and behold, we received a magic package addressed to Dr. Weil containing the drug in powder form. We were temporarily stymied; we couldn't just swallow it *Alice in Wonderland* style. I emptied the powder into an old-fashioned brown vitamin bottle and took it down to the College House pharmacy at Harvard Square, where I asked the kindly druggist if he might put the chemical compound into capsules for one gram doses. "I'm doing an experiment on the nutritional requirements of fish," I glibly improvised, thinking on my feet. "I need capsules for time release." In Boston, no one says no to a Harvard man, not where science is concerned. Two days later, for all of five dollars, I had one hundred rocket fuel blasters encased in gelatin.

It wasn't that I was a teenage drug addict. I had never taken anything, not even marijuana. Aside from some fine French wine my parents shared with me, my consciousness had not been altered at all. But I wasn't opposed to it. This was science, and I saw myself as a scientist and chemist. Andy and I reached out to Dr. Timothy Leary, who was a member of the psychology department. In 1960 Leary was an unknown figure in the media. He was, however, gaining an underground reputation as a cult figure in the about-to-emerge "mind field," having traveled to Cuernavaca, Mexico, that summer to take psilocybin mushrooms, an experience that he said changed the course of his life

In the aftermath of that Mexican epiphany, Leary and his chief associate, Richard Alpert, had begun a program that fall known as the Harvard Psilocybin Project, testing the psychedelics on young people from the disparate constituencies of the Andover Newton Theological Seminary and the Concord State Prison. Harvard students were considered off-limits for his experiments. Never taking no for an answer, we decided to try to meet him anyway.

I rang Leary up, and he promptly invited us to his office, a shingled cottage on the western edge of campus. It was fall, and the leaves were splendid, a true explosion of colors, earthy and at the same time not of this earth. Leary greeted us and sat us down in a very Harvard-y book-lined study that did not look at all what I imagined the cutting edge of mind science to be. Forty at the time, he wore an Ivy League tweed herringbone jacket and a button-down Brooks Brothers shirt. Regal as a Roman senator, Leary wore his salt-and-pepper hair combed forward to conceal a receding hairline.

Leary lit a cigarette and, thrilled to have an audience, told us about his work in a windy voice that was both learned and puckish. Eager beavers, we offered him our big cache of mescaline if he would let us join his experiments. "I really can't talk about that," he begged off, almost with a wink. "Scientific privilege." Then he added, "I can help you to do this, to go on a trip. But all of this is unofficial."

Leary explained to Andy and me the importance of set and setting. "Don't try this alone," he warned us. "Not the first time. Find a good friend, a trusted friend. But only one of you take the drugs. The other acts as ground control, a reality check, if you will."

Because I was the more reluctant psychedelic virgin of the duo, Andy decided to go first. I would be ground control. We went back to Claverly, and he popped some pills with a water chaser. Then he lay down on the tattered sofa and waited for whatever was to come. We chose Bach as our mood music. Aside from playing DJ, I did all the worrying for both of us. What if the pharmacy put something else by mistake into the capsules and Andy was poisoned? I started counting the steps from the dorm to the University Health Services' emergency entrance. Or what if he went psycho and had to be restrained?

As time passed, Andy's initial smile became more and more luminous. No longer was he a mere subject in a mind drug experiment; he was becoming an initiate in an ancient Eleusinian ritual. As he sat up on the couch pillows with his head thrown back, his mouth fell open in orgasmic rapture. "Ron, you can't imagine what I'm seeing. Paradise."

This went on for hours until I changed the Bach to jazz, as much to reassure myself as to rouse Andy. Finally he opened his eyes

"I'm here, Ron. I'm drifting down."

"Are you all right?"

"Fine. You can't imagine where I went. You must try it."

I nodded, but I knew my intent was half-hearted. Was the trip worth the anxiety? During the fall and spring semesters of my sophomore year, many of the boys on our third floor of Claverly tried the mescalito. Some were blasé, others over the edge, like Dennis Milford, a Gary Cooperish fundamentalist Christian from the heartland. He not only saw Jesus; he had a long dialogue with him and left the drug trip so confirmed in his faith that even Harvard's secularity could not shake him.

By April I was the last man standing. Andy pressed me to the task, and one fine Saturday afternoon I lay on the "drug couch" and gulped down the pills. Andy put on some Bach, and I waited nervously for my mind to be blown. Nothing happened. Then Andy suggested a stroll along the Charles. They were having a kite festival, sort of like those in Japan where giant koi-like kites soar like huge flying fish. In Cambridge the kites were far less imaginative, but what started out as plain box kites soon became a circus of twirling colors, sort of an update of Seurat's painting *A Sunday Afternoon on the Island of La Grande Jatte*. The mescaline genie was finally out of the bottle. The river was at once liquid and solid. I thought I was witnessing a scientific miracle. The setting sun seemed like Hiroshima. I needed to retreat to the safety of the couch, and gradually I glided down.

I felt privileged to have been introduced to the world of psychedelics, but I had to focus on the end of term and mundane things like exams. There were lots of high jinks to cut the tension of studying night and day. My contribution to this gaiety was to place a garbage can lid loaded with rocket fuel powder in Andy's room when he was napping, ignite the mixture, and close the door. What followed was a very big bang, with smoke and flame jetting over the transom. The door opened, and Andy stood there in a cloud of smoke, staring wide eyed and unblinking. "I can't see!" He cried. "Call the hospital. Please!" he pleaded. Then I saw him wink at his roommate.

"You devil," I yelled. "You had me!" Two years later, he would really have me. And it would be no laughing matter.

Meanwhile, Harry pressed me into working for him in his grand new Fifth Avenue emporium during the busy Christmas season and over my spring break when the store was packed with ring buyers and gift givers for the wedding blitz coming in June. For me, it was culture shock, entering Dad's magnificently palatial, perfectly ordered, and dead-quiet salon, the total opposite of my Clavitorium with its explosions and drug trips. The salon had ornate paneling painted dove gray. There were hexagon vitrines set in the walls.

Because Dad believed in muting the ambience so that his stones alone would shine, the only touch of color was a black, gray, and gold Aubusson carpet that covered the floor from wall to wall. The grand, hushed effect rivaled that of Napoleon's tomb in the Hôtel National des Invalides.

At the entrance of the store was a prim receptionist at a kidney-shaped antique desk who buzzed in the clientele, who would shop downstairs or be escorted upstairs to Dad's office in a tiny, diamond-shaped private elevator. Dad would greet the elite by rising from his Louis Quatorze desk, with classic views behind him of Fifth Avenue.

In 1962 Jackie Kennedy would organize an exhibition of Dad's Hope Diamond at the Louvre, which was the blockbuster museum show of the decade. There it was, with a plaque reading DONATED BY HARRY WINSTON, the greatest diamond in the world in the greatest museum in the world. That winter, the Kennedys invited Mom and Dad to a state dinner at the White House. How, Dad continued to ask me, could I resist all this?

He and Mom put the burning question to me countless times over dinners at the Colony, Le Pavillon, and La Côte Basque, Manhattan's most exclusive restaurants, where we'd drink the finest wines and be surrounded by gorgeous women all wearing Harry's gems. How could I say no to all of this?

But my heart belonged to Harvard, where I majored in both Chemistry and English Literature. It may have seemed like a strange combination, but I was able to find poetry in the periodic table, and at the same time I could find chemistry in the language of the poets. I guess I must have been inspired by my mother's father, dear old Winkie, who was both a doctor and a bibliophile. I took courage from Mother's tales of how Winkie would do dangerous chemical experiments and how he had once blown his wire-frame glasses off trying to distill ether. Those explosions of mine were thus mitigated by the fact they had genetic roots.

I was still very much a dreamer, and the idea of going into the family business just didn't seem like the stuff dreams were made of. "I need you, Ronnie," poor Dad would plead to me at the Colony. His pleas was both flattering and frightening.

Mother would look on anxiously and approvingly. "Daddy's worked so hard," she would say, ladling on the guilt Jewish mothers are so famous for.

"What do you want to do?" Dad would ask when I skirted his entreaties.

"I think I'll try science for a while," I'd say, diplomatically leaving the door open, fanning Dad's hope that "a while" would end soon.

I could see from his furrowed brow his barely suppressed thoughts that "I knew I should have never let him go to

Harvard." What he did say was, "You know, son, you can do both."

There was a long pause, then his own guilt trip, scarier to me than any mescaline trip. "Ronnie, I'm not getting younger." There it was. The threat of his mortality.

In the Edward Albee play *A Delicate Balance*, two of the lead characters are named Harry and Edna. Albee used to visit Stonwin to play tennis as a teenager. His adoptive parents, theater heir Reed Albee and his towering wife, Frankie, were two of my parents' closest friends. The specter of death was a powerful force in both families' dynamics, and Edward put it at the center of his play.

In general, my father was a denier of death. I couldn't blame him, having lost his mother so young and witnessing his father basically choking to death. If people become doctors to learn to thwart the grim reaper, Harry Winston may have thought that enough money and fame could similarly overpower the devilish force that was trying to destroy him. If not, the worst-case scenario was that his name, his legend, and his eponymous business would live forever.

"I'm just getting started," I heard him boast to his Swiss staff when visiting Geneva. But I knew, and I think he did, too, that life did not begin at sixty-five. Three Winston cousins already worked for him. They were capable, but none were take-charge types, not like Harry. There was no force of nature like Harry, least of all my brother Bruce. By my second year at Harvard, Bruce was already on his third prep school after Riverdale. Mother referred to Bruce as a *spielkatz*, which in German meant "playcat." Bruce was charming and likeable, with a Winstonian warmth that won him lots of friends. Bruce did know precisely what he wanted to do, which is not to work. He declared his commitment to leisure at an early age. He would take my father's wealth and use it to enjoy his life. Worry, that was my job. In the family game of business tag, I was "it." I was to be the worker bee. What would my family have thought about my "consciousness-expanding session"? I shuddered to think. That would have blown their minds more than it had blown mine, and in a far worse way. I never mentioned it to anyone outside our pump house circle in Claverly.

That circle was dispersed in my third year at Harvard. In the fall of 1961, my premed friend from back in Riverdale, Tom Garvey, and I shared a suite at Quincy House. Andy Weil went to Lowell House, so we saw a lot less of each other. Accordingly, my interest in mind expansion diminished. I kept at my rocket work by going down the road to MIT, where a young rocket man named Franklin Kosdon became my collaborator. When my Harvard pals were out dating on Friday nights, Franklin and I were static firing our rocket motors in the basement of Building 25 at the MIT Rocket Research Laboratory. I developed a formula for solid propellant, an effort that paralleled that of the federal government. While the government spent $5 billion a year on their efforts, we spent $50.

We got a huge bang for our buck. The apostate German rocket scientist Wernher von Braun, father of the US lunar project, came by our lab while visiting MIT Professor George Kistiakowsky, President Kennedy's chief science adviser. The huge-headed Prussian genius looked approvingly at our bulletproof steel rocket test cell. "That was how we began in Germany," declared von Braun. Although his bombs may have blitzed London during the war, von Braun was a personal hero to me, and I hung on his every word. The rest of the country caught up with my adulation when von Braun's Saturn V rocket landed Americans on the moon.

In addition to von Braun's benediction, in 1961 and 1962, Franklin and I won the American Rocket Society's award for the best research study in space science for two versions of our paper "The Development of an Isocyante Solid Propellant." Our first award was given at a Manhattan cocktail event hosted by Senator Jacob Javits, who was not only one of the most powerful men in government but also a friend of my father. I had never felt more vindicated than at this party, which Mother and Dad both attended. This was the beginning of the space race with Russia, and Washington attached its highest urgency to winning it. In other words, science guys like me actually *mattered*. "That's my son," I could hear my father boasting across the room. "I encouraged his work." *Sure, Dad*, I thought, with a smile on my face.

Our second award was presented in Los Angeles, by then vice president Lyndon B. Johnson. This was also my first trip to the West Coast. No one had ever won the rocket society's award twice, plus, this time we received a prize of $1,000, which was enormous money in those days. We were put up in a hotel in downtown Los Angeles, and we weren't even taken to Hollywood, or even to Santa Monica to see the Pacific Ocean. I suppose they thought we were way too serious for that. I did get to see the snow-peaked mountains that ringed the L.A. basin.

What an honor it was to meet LBJ at the black tie hotel ballroom event. "Good work," he drawled to me. "We need young men like you." But Harry Winston needed me more. Dad arranged for me to see the location of my grandfather's original store on East 5th Street. Now it was a pawnshop, in a neighborhood where winos staggered around in the streets. The JACOB WEINSTEIN—JEWELER sign had been gone for some forty-five years, but the sense of history was sobering. I recalled Dad's words, which he intoned whenever he took a major business gamble. "Why not? After all, it all came from nothing." Here, then, was that nothing, in this downtown slum. I tried to imagine my family's own poverty at the time and their hard life together, with Aunt Dora taking care of Dad and his father. But I was unable to envision it. I was young and excited about my own success.

Back at Harvard, I wasn't a full-time lab rat. I was punched for the DU Club (later to become the Fly Club), an agglomeration of polo-playing preppies and Euro-types who were the total opposite of the brains from the Bronx High School of Science, my first Harvard friends. Many of these rich and social boys had gone to Le Rosey in Switzerland; they gave great parties. Harvard was its height of its mystique, thanks to President Kennedy, the ultimate Harvard man, and his Camelot administration, which was heavily drawn from Harvard. To the legions of college girls in Boston, every Harvard man was a simulacrum of JFK. The very word "Harvard" was a verbal aphrodisiac to any girl looking for Mister Right. Such was the power of the JFK stardust.

I kept my merchant-prince identity to myself. In junior year, my fellow princes, Richard Marcus and Bob Sakowitz, of the grand Texas department stores, and I found ourselves in the same classroom for the first time, Government 180, Deterrence and Defense, a course on global political and military strategy taught by a relatively unknown professor with a German accent named Henry Kissinger.

At Christmas of 1962, I went to a party in New York that reunited a lot of friends from La Bande in the South of France. One of these was a sporty, gamine girl named Nikki Jaeger. Nikki always seemed to be at the forefront of cool, a lightning rod for adventure. Nikki asked me for a ride up to Cambridge, then explained the purpose of her journey. "I have a friend, Professor Richard Alpert," she said. "Do you know him?" I said I hadn't had the pleasure but certainly knew who he was. "He's doing some great work on drugs," she explained, then added, with a tinge of pride, "He invited me to be part of the experiment." In the time since Andy and I met Leary, he and Alpert had actually gotten called on the Harvard Crimson carpet for experimenting with undergrads. Maybe that's why Alpert was importing people like Nikki, because Harvard students were off-limits.

I was immediately charmed by Alpert. He was like Einstein, minus the hair. He had an intense, wide-eyed way of gazing at you, and was an intent listener. Alpert shared a quick drink, then spirited Nikki away. "Come, Nikki, we have work to do," he said.

A week later Nikki rang me up about the "work." "I had a drug session," she said breathlessly. "It was wonderful. Professor Alpert is the greatest guide. He taught me so much about my life and myself. You should try it." I had not confided in Nikki, nor anyone else outside Claverly about my own experiences. Later that spring I ran into Alpert on Mt. Auburn Street, Harvard's main drag. He put his arm around me and greeted me warmly, flattering me by remembering my name. He asked me about my classes and seemed so genuinely interested that I spontaneously invited him to a Quincy House production of *Cat on a Hot Tin Roof*, on which I was assistant director.

Much to my surprise, he said yes. Again, I was proud of myself, that this brilliant professor and cult star of the Harvard underground had accepted my invitation. But just before showtime, our little production lost its female lead. A nice girl from Denver named Patricia Elliott stepped into the breach, and it was my job to prepare her. This was her first major production, so it was the blind leading the blind, except that at least she had talent. Patricia would go on to win a Tony award on Broadway and star on the long-running soap opera *One Life to Live*.

On opening night, I was nervous as hell about both Patricia and Alpert. She was flawless. During the standing accolades, I could feel Alpert's shoulders touching mine. "Really good," he said. "Something magic about first times." I wasn't sure if that was a veiled suggestion, but Alpert did invite me to his home the next Friday. Friday was normally rocket firing night at MIT, but I skipped it. This was the first time at big, cold Harvard that I had the chance to make friends with a real professor, and a famous one at that.

Alpert's house in Newton was quite modest for a man of his wealth and taste. His father was the president of the New Haven Railroad and was a legend on Wall Street for getting the trains to run on time. I sat on the sofa. Alpert put on some Maynard Ferguson. He sat in an armchair and beamed like a holy man. His gaze was both piercing and beatific. Out of the blue, Alpert suggested we take a trip. A literal one. "Let's fly out to the Berkshires and have dinner there," he suggested as casually as inviting me to the Greek taverna on the corner of Massachusetts Avenue.

"There are no flights at this hour, are there?" I replied dumbfoundedly.

"I have my plane down at Belmont Field. I'll fly us." Then Alpert pulled a bottle out of his tweed jacket pocket. It looked like an aspirin bottle. Tipping two tablets into his palm, he extended his hand to me. "Here. Take these."

"What is it?" I asked.

"Psilocybin," he said softly. I hesitated. He took the tablets himself. Then he put two more in his hand. "It's okay," he said with the reassurance of a skilled surgeon. "You're with me. I'll guide you."

A trip *and* a trip. I took the pills and swallowed them.

As Alpert drove us to the local airport, my only thought was that I prayed he knew what he was doing. The Cole Porter lyric ran through my mind: "Flying so high with some guy in the sky is my idea of nothing to do."

The plane was a single-engine Cessna. "Hop in," Alpert said. I began to feel the same visceral vacuum, the tingling in an empty gut, that I had when I did the mescalito with Andy Weil. "Nine, seven, four, oh . . ." Alpert relayed a flight plan by radio to the control tower. The words became unintelligible. I was out of it. We took off, and as Alpert made a left bank, I felt the world beneath us spin one way and the plane the other.

"Dick," I said, taking the liberty of familiarity I would have normally never done. But this wasn't normal. This was not of this earth. "Dick, I'm scared!"

"Hang on to me," Alpert said, extending his right hand to me while flying with his left.

We landed. Descending from the plane, I was amazed that I could still walk. We had dinner somewhere, but I can't remember a thing. On our way back, driving to Alpert's Newton house, we passed an orchard in full spring flower in the moonlight. Van Gogh came to mind. We stopped at a roadside grocery. The colors floored me. The first radishes of the season seemed to dance in their stalls. The counterman's face haunted as it became distorted with hideous features. "Dick, he looked horrible," I said in the car.

"You weren't looking at him. You were looking at his mask," Alpert replied. "He was in his role of selling. That's what you saw, and it was ugly. You must try to see his inner face. The drugs will help you."

Alpert, who took me back to his house and gave me more psilocybin, was in his role of selling as well. He put on Mozart, and the wallpaper began to undulate to the sound of the violins. Alpert stretched out on the couch, like a reclining Buddha, and just as serene, except for those high-powered big eyes behind huge glasses. He never took his eyes off me. I watched as he sipped a beer, cool and slow. Then he came over and put his arm gently around me.

I was way too out of my mind, my regular mind, to go into a homosexual panic, but even in this dream state, I knew something was wrong with this picture. I needed the professor, just to keep me from flipping out, and I honored him, because of his brilliance and position. But making a move on a student, on a subject, was clearly out of line, and I just said no, as nicely as I could.

Meanwhile I was engulfed by a new wave of hallucinations, these involving my parents. I was in the middle of a forest fire, a massive conflagration, with my father running down a lane into the flames, then whipping me nearly to death for starting the fire. Upon reflection, this surely was a flashback to the first experimental blaze I started as a boy at Stonwin, and while Dad was mightily displeased, he never touched me. Later I imagined I was dead, buried in a cathedral, while outside my father calmly spoke to my mother, holding the leash of a dalmatian as if they were at a garden party. Somehow, thank God, I finally came down and made it back to the brick and mortar reality of Quincy House.

I later told Andy Weil about this trip, and he was riveted to the point where he insisted, pleaded, that I introduce him to Alpert. I took Andy out to Newton and presented him to the professor, who was beginning the deep spiritual conversion that culminated years later when Richard Alpert, Jewish prince, became Ram Dass, enlightened seer. The Newton digs were becoming a utopian haven, with lots of comings and goings. It was a pigsty. Alpert apologized. "After being high for days, nobody wants to do housework. Stoned or not, you've eventually got to do the dishes." Amid the crash-pad squalor and the haze of pot smoke, there was a great deal of provocative sexual experimentation going on. I kept my distance after that visit, but I did find out that Andy couldn't get enough of what he had seen. He made numerous efforts to convince Alpert to let him join him in his research, but he was inexplicably rebuffed.

At the end of my senior year at Harvard, in May 1963, I went home to Stonwin to unwind after final exams. I was looking forward to getting my degree in two weeks, proud of my upcoming validation as my dad's college man. I had just gotten out of the swimming pool when I got a call from Andy Weil. He told me he was coming down to New York and had to see me. Couldn't it wait until we were both back in Cambridge in a few days? I asked him. No way. It was a matter of "great urgency," he insisted. "By the way, Ronnie, are your parents there with you?"

"Yes. Why?"

"Just thought I'd ask," he said. "I'll come out to Scarsdale. I'll see you at Stonwin tomorrow, midday."

I knew Andy was aggressive, but I had never seen him this strange and pushy. I wondered what he wanted but was unable to get any hint of it from him on the phone. The next day he arrived by taxi, accompanied by Lee Auspitz, one of the Claverly gang and another mescaline initiate. Unlike Andy, Lee was painfully shy and had a hard time speaking at all. I took my buddies upstairs to my bedroom. There Andy dropped the bomb, telling me that the Food and Drug Administration had a file on me and my drug use. "You're in the dossier," he said, adding that the *Crimson*, of which he was an editor, was about to do a scoop on me and Alpert. The *Boston Globe* was also preparing a story.

"Big deal," I said with bravado. I never knew when Andy would be pulling one of his celebrated pranks. But I didn't think he'd come out to Scarsdale just for fun.

"You're the star witness against Leary and Alpert," Andy said gravely. Lee remained silent, glumly serious.

"What did I do?" I asked.

"It's not what you did. It's what the two professors did, giving drugs to undergraduates. They knew they were going to get in trouble, and they pushed it. With *you*."

I wanted to know what Andy wanted from me. "Come clean, and nothing will happen," he said. I didn't think I had done anything illegal, and I hated the idea of ratting out Alpert and Leary. "Harvard needs to talk to you," Andy pressed.

Finally, Lee chimed in, dipping his chin as if he were apologizing for opening his mouth. "Look, Ron, if you confess, it will be considered a youthful indiscretion. It'll be forgotten."

"I get the picture," I said, wanting to get them out of my house as quickly as possible. Andy kept snooping around, looking for my parents. I didn't want him to talk to them, but, sadly, Dad was sitting downstairs in the library reading his *Value Line* stock report, which he did every Saturday.

Dad was instantly suspicious. "Why did you come to see Ronnie?" Dad put it to Andy.

"Perhaps you'd better ask your son," Andy replied in a tone that would raise anyone's suspicions, particularly those of Harry Winston.

"Come into the library, everybody," Dad ordered. This audience with the pope of Stonwin was exactly what Andy had come for. "Ronnie, are you in trouble?" Dad asked me outright.

"Not exactly," I hemmed.

Dad turned to Andy. "Is my son in trouble? He needs to graduate."

"Well, Mister Winston . . ." Andy paused. And then he spewed out the whole story with the added emphasis that Lee and he were here to help me. I had only seen Dad so shaken up during the Nina Dyer scandal, when he saw his own reputation on the line. His face was furrowed with a panic.

"Have you been taking drugs, son?" he queried me.

"I took a psychedelic a year ago," I confessed. "They were experimental chemicals, not drugs."

"What's a psychedelic?" Dad was confused. I tried my best to explain the difference, but I failed. His understanding wasn't any different than if I'd been arrested nodding out on a heroin overdose in some needle park. "You realize you're doing something illegal." Dad found me guilty on the spot. "I'm calling Harry." Harry was the great lawyer Harry

Torczyner, who was Dad's go-to for any trouble in the Winston realm. Born in Antwerp, Harry T. had once run for mayor of New York, with a poster portrait of him by Karsh plastered all over the city. To me he looked like a Mohawk Indian in a bespoke suit. Harry T. rounded out the Little Harry Society, which included Harry W. and Harry O(ppenheimer). An attorney for René Magritte, Harry T. had a serious art collection, which focused on the surrealists. My case was right up his alley.

Having learned all he needed to know, Dad sent my two troublemaking "friends" to LaGuardia in his chauffeured Cadillac, shaking their hands warmly when they left. The information Andy told me was in the files was a pure parroting of what I had confided in him over the past years. I was overwhelmed by his betrayal and deeply confused by it. Andy was behaving like a jilted suitor. Wanting to penetrate the psychedelic inner circle at Newton, which was perhaps the first hippie collective, he had tried and failed to be of use to Leary and Alpert. Rejected, he could wreak his revenge, getting them thrown out of Harvard, and getting me thrown out in the process too.

Harry Torczyner arrived late that Saturday from his own nearby Westchester country retreat. Wearing the orange boutonniere of a *legion d'honneur* awarded to him by the Ivory Coast, he listened to Dad's precis intently, frequently raising his trademark monocle to observe Dad's frenzied expression more closely.

"This is very serious," Dad concluded, turning to nod gravely at me. "Harry, what do you think?"

"Mister Winston," he said with a flourish. "I do not make instant coffee."

What followed were long hours of serious legal discussion on issues of obstruction of justice, self-incrimination, narcotics statutes, everything. I considered Harry T. a friend. I would sometimes visit his office on my own when I was in New York and turned to him as a mentor in contemplating my career plans, though of course he had a strong bias in favor of my joining my father. I tried to convince him that what I had done was not illegal, but the master wasn't buying my plea. He became particularly concerned when I told him that I had a bottle of the pills Alpert had given me in my desk at Quincy House. My father turned green.

"Does anyone know of their existence or whereabouts?" Harry T. quizzed me. When I said no, Harry T. spoke, "Then you must go back to Cambridge immediately and eliminate the evidence."

"Evidence!" I exclaimed. "I'm not guilty of anything!"

My father stood up. "Ronald," he said. This was a name he used only in the direst circumstances. "Ronald, you must listen to Harry," Dad said, clenching his fists as if he were about to hit a table. Or me.

With the two Harrys ganging up on me, I could see I was fighting a battle I could not win. I took a shuttle early the next morning back to Boston, then a cab to Quincy House. I waited outside until I knew Tom Garvey and our suitemates would be away from the room. Then I sneaked in and found the pills in my drawer. I flushed them down the toilet, twice for good measure. Then I beat a hasty retreat back to Logan Airport and caught the next shuttle to La Guardia.

Back at Stonwin, the two Harrys had already planned my next move, which was to speak to the Harvard dean of students and throw myself upon his mercy, but I wasn't sure

Dean John Usher Monro had any. A stern Yankee, he harked back to the pilgrim Harvard of Cotton Mather. Where spiritual enlightenment was concerned, these pilgrims hadn't made much progress. Maybe some students and professors had become liberals, but the essence of the place remained as Puritan as Hawthorne's Salem. My so-called psychedelic crime was, apparently, akin to witchcraft, and witches were burned at the stake. I could imagine the statue of John Harvard in the yard stamping his bronze-buckled shoe in intolerance. Just as Hester Prynne was forced to wear a scarlet A, Harvard would want Leary and Alpert, and maybe me, too, to wear crimson MDs, for "Mental Deviant."

I dutifully called the dean's office and made an appointment for the next morning. I again grabbed the first shuttle and arrived at University Hall at eleven. All I remember was darkness in the dean's office. Monro looked up at me from his paperwork. He resembled a classic preppie thirty years out of college. His dark bushy eyebrows had a satanic aspect, but how could they not, under the circumstances?

"Sit down, Ron," Monro tried to be friendly. How was the term?" "I'm done," was all I could say.

"Let's cut to the chase." His tone turned serious. The room turned black. He explained how "the University" needed to know about the "activities" of Professors Leary and Alpert, specifically involving undergraduates.

I remained silent.

"We have reason to believe you can help us," Monro said ominously.

I still didn't say a word.

"Well" sighed Monro, raising his Satanic brows.

"I don't wish to discuss it," I balked.

"Think very hard about your decision," he pressed.

"I don't have anything to say."

"That's *your* conclusion. But from *our* point of view, you can kiss your diploma goodbye."

"What do you mean, sir?"

"You won't graduate. Not now. Not ever."

I felt I was up against Torquemada, facing torture, the stake, the noose, but in my case I didn't even get a hood. I could see myself swinging from the gallows. "I did do a drug experiment . . . with Professor Richard Alpert," I confessed, then added, trying to save him. "It was at *my* request."

"When?" The dean's eyebrows were twitching.

"April. 1962."

"Thank you," Munro said triumphantly. "We will let you graduate."

I felt soiled, sick. "I'd like to add a few words, sir."

"Go ahead."

"I believe this work is extremely valuable in understanding the mind, sir. The drug research has value in opening the doors of perception." I tried to seem smart by alluding to the Huxley book. Munro took it as the crack of a smart aleck. He said nothing. The meeting was over.

I walked in a daze into Harvard Yard. I was still a Harvard man, but what kind of man was I really? I had never felt worse in my life. I shuttled back to Scarsdale. If the plane had crashed, it wouldn't have mattered to me. The first thing I did back at Stonwin was to call Richard Alpert. I shamefully admitted to him that I had been strong-armed into siccing the attack dogs of Harvard on him and Leary.

"I see," was all he could say. He remained serene as ever.

"They weren't going to let me graduate," I tried to explain.

"Nice guys," Alpert said. "Monro?"

"Yes."

"Okay, Ronnie," he said. "Thanks for the warning." He was always the gentleman. I wish I could have been as heroic, as committed to a cause as he was.

Harvard got what it wanted. Its centuries of tradition would not be shaken. The rogue professors were dismissed. The inciting incident was violating their pledge not to provide drugs to undergraduates. I was that undergraduate, and now I was that graduate. I had the most prestigious diploma in the land, but at what cost? I was demoralized. Andy Weil was surely exhilarated, his vengeance complete. Leary and Alpert, expelled from the Eden of Harvard, unleashed their Eden of the Mind on the entire world. Psychedelics, especially LSD, would become a cornerstone of the culture of the sixties. At least I had been there at the inception. Now I was a Harvard man for life.

CHAPTER TWELVE

My Brilliant Career

Nineteen sixty-three was a very turbulent year for the world, and for me, because, fresh out of the trauma that was Harvard, I was racked with indecision as to what to do with the rest of my life. The empire that was Harry Winston was waiting for me, but I was one highly ambivalent emperor-in-waiting. Here I was on the cusp of the Age of Aquarius, when freedom was everything and not just another word for nothing left to lose. So to consider giving up that freedom for the ultimate gilded cage that was my family business was a choice that I didn't even want to contemplate.

My parents had other ideas, ideas that were rooted in the traditions of the Old World and in the dynastic territorial imperatives of big business. Not that their ideas were spoken. The ideas of Harry and Edna Winston were never spoken. They were masters of the art of understatement. But what they had in mind was marrying me off to the most eligible heiress in their world. This was Mary Oppenheimer, the daughter of Harry Oppenheimer of De Beers. Mary, just about my age, was the Diamond Princess. And I guess, by default, that made me the Diamond Prince, a cringe-inducing thought. It was a match made, if not in heaven, at least on Charterhouse Street.

The union would be the ultimate testimony to the entente cordiale forged between the two Harrys after their fierce competition throughout the fifties. Their truce had been symbolized by the Regency desk Dad presented to Sir Ernest Oppenheimer for his fiftieth anniversary in the diamond trade and to celebrate De Beers's new headquarters in London. A desk was one thing; a cradle would be something else. Harry and Edna had been busy talking to Harry and Bridget about my spending my first post-Harvard summer as the Oppenheimers' guest in South Africa. Dad presented me with the great news that I had received this invitation that I could not refuse. "You'll love Brenthurst," he told me, referring to the Big O's famous Johannesburg estate. "You can learn diamonds form the source," Dad continued, "and see something of the mining. It's a wonderful chance to bring the two families together." Not a word was uttered about Mary, but she was definitely the elephant in the room.

My deep aversion to any parental fix-up notwithstanding, I agreed to go. I loved the idea of seeing South Africa. In terms of matrimony, where Harry was concerned, it was like Tina Turner's wail, "What's love got to do with it?" It was a long journey, first to London, then overnight to Johannesburg. I awoke to see the ridges of the mile-high city in the range known as the Witwatersrand gleaming in the morning sun like the gold on which the city was built. I noticed Jo'burg's trademark, huge man-made mountains of earth that had been excavated in search of gold, and, later, diamonds. About $300 billion worth of gold had been dug from this hallowed soil, and countless billions worth of diamonds. And here I was going into the heart of it, to the home of the mogul who controlled the sale of 80 percent of the world's diamond supply. A chill went through me at the thought of such power. I hoped my journey into this heart of diamonds wasn't also going to be into a heart of darkness.

I was met at the airport by a very British chauffeur and taken by Rolls-Royce to the very British baronial estate in the exclusive suburb of Parktown, across from the world-famous zoo, whose giraffes I could actually see from the road. We drove through downtown Jo'burg, with its modern skyscrapers, a little Manhattan on the veld. Except this was Africa, and oddly enough I didn't see many Africans, Black Africans that is, just lots of white men in business suits going in and out of those high-rises. I could have been on Wall Street. But I wasn't, and, coming from the most disruptive year yet of the civil rights movement, with the tragic violence at Selma, Alabama, and Dr. King's March on Washington, I was fully aware of the profound underlying tensions of apartheid that had kept Black South Africans in their place and the whites in their place, which was on top. And if there was a pinnacle in South Africa, Brenthurst was it, and here I was.

During World War II, the Oppenheimers had actually moved out of Brenthurst and donated it to be used as a Red Cross hospital that became Africa's first plastic surgery center for combat wounds. I was greeted by the lady of the house, Bridget Oppenheimer, who was anything but the type who would have sought cosmetic plastic surgery. She was as plain and simple as her grand home was fancy. A native Jo'bergian, Bridget McCall had been educated in England and served in the South African Army during the war, where she met Harry, back from fighting Rommel in the North African deserts.

There was still something militarily proper and no-nonsense about Bridget, who was extremely tall and towered a good head over her husband, who was about the same size as my father.

Before I could even unpack, Bridget took me out on maneuvers, giving me a grand tour of the Brenthurst gardens. "Your mother tells me you love flowers," noted Bridget, who led me through splendorous fields of grass, lush beds of roses, and stately avenues of plane and eucalyptus trees. An army of silent gardeners tended to a botany text of local vegetation: *Protea, Clivia, Canna, Agapanthus*, shrimp plants, wild rhubarb. "Ronnie, are you winded?" she asked me as she put me through my paces. "We're six thousand feet high." I told her that I was a runner and was in pretty good shape. "Quite," she said, discreetly looking me up and down as she took me into the manor for lunch with her husband and daughter.

"Welcome to South Africa, Ronnie. How is Father?" That was how I was greeted by HFO, as Harry was known in circles of power. Then in his midfifties, he was tiny but grand and spoke in an often unintelligibly soft accent that had been cultivated in his English schooling at Charterhouse, then Oxford's Christ Church. With the death of his father Sir Ernest in 1957, Harry O. sat astride the colossal cartel. But he didn't seem at all like a ruler. He was shy and tentative, often punctuating his comments with the very indecisive and nonregal phrase "Don't you think?" and tilting his head like a little sparrow waiting for your response.

There was no intimidation whatsoever, until you contemplated how powerful this man actually was.

My "blind date," Mary Oppenheimer, soon joined us at the lunch table, where we were catered to formally by white butlers. She apologized for being late, noting a problem with one of the horses at the Brenthurst stables. Lacking her mother's height but not her English reserve, Mary shared her father's understated, unintimidating aura. Just back from her first year at the Sorbonne, where she had gone following her graduation from Heathfield, England's fanciest women's boarding school and the female Eton, Mary was plain beyond plain. Though completely polite, she was so steeped in boredom I thought it might have been an affectation to make herself seem more mysterious. The only thing that seemed to raise her blood pressure beyond that of a cadaver were her horses, a passion that was furthered no doubt at Heathfield, which was located in Ascot, home of the famous royal thoroughbred racecourse. There was no evidence, however, that anything in Paris had rubbed off on her.

After lunch, Mary drove me around in her Aston Martin, giving me a grand tour of her city, albeit not of places like Soweto (short for South Western Townships), where just a few years before over sixty thousand blacks were uprooted from white areas and "resettled" into notorious vast ghettos. We talked horses, not apartheid, and we talked diamonds. It was winter in the Southern Hemisphere, and there was a chill in the air and probably also in our very proper, superficial conversation. What interested me most were those gold dumps, the hillocks created from mining the "reef' as the local Afrikaner turf was known. Mary told me how you could walk underground through hundreds of miles of connected tunnels. That fascinated me.

When we returned, I found HFO reading Thackeray, which somehow I sensed was an affectation designed to impress this Harvard man by an Oxford man who probably would have preferred the *Financial Times*. He sat in a high-backed chair perfectly suited to an English club. The walls of this high-ceilinged living room, painted in a faux *bois* verdigris, were hung with paintings of wild game and Xhosa tribesmen. It was all very late Victorian colonial. When Dad later took me to London to visit HFO's boardroom there, the decor was almost identical.

HFO plotted out my stay. "I want you to see the game," he said. "Not what you see in zoos. But that's next weekend. Tomorrow we'll show you a mine which is very important to Anglo." "Anglo" was HFO-speak for the Anglo American Corporation that controlled over half of the country's gold mines, not to mention its leading steel manufacturer, its entire petrochemical industry, and most of its insurance companies. Diamonds were only part of the Oppenheimer story.

Mary went back to her horses, and I went over to Kimberley, home of the Big Hole, the largest diamond mine on earth. Accompanied by one of HFO's lieutenants, I was billeted at the Kimberley Club, another colonial extravaganza founded in 1881 by Cecil Rhodes. Here I was waited on elegantly by African waiters in white jackets, feasting on springbok at night and a heroic English breakfast in the morning. Claridge's had nothing on these people. After that early feast, I visited the Big Hole, which was a major tourist attraction but no longer an active mine. The Hole, a quarter mile wide, was now filled with water, a smaller version of Crater Lake. There were still reputedly diamonds there but getting them would be an operation akin to raising the *Titanic*. What I did see was testimony to the backbreaking labor of thousands of tribesmen who had toiled for over fifty years extracting diamonds to enrich white capitalists.

Then we went to a working mine, the Dutoitspan, where I was outfitted in the miner's gear of a white sou'wester rubber raincoat, paratroop boots, and a helmet with a clip-on flashlight. "What do I need this for," I asked my guide. "It doesn't rain inside."

"You'll see" was all he said.

I then was sent down three thousand feet on a journey to the center of the earth in an open elevator that was little more than a giant iron bucket. As the shaft got darker and darker, the bucket clanged against the walls, and water began spraying out of the seams so violently I could barely see.

I was plunging to the three-thousand-foot level, losing the normal sangfroid on which I prided myself. I had flown planes, blown up chemistry labs, launched rockets, but nothing like this. I felt like the devil falling from heaven in *Paradise Lost*. What a fiendish place to work. The air was black, thick, humid. When the bucket stopped, I staggered down long corridors passing teams of miners padding down the access tunnels. The rock above was in the shape of a cathedral arch, but unlike those cathedrals, this one was unstable and kept collapsing. Huge rumblings shook the tunnels. My guide explained it as the sound of diamond-bearing rock falling into slots called drifts. From there it was mechanically extracted then pulled up to the surface to be concentrated and sorted. This technique of self-collapsing ore was known as block caving. I was caving fast, overwhelmed by the claustrophobia of billions of tons of earth and rock bearing down on me. What a nefarious process to produce something so brilliant and ethereal as a diamond. I longed for the sweetness and light and open air of Brenthurst and its magic gardens.

However, before I could return to paradise I was flown around the Oppenheimer empire, visiting one mine after another, some underground, some open pit, and some just diamonds lying in the beach sands of the skeleton coast of nearby Namibia. This vast network of mines that was De Beers was controlled by one man, my host, HFO. I was in awe of my father's guts and daring to try to challenge this colossus. And this was the business, the family business, that I was being groomed to manage. "Groomed" may have been a Freudian slip. The weight of the rock in those dark mines became the metaphor for my contemplation of my own future.

Once I had completed my mining course, HFO sent me on a wildlife course. Just watching HFO's herd of springboks, hundreds of them, prancing in dawn's first light on the fields of Brenthurst made me feel guilty forever about that feast at Kimberley. Noting how inspired I was with the lyric beauty of his land, HFO dispatched me in one of his planes, sans Mary, to the Mala Mala Game Reserve. This was long before Mala Mala had become a luxury tourist destination, and I seemed to have the wilds, and the big game, all to myself. I slept under a baobab tree, so soundly that the next morning my guides told me a leopard had been stalking prey not more than twenty steps from me. And I thought those growls were my stomach.

My moment of truth came once I returned from my safari. Harry and Bridget were going off to Durban, on the Indian Ocean, for an important race weekend to watch their horses run. "You children will just have to make do for yourselves," Bridget said. Brenthurst seemed remarkably cavernous without them. I had no idea what to do with Mary, so I was relieved when she suggested going to a squash tournament at the nearby Sandton Sports Club. I had played a little squash at Harvard. The English version was with a squishy soft ball, as opposed to the hard American one. Squish, squash, whatever. It was less boring than cricket.

After the matches, Mary connected with two of the players she knew. They were straight out of central casting—big, ruddy, powerful. They could have been poster boys for the Grenadier Guards, fine specimens of Anglo-Saxon manhood. Mary, whose offers no one could refuse, invited these two hunks back to Brenthurst for drinks and sandwiches. Having discharged all the servants for the evening, Mary played barkeep and mixed several very powerful rounds. For the first time, I saw her loosening up. Maybe a little too loose, I shuddered, when she suggested we play cards, not at a table, but sitting on the rug. Mary sat herself cozily between the two handsome swains, while I sat demurely across from them. After a few hands of blackjack, Mary changed the game to poker. Strip poker.

The first hour was slow, an attrition of ties, shoes and socks, bracelets, necklaces, stockings. Then more drinks, and fewer clothes. I wasn't much good at poker but I was certainly more adept than Mary and her pals. At a certain point of play, I took stock of the situation. Here was the true African Queen, one of the most eligible girls on earth, drunk and sprawled on the floor in nothing but her bra, garter belt, and panties. The rest of her attire—hosiery, shoes, skirt, blouse, jewelry—lay in a pile. The squash men were in their skivvies and one sock apiece. If this was the British Empire, the sun was surely setting upon it. How long, I wondered, would it be before the bacchanal melted into the way of all flesh? However innocent I may have been, my father would have blamed me and never forgiven me if anything untoward transpired. This was no way to treat a lady. I got up.

"Where are you going?" Mary asked.

"To the loo," I lied. I grabbed what few clothes I had lost and made for my room. I don't think the party even noticed, as no one came to retrieve me. I lay in my antique bed contemplating the end of the nonaffair and the end of the merger of the two Harrys. So much for the fairy-tale romance between the diamond king's daughter and the jewel merchant's son. A few days later, when the Oppenheimers returned from Durban, I got creative. I concocted a story about a new big diamond that Dad had bought from non–De Beers sources. "They want me back in New York to do public relations," as I explained the necessity of an early exit from this paradise.

HFO nodded understandingly. "Duty calls," HFO said, a bit wistfully. "You must, Ronnie. You must." In departing, I knew that the De Beers–Winston relationship would be based not on family ties but on purely commercial exigencies. Mary Oppenheimer would go on to marry two years later, not to one of the squash studs but to an equally sporty English rugby player named Gordon Waddell. That marriage having failed, in 1973 she married yet another sportsman, a Springbok show jumper named Bill Johnson. Her third husband, Hank Slack, whom she married in 1978, worked for her father at Anglo. She became South Africa's doyenne of thoroughbred racing and a major patron of the arts. I never looked back in regret.

My parents were happy to see me back home, particularly Mother. The thought of her firstborn being away from her half the year in Johannesburg was probably more than she could have stood. Dad never asked me why the match of the century did not take. He may have already found out the truth from HFO. Dad always played his cards close to his vest. It came with his territory. The only part of the trip I did talk to him about, and waxed enthusiastic over, were the mines. "Dad, you must see them someday," I told him, knowing full well he would never descend into those dark and hellish pits. "Because only then can you understand why diamonds are so expensive. They're damned hard to get."

Not long after I returned to New York, I got that dreaded "Greetings" letter from my local draft board. Lacking flat-feet, a bad back, or obvious psychological troubles, and no longer a student, I was prime cannon fodder for Vietnam. I had discussed this with Dad before, and he had minimized it. "Don't worry, Ronnie," he assured me. "I've got friends in Washington." Friends like John McCone, head of the CIA, Senator Jacob Javits, Jackie Kennedy herself. Of course when the actual letter came, Dad proved to be both speechless and impotent. He was incapable of action, of pulling strings for me. I would have to pull my own, a task I sprang to with vigor following the probing indignities of my induction physical down on Whitehall Street. Because I knew a lot about rocket propulsion chemistry, I was able, through my own MIT connections, to find a position as a summer researcher at NYU's engineering faculty, which was doing fascinating work on the use of boron and fluorine compounds to improve the range of ballistic missile for our despised military-industrial complex. That summer led to several years of research work and a strategic skills deferment. Dad was deeply impressed with my resourcefulness in pulling this off without his aid.

I had by then become interested in a completely different field, the research work of the famous eye surgeon who was the father of a girl I was dating. Dr. Irving Leopold was the head of ophthalmology at Mount Sinai Medical Center on Fifth Avenue, the hospital that had rejected my poor grandmother and sent her to her death. I tried not to think of that and to instead focus on helping the courtly and brilliant "Irv," as I called him, in his work saving sight. He put me to work on an enzyme that could dissolve cataracts in the eye, and thus avoid surgery. Irv had me doing experiments on mice, then graduated me to rabbits, injecting their eyes with a solution while they were held, screaming, in a restraining cage. One morning I found one poor bunny with its eye out of its socket, clinging to its wet cheek. I loved animals too much for this, even in the name of science. I quit.

I took some biochemistry courses at Albert Einstein College of Medicine, but my father never let me forget that he was waiting for me, that he *needed* me. What good was a family business without your family? The other member of our family, brother Bruce, had already let Dad down. My younger sibling still seemed to want to do nothing but play. Dad had done everything he could to try to get Bruce to learn the business, sending him off to a glamorous apprenticeship in Antwerp to the Van Blerk family, the royalty of rough stone polishers. Every time Dad called Robert van Blerk, the patriarch, to speak to Bruce, Bruce was never there. Van Blerk, embarrassed by Bruce's lack of seriousness, covered for Bruce by saying he had gone out for a smoke. Then he called Bruce, who in fact had never come in at all, and told him his father was looking for him. Bruce would then come to the workshop, call Dad, and leave again.

Bruce's next plum apprenticeship was in the Harry Winston Geneva European headquarters, which was known to the employees there as "SA" or *société anonyme*. Bruce was as anonymous there as he had been in Antwerp, although he was a well-known habitué of Geneva's best restaurants and nightclubs. Sometimes he would call Dad's Geneva secretary, Francine Rieux, and say something like, "Bonjour, Francine. I was thinking of coming over to SA today. What time is it, anyway?"

"It's four in the afternoon, Bruce."

"Oh? Oh well, I guess it's not worth it," Bruce would say. "I'll try again another day." And so it went. Bruce rarely came in at all, and Dad had pretty much given up on him as a diamond man.

But it was the real diamond men in Dad's life in his all-profitable European theater that gave me far more concern for Dad's future than Bruce's devil-may-care indifference. These were three devils who did care, and I developed a terrible apprehension that his dependence on these men contained the seeds of destruction of the Harry Winston empire. I had met them on my own summer visits to Europe, and they, more than anything else, prompted my conversion from a profound aversion to joining Dad to a filial protectiveness that impelled me to stand by his side.

I've already introduced you to the serpentine master salesman Manfredo "Fred" Horowitz, the confidant of the postwar Euro-industrial plutocracy who would do literally anything to make a sale—including putting his own wife in the package as part of the bargain. In the fifties, Fred was joined at Harry Winston by two slick operators named Albano Bochatay and Serge Fradkoff. These three master salesmen all became multimillionaires working for my father. I came to see them as the three horsemen of the apocalypse. Fred was the least of the three evils, and he seemed to know that his two successors were too much to manage, for even him. Accordingly, once Bochatay and Fradkoff arrived, Fred moved his own office out of the Harry Winston building overlooking Lake Geneva and its *jet d'eau* to a small bureau around the corner on the Rue Ceard. There was only so much intrigue even an intriguer like Fred could take.

Bochatay came to Harry Winston in 1952. No man could have been more self-made. Bochatay was from a tiny village in the rugged canton known as the Valais, home of the Matterhorn. He knew as a boy that there had to be something else, and he left his cow town for Geneva as a teenager, going to work in a jewelry shop called Gübelin, changing his birth name of Marius to the made-up Albano, which had sophisticated Italian overtones. Bochatay was handsome, like the young Roger Vadim, and learned to dress dashingly and sell charmingly.

Eventually word got around Geneva and to my father about this supersalesman in the making, and Dad invited him to the office. "You've heard of me. Why have you never called me?" Dad asked him.

"Because, Mister Winston," Bochatay replied with all his charm and cunning, "I wanted you to call me."

Dad hired him on the spot. The day was Bochatay's thirtieth birthday. It was the greatest gift he could receive. His dream had come true. He had arrived. When I first met him he was ensconced in our office with stunning views of Lake Geneva. He never looked outside. Instead, he set his desk in front of a mirror, before which Bochatay was perpetually preening, during his endless phone calls to Arab princes and their retainers.

The third key member of Dad's European team came a bit later. This was Serge Fradkoff, who was as dark and scowling as Bochatay was charming and light. Serge presented himself as the wizard of the Casbah, a *pied noir*, or North African Jew from Tunis. Bochatay would later insist that Serge was actually a Polish Jew from Lodz and was passing as a Tunisian to give him more mystique. Besides, Harry Winston already had its Polish Jew in Fred Horowitz. As a Tunisian, Serge would provide geographic distribution.

Wherever he was from, Serge was faster than a speeding bullet, with formidable mathematical and memory skills that rivaled those of my father. He was tiny and actually did resemble Harry Winston to a degree that the narcissistic Serge liked to pass himself off to people who didn't know better as Dad's illegitimate son. He also passed himself off as one of the great bridge players of Europe. What a talker he was, but such were the ways of the casbah. Serge had come to Dad through Jacques Timey, a Russian émigré who had built a precious stone business in Geneva after the war and whom Dad trusted implicitly, though perhaps too much.

The world of Harry Winston outside America was divided into three parts: Horowitz had the European tycoons and royalty, Bochatay had the Arabs and Imelda Marcos, and Fradkoff had the wealthy European Jews who survived the war and, most important, the less glamorous but highly profitable rough diamonds, which he traded in Antwerp. I guess Serge troubled me the most, if only because of his insinuations that he was my half-brother. The more successful he got, the more he began to develop his "style," which was a Jewish version of a Times Square pimp in *Shaft*. He carried a big pocketbook, sported even huge, jewel-encrusted belt buckles and wore a full-length mink coat that instead of enlarging his small body drowned him in a sea of fur. He also began buying racehorses, competing with the Rothschilds and the Hunts in derbies across the continent.

Bochatay, too, had his affectations, but they were all about refinement, not flash. He collected fine art, bought a chalet in Gstaad, married a beautiful French woman, and lived in increasing splendor in a chateau on Lake Geneva. No salesmen could have ever lived higher on any hog than Harry Winston's. Of course, they all hated each other, and they probably resented Dad, who could barely control them but didn't seem to mind that they were getting rich off him. "They serve a purpose," was all he would say about them. They were multilingual, while Dad could barely get through a French menu, so he depended on them for communication to the world of wealth who wanted his status symbols. The problem was that this troika didn't work together, but rather stumbled along, each veering in his own direction, all drunk with the love of money.

This was the background against which I began working for Dad in New York in 1966. Not that I was living like a Bochatay or a Fradkoff. In fact, Dad didn't pay me a cent for the first two years. He regarded what I was doing as an apprenticeship, like one of the ancient diamond cutters' guilds. He did give me a tiny office adjacent to his gray-and-white master suite overlooking Fifth Avenue that had two exposures, one east across the avenue to Tiffany's, the other the all-important north to Central Park, which provided the most serene daylight for viewing gemstones. Except for two small English landscapes on the south wall, there was nothing to distract the clients from the treasures Dad presented to them. He sat at a great Louis Quatorze desk in a cane-backed French armchair with a thick leather cushion to raise him up. When Dad needed me, he would buzz his secretary, Elinor Wurtzel, whose daughter Elizabeth would also go on to Harvard and become a writer (*Prozac Nation*). Elinor would trot into Dad's office and up to his desk, like a retriever.

"Yes, Mister Winston?" she would say.

"Have my son Ronnie come in," he would reply.

Elinor would then trot into my office. "Ronnie, Mister Winston would like you to come in and see him." Again, it was like medieval times. Dad somehow couldn't pick up the phone and call me directly. I don't think he ever dialed anyone.

In my early working days, I would spend vast amounts of time sitting silently at the south end of Dad's desk, while his clients would sit across from him facing Fifth Avenue. When he wasn't selling, Dad spent a good part of each day with his controller, Jerry Schultz, planning fiscal strategy and going through the mail, particularly the checks that arrived from around the world. After three months of this I was bored and fidgeting. I would pick the brass brads out of Dad's imperial desk and put them in my pocket, like worry beads. Later in the day, when Dad was downstairs in the sales salon with the late afternoon press of clients, I would hammer the brads back in.

Not that Harry Winston was having the time of his life either. I could see his own inner conflicts when I would start my day every morning by walking over to my parents' 927 Fifth Avenue co-op from my rent-stabilized walk-up on East 73rd Street. The courtly Irish doorman would whisk me to the ninth floor in the oak paneled elevator. I would then invariably find Dad in the dining room in his navy blue and burgundy embroidered silk dressing gown, ensconced in his favorite white Scalamandré silk armchair, reading the financial pages of the *New York Times*.

He'd be gulping down copious drafts of coffee from a giant cup, trying to rebalance after the excesses of the night before. I was amazed at how much this little man could drink. "Good morning, Ronnie," he'd say. "I see where there's a new railroad bond, Missouri Pacific. Pays eight percent. I think I'll buy some for you boys." As he spoke, I noticed his bare ankles above his brown leather slippers. They were obviously swollen. Not a good sign, though I didn't dare comment on them. Dagmar, the housekeeper, would bring me bacon and eggs, and Dad would expatiate on the stock market as I ate. Then, once he'd wolfed the food down, he'd fold the paper and stand up. "Time to go to work. Have to make a living."

While Dad scuffed down an endless hallway to change in his bedroom, I'd wait in the library. Mother was invariably deep in sleep, never to arise before ten or ten thirty. Once I made a comment on this that I would come to regret: "Only the dead sleep longer." Soon Dad would emerge in his tuxedo-style dickey with the inset studs. He always wore black elevator shoes with perforated leather toes. He often looked sewn into his office garb, and the outfit could drive him to distraction; he'd furiously rip off his collar the moment he got home and throw it to the floor. To complete the morning dress, his maid or butler would hold his gray Chesterfield topcoat, while Harry, holding his suit sleeves like a child, would kip into the Chesterfield. I could just imagine his mother, Jennie, saying to Harry as a child, "Now, darling, hold onto your sleeves. You don't want to catch a death of cold."

We would then be driven down Fifth Avenue one mile to the office at 56th Street in the green Cadillac with the "VV 155" plates. When we arrived, the receptionist would come out from behind the kidney-shaped desk at the entrance to greet Dad and take his coat, a ritual that was repeated every single day of the workweek. Then the uniformed security guard would hold the door of the elevator that went only to his office. Once the elevator door closed, and no one but I could see, Dad would wince and pass his hands over his eyes as if to expunge all the pain in his life. "My office," he intoned to himself. "My monster. My Frankenstein." Small wonder I was ambivalent.

CHAPTER THIRTEEN

Foreign Intrigues

The part of my apprenticeship that I found most compelling was accompanying my father on his European excursions. I particularly enjoyed Geneva, for its food, its sophistication, its Alpine beauty, and the opportunity it gave me to use my French. The Swiss office was trilingual, all fluent in English, French, and German, and a lot of the dialogue went right past my father, who only spoke diamond-ese. Naturally, when Harry Winston spoke, everyone listened, and very carefully. The Geneva office was, on its surface, a gay place full of bonhomie and high spirits at the astronomical revenues the troika of Horowitz, Bochatay and Fradkoff were generating.

Dad was proud of this elite corps. They had no equivalent in the New York office. Perhaps if he had had these three dynamos fifteen years before, he would have realized his dreams of independent diamond mines and become free of the dreaded necessity that was De Beers. But in the challenging days of the early fifties, when Dad tried to take on the Oppenheimers, he had no backup. "I was alone. I didn't have you," he often lamented to me.

Behind all that bonhomie, I sensed an increasingly sinister ambience, particularly in Bochatay and Fradkoff. There was nothing tangible, just a slight whiff of putrescence. Because of the old-world formal and ever-polite dialogue I had with my father, I could not come right out and ask Dad how could he trust these men. Whatever Harry Winston's standards were, he also had a need for yes-men.

The vehicle of treachery in Switzerland was an instrument known as the blind transfer, which was integral to the vaunted secrecy of Swiss banking. Money in Switzerland was rarely moved by check, the way we do it. Instead the lucre went from Account X to Account Y without a name or often even a reference number attached to the transaction. Sometimes there would be nothing but a code name, like "torpedo." Thus, when Bochatay returned from one of his trips to Riyadh and ostentatiously showed me a check made out payable to him for $26 million, I instantly feared that in the maze of blind transfers from Bochatay to Winston that somehow Harry would not get his full due.

It was up to Bochatay to deduct "commissions and expenses," which could easily have included bribes, kick-backs, call girls, whatever, and then come up with a sum for the company, which may have been $20 million, give or take. In addition to the rake-offs, Dad established an off-the-books pool to further pay "the boys" as he called them, basically 25 percent of the overseas operation, which included the Geneva office, the new Paris store, and, the Saudis. These monies went into the boys' numbered Panamanian accounts, and I strongly doubt any taxes were paid. Maybe I was just too square to appreciate the cloak-and-daggerness of it all, but what it came down to was that I sensed they were stealing my family's money.

Bochatay had us over a barrel (of oil) with the Arabs, because we were officially on the Arab blacklist. This wasn't because of Harry Winston's Jewish heritage but because the firm had an alleged relationship with Israel, in the form of a small cutting and polishing factory of postwar Antwerp émigrés in Tel Aviv's diamond district of Ramat Gan. Dad didn't even own the factory but merely sent certain stones to be worked on there. Virtually everyone in the diamond trade used Ramat Gan, which had come to surpass Antwerp as a cutting center, but somehow Harry Winston was singled out and made the list. I suspected that Bochatay might have had a hand in this, as the blacklisting prevented the firm from dealing directly with Saudi retail customers. Instead, Bochatay brought the mountain to Mohammed, mountains of jewels that he transported to Riyadh to sell for mountains of money, of which he surely took a few molehills of his own.

Harry Winston had begun selling to the Arabs in 1955, starting at the very top, with King Saud, who had just succeeded his late father Ibn Saud on the throne the year before. Ibn Saud was considered the father of modern Saudi Arabia, as well as the father of dozens of sons and daughters conceived with his harem of wives and concubines. This extensive royal family was also the basis for the massive gift-giving of Harry Winston jewels. Originally known as Abdulaziz, Ibn Saud was a Bedouin warrior chieftain from Arabia's eastern desert who, in 1902 at age twenty, stormed Riyadh's Masmak fort, killed the governor, and proclaimed himself the ruler of this key city. His next conquest in what would ultimately be his dominion of the entire Arabian peninsula was the city of Jeddah. Jeddah proved to be a bloodless siege, thanks to the diplomacy of a vizier named Ali Riza Pasha, who sallied forth from the gates of Jeddah and, with great pomp and ceremony, awarded Abdulaziz the keys to the city. Many lives, on both sides, were saved.

The future King Ibn Saud never forgot this display of hospitality and lauded many gifts and business opportunities on Ali Reza and his clan. One of these positions was Ali Reza's being appointed the crown jeweler of Saudi Arabia, along with a key adviser to the king on many other matters of economy and infrastructure. The Ali Reza family, originally Persian émigrés, were educated, sophisticated, and wealthy at a time when the Sauds were uneducated and savage tribal leaders. Ali Reza had the first Rolls-Royce in the kingdom when there were hardly any roads and most Bedouins traveled on camels. He cut a very stately Western figure and spoke the King's English.

In the midfifties the Arab oil wealth began to gush; the postwar boom had made the world car crazy and gas needy. The royal family accumulated vast dollar reserves, and with the funds came the desire to spend. Spend on palaces, spend on conspicuous consumption, and spend on jewelry. King Ibn Saud himself was Dad's first Arab client, arranged by Ali Reza's equally elegantly assimilated son and successor, Ali Alireza, who met with Dad both in New York and Geneva. In 1955 Dad got a formal invitation from the Royal House of Saud to send an emissary to Riyadh with his latest collection of stones and jewelry for a special private showing to the new King Saud. Worried that his own Jewish background might scotch a deal, or worse, Dad dispatched his very all-American salesman Charlie Steiger as his emissary. Charlie could be a boisterous frat boy, but he could also be as discreet and polite as a statesman.

As a boy, I can never forget Charlie's return and his recounting of his exotic adventures. "Chief," he related to Dad, "you can't imagine the life there. When I got off the plane, we drove into Riyadh, and as we approached a square surrounded by mud ramparts, there was a pack of wild dogs baying and jumping at something held against a wall. As we got closer, I could see what it was—there were four or five pairs of hands manacled to the wall with blood streaming down. God help me, Chief, the dogs were devouring those hands. Thieves, the guide said." Right then and there Harry Winston knew he had done the right thing to send good-time Charlie in his place.

Charlie eventually showed the king the jewels, which were mostly big yellow off-color diamonds, twenty, thirty, forty carats. The king asked Charlie to bring them back in the morning, so he could inspect them by daylight. In the meanwhile, he invited Charlie to a typical Arab feast. They drove far out into the desert in a fleet of Cadillacs to an oasis where tents had been set up and laid with rare Persian carpets and fine silk pillows. Although the Saudis by then lived in palaces, they loved returning to their Bedouin roots.

King Saud strode in and motioned to Charlie to be seated next to him. Several whole lambs roasted on spits inside the vast tents. The cooked but uncarved meat was brought before the king, who with his right hand proceeded to pull huge chunks off the carcass and serve his guests, intermittently using that same serving hand to wipe the oozing pus out of his infected eyes, as well as to swat the flies that were attracted to the pus. Rice was then served by the monarch, again right-handedly and oblivious to concerns of sanitation.

"Chief," Charlie said, "you can't imagine how disgusting it was. But what else could I do but eat?"

"You were brave, Charlie," Dad told him. "Brave."

Brave, as well as good. Charlie sold virtually the entire collection, and his visit started a steady stream of income to Harry Winston that would become a fiscal Victoria Falls. By 1960, however, Bochatay began to subsume Charlie's business, and that's when even bigger money began to roll in. Working with the House of Saud was much easier from Geneva. The trip was shorter by many hours, the reimportation documents simpler, and the blind transfers, impossible in the United States, were, to say the least, convenient. No one could sell Arabs like Bochatay. In 1964 the royal family forced Saud to abdicate, largely based on their horror at his lavish spending. He was replaced by King Faisal, who proved to be anything but ascetic. In fact, in those first two decades, our glory years, Harry Winston may have sold as much as $400 million worth worth of stones and jewels in Arabia. Alas, King Faisal was assassinated in 1975, in a further regime change arguably provoked in part by the Winston jewel purchases. Nonetheless, the appetite for diamonds in the Gulf has never abated.

The way the business worked was very interesting to me. I watched closely how Bochatay befriended much of the royal family when they visited Switzerland in the summer, to be ready to sell to whoever took the throne. All of his sales were fostered by Ali Reza and his Alireza Crown Jewelers. The refined Ali never himself appeared at court with Bochatay but left the negotiating to his right hand, Sheikh Ye Ye Tofic, who sounds like a sixties French rock star but was a cultured and smooth-as-silk diamond diplomat. Our jewel collections that we would show to the Saudis were exported from Switzerland under a temporary exit permit known as a carnet, which allowed them to be reimported to Switzerland without duty, as they had originated there. Bochatay, with one or two handsome assistants (looks really counted in selling jewels) would then fly then to Riyadh, though sometimes to Jeddah. Although diamonds and jewels in Arabia were subject to a huge duty, even for temporary importation, Bochatay was always met by an emissary of the royal family in the middle of the night when the flights would arrive. A mere wave to customs, and Bochatay's cases were never even opened. It was a perfect example of the old adage, highly subscribed to in Arabia: "For my friends anything, for my enemies the law."

Bochatay never brought more than $200 million worth of jewels per visit, which seems like a king's ransom but was actually the limit of our Lloyd's of London policy, $200 million at any one place at any one time. We could thus have two robberies, one in New York and one in Paris, and collect $400 million. But it never happened, so we just paid a lot of insurance premiums. Charlie Steiger was once robbed in Chicago at gunpoint, and there was a Bonnie and Clyde shoot-out outside Paris's Hôtel Plaza Athénée, where thieves had smashed a gem-loaded vitrine in the lobby and made off with the treasures, killing a hotel guest in the cross fire. Saudi Arabia in those days was a police state and safer than Disneyland.

Past customs, the waiting game would begin. The hotels then were fairly primitive, and because their message services could not be trusted, Bochatay and his men never left their rooms, where they might be holed up for a week or more, waiting for *the call*. It was like being under house arrest, and given the Saudis' otherworldly sense of time and absolute lack of any sense of urgency, it could be frustrating beyond belief. So Bochatay learned to wait for the palace to ring, just as he had waited for Harry Winston to hire him. Bochatay, who was amazingly self-confident, knew that once he got before the royal buyers he could sell and sell and sell. Sometimes, however, the palace would ask Ye Ye to show the collection alone. As Bochatay described it, "then I am blind" and would have to continue waiting in the hotel for the outcome of a game he wasn't being allowed to play.

Most of the time, though, Bochatay got his audience. When this happened, his hotel phone would usually ring at two in the morning. Arab kings are night people. Daylight is shunned because of the intense Arabian heat, a cultural tradition that did not die with air-conditioning. Bochatay, like a fighter pilot, usually slept in most of his clothes, ready to jump at a moment's notice, which was all he would get. The assistants would then scramble to get the jewels from whatever safe they were in, packed in blue leather valises, something like pilots' flight cases, sporting the gold HW logo inside a hexagon. Then they would go to the palace and be set up in a grand drawing room. The valises would open up to trays, each with a spectacularly luminous display of stones laid out like bonbons at Fauchon. The jewels would be taken out of the trays and spread on velvet pads on several tables. Selling was usually cued to a particular family event: a wedding, a birthday, the birth of an heir. Jewels were bought not only for the bride or birthday girl but also for the whole family. There was democracy in royalty, in that if the king bought a jewel for one of his many wives, he would feel compelled to buy jewels for all of them.

At anywhere from three to five in the morning, the king would enter the palace viewing room, circle the glittering tables, and greet Bochatay. The royal buyer would quickly pull $10 million worth of gems aside, whisper something to his aide-de-damp who followed behind him, and leave. On other occasions, the king might hold a *majlis*, or court audience, with Bochatay, talking politics interspersed with a bit of bargaining. Ye Ye would be the clean-up man in those situations, acting as a go-between to solidify the price.

In these showings and negotiations women were never present. This was a kingdom where women were forbidden to drive or walk the streets without a man. The king did the buying, the women the receiving. However, on one of Bochatay's Arabian nights, he told me how this rule was broken. One of those endless early mornings in Riyadh, Bochatay was awakened from his half-sleep by a call from an aide-de-camp he did not know. This man introduced himself and said King Faisal's wife, Her Majesty the Queen, would be honored to receive the representatives of Harry Winston for a private viewing. Bochatay and his aides sprang into action, prepared the collection, and were chauffeured to the palace. As the aides waited in an antechamber, Bochatay alone was ushered to the queen's private quarters, which he described as a garish fusion of Arabic and French. The queen sat on an embroidered pillow on the floor, surrounded by fifteen to twenty ladies in waiting or sisters or courtesans. How could he know? They were all veiled.

Bochatay sat on the floor opposite the queen, showing the jewels with tact and savoir faire. Very tan, he wore his trademark light gray shantung silk suit with a bright Hermès tie and a pocket handkerchief puffed up in his jacket like a freshly picked peony. He must have charmed the queen, for he described to me how she dropped her veil and signaled all the other ladies to follow suit. It was straight out of Scheherazade of The Thousand and One Nights, but this night was completely real. Seeing King Faisal several days later, he didn't dare mention his visit, Bochatay said. Perhaps the king knew, perhaps not. Because of the hermetic nature of palace intrigue, Bochatay knew discretion was the only approach. Though the queen bought nothing that night (queens never bought but were only bought for), Faisal bought far more this trip than was expected. Had someone whispered softly in his royal ear? Don't ask, don't tell, was the only policy, for profit and survival.

Upon returning to Geneva, Bochatay would report to Dad on the results of the trip, which was invariably a great success. During the sales mission itself, radio silence was always observed, since we assumed all the lines were tapped. Back in Europe, Bochatay would send Dad a telex in New York detailing the inventory sold, the cost of each item, and the selling price achieved, all of which was encrypted in one of the Winston codes, which were straight out of the cloak and dagger of the ongoing cold war. The sales prices were all on Bochatay's honor system, so no one really knew what he had actually gotten. Fradkoff, Bochatay's codirector of Harry Winston Geneva, would find out via this telex what his supposed colleague but actual archrival had accomplished. It often drove Fradkoff crazy, because he knew how much "play" there was in these figures, and it takes a thief to catch a thief. Yet because there was honor among thieves, Fradkoff never called Bochatay on any of his suspected transgressions.

Bochatay had equal reason to covet Fradkoff's earnings both from rough and from the increasingly wealthy reconstructed

Jewish families of Europe, who saw Fradkoff as the landsman that Bochatay could never be to them. Meanwhile, Fradkoff was becoming every day more and more a Jewish prince of the realm, undoubtedly aided by his relentless allusions to his Winston family bloodline. Just as Bochatay had eradicated his Valais peasant roots and entrenched himself in the top Geneva men's clubs as well as the Eagle Ski Club in Gstaad, Fradkoff was entrenching himself in the sport of kings, horse racing, sharing ownership of steeds with the oil billionaire Hunt brothers of Texas. The European press took notice and anointed Fradkoff the young genius of horse studs but never mentioned that he also worked for Harry Winston. Dad did not speak about this subject, but I'm sure it rankled him.

The rough dross that Serge Fradkoff turned into gold was the result of my father's twenty-five years of diamond wars with De Beers. By the late 1950s, just as we were establishing our hegemony in Saudi Arabia and just before the death of patriarch Sir Ernest Oppenheimer, Dad and De Beers had concluded their own kind of truce, which was evidenced by Sir Ernest's giving Dad the most privileged selection of top-grade rough at the De Beers sight in London every six weeks. In addition to this, Sir Ernest threw in a very lavish allotment of "specials," stones that weighed over fourteen carats that could be counted on to yield some very luscious large cut diamonds for the Bochatay market, stones, to use Victorian parlance, "of the first water." These stones were not offered to any other dealer in the world.

Although Dad was jetting back and forth to London many times in 1956 and 1957 to conclude the armistice, it was never reduced to documentation, given De Beers' fear of getting ensnared in American antitrust laws and jeopardizing its monopoly over the diamond trade. Any contract generated by De Beers would be instantly subpoenaed if one of the parties was an American. So impenetrable was the wall De Beers had built around itself that every overseas call to the Charterhouse Street headquarters was fielded by an operator whose first question was whether this call was from the United States. If so, the woman would apologize in her best British accent that she could not make the connection. De Beers was a cathedral of secrecy. Then again, so was my Dad. It seemed to go with the trade.

All business with De Beers Diamond Trading Company had to be conducted through outside brokers who did the negotiating, provided the billing, and received the cash transfers to pay for the diamonds. Actually there was no real negotiating, except for the special stones over fourteen carats. Aside from that, *hondling* (Yiddish for bargaining) was verboten. The uncouth, unchic Orthodox New York, Antwerp, and Tel Aviv diamond men made de Beers a fortune, but that still did not prevent the lofty cartel from lording it over their rough dealers, even going so far on occasion as to schedule a fall sight on Yom Kippur, forcing these religious clients to travel and conduct business on the holiest of Jewish holidays.

At the beginning of my apprenticeship, Dad would take me with him to De Beers. It was incredibly boring, and I was beside myself for not having a desk to pull the brads out of. We would go to London and stay at Claridge's, which was the good part. Dad would always bring his right-hand diamond man from Geneva, Nick Akselrod, and we would take a chauffeured car to Charterhouse Street and sit in a big conference room and just look silently at the goods, diamonds galore, for what seemed like hours. They all looked the same to me. I realized I had a lot to learn, but I wasn't sure I wanted to.

We would meet with the indomitable E. M. "Monty" Charles, who was the master of all sights. I say indomitable because Monty was one of the few Brits to survive the Burma death march in addition to a year of torture in a Japanese prisoner-of-war camp. Monty had been close to the Oppenheimers, who liked to stay at a classic country inn owned by his family. Monty had worked there as a bellhop. The Oppenheimers lured the young Monty away from the inn to work in London as a diamond sorter. After the war, he rejoined the company and rose to the very top.

Monty's negotiating style dealt from the strength and unequal bargaining power De Beers possessed. But at least he would create the illusion of trying to make a fair deal with Dad. The basic attitude was take it or leave it, and if you leave it, we have many clients who will love to take it. Looking more like the maître d' at an exclusive Mayfair Italian restaurant than a typical buttoned-up-and-down syndicate leader, Monty would literally dance around Dad as we sat at a table examining $15 million in gems.

The theater was all Monty's as he played at humor, but his actions were deadly serious. Pay up, or you don't get the big stones, the stones that were the forte and trademark of Harry Winston.

To distract myself, I looked through the window at an office worker in his bureau across the alleyway who pulled a whiskey bottle from his desk drawer and toasted me numerous times as he proceeded to drown his own tedium in spirits. I admit it made me a bit jealous, so bored was I.

After a good two or three hours of diamond fisticuffs, Dad, Nick, and I would be invited to lunch in the Diamond Trading Company boardroom, which was dominated by a long, high table set with the finest crystal and silver. This was off-limits to all other diamond dealers except Harry Winston, so it was supposedly an honor and a privilege for us to be there. The room was paneled with blond oak, and the walls were festooned with the South African equivalent of Currier and Ives prints featuring prides of lions, herds of elephants, rhinos and giraffes, a veritable Noah's ark of African wildlife.

After being plied with several sherries, Dad, who eschewed the harder stuff for these high-toned midday feeds, would slip into his raconteur mode and regale the stiff Anglos with tall tales of his youth in California and his famous clients, the tycoons, the kings and queens, the stars. The diamond men loved it and loosened up. The rich American market from which De Beers was excluded was both terra incognita and promised land, and Harry Winston held the keys to this El Dorado. They sat at the feet of the man who had singlehandedly created the market for big stones, and I unexpectedly felt an intense surge of pride.

After the lunch, we would be chauffeured back to Mayfair and Claridge's, a long ride during which I had to endure Dad's endless jeremiad against the syndicate, and particularly against Monty Charles. I can still hear Monty's laugh, half-facetious, half-threatening, goading Dad into another purchase at terms he hated. Dad didn't like to be goaded. "All they understand is a club," Dad would rail, then add, for good measure, his battle cry from the mean streets of his childhood. "The bigger they are, the harder they fall." I felt put upon that I was the one he was looking to continue his battle against the Goliath of Charterhouse Street. If I couldn't join them by marrying Mary Oppenheimer, then I would have to beat them at the game they owned. Tall order.

Aside from these visits to Europe, I was fermenting with unrest, seething with energy with no outlet. My friends were becoming doctors, lawyers, bankers, writers. The choice I had made, or rather was sliding into, was rankling me. I had never committed myself to the diamond business and to Harry Winston. My decision was more or less a sustained try-out that gradually immersed me irretrievably in Dad's world. After over a year of pulling nails out of the desk, I asked Dad directly to give me something real to do, a task, anything. Harry Winston simply could not delegate. He just wanted me squarely at his side.

Finally, through Dad's English friend and colleague Chester Beatty, I was able to get myself a mission of my own. I was going off to Mali, the newly independent (from France) sub-Saharan country in West Africa where Dad and Chet were investigating the possibility of starting their own diamond mine. The Kéniéba diamond fields of Mali didn't yield many diamonds, but what they did yield was prime—giants of fifty to two hundred carats. A diamond mine in Mali would have been one of my father's life dreams, and here I had the chance to be instrumental in helping make that dream come true, because third world–phobic Dad, for all his dreams, wasn't about to go to this darkest corner of the Dark Continent.

We had been talking diamond exploration with the Selection Trust, whose Chairman was Chet Beatty, ever since the early 1950s. Dad had gotten to know the company through his non–De Beers diamond purchases in Sierra Leone. Dad always tried to encourage a friendship between me and the scholarly, avuncular Chet, who had a penchant for opera and a passion for cancer research. "You speak the same language," Dad would say. Alas, I could barely understand Chet, since he spoke as if he had a mouthful of mashed potatoes. Instead, I was content to spend evenings at his Mayfair town house drinking vintage French wines and staring at his *Sunflowers* by van Gogh.

Bamako, the capital of Mali, was a long, long way from Mayfair, though I, unlike Dad, loved the third world and being alone in it and beyond his long shadow. From teeming, brutally hot Bamako, I set off for the exploration site in the alluvial diamond fields, which were lush and jungly, compared to the desert sand dunes in the northern part of the country. Water buffalo, hippos, hyenas, and elephants crowded the river banks. This was the wild kingdom. The diamond site itself looked like a Paleolithic excavation more likely to yield dinosaur bones than a wealth of precious stones. Yet the potential was there for this to become a field of dreams.

Hundreds of skinny, frail workers were digging holes and filling burlap sacks with gravel that would then be sorted and probed with tweezers in search of treasure. These were diamonds in the rough. The workmen were all Black Muslims, so, so different from Malcolm X and his cohort who had captivated the public's imagination back in America. Mali was one of the world's poorest nations. My own dream was to discover diamonds that would make this beautiful land a lot richer and make Harry Winston richer too.

After years of exploration, none of these dreams materialized. But I was young, and hope sprang eternal. From Kéniéba I returned to Bamako, where I was debriefed by both the British and American ambassadors who were eager to learn what was going on in the hinterlands, particularly if there might be a fortune in it. When Harry Winston spoke, people listened, and I felt like a little big shot at all the attention I was getting. Once I was in the embassy circuit, I began to meet all kinds of interesting expats, including several junior American embassy secretaries who were planning an expedition into Mali's largely uncharted interior. There were three women and two men, and they needed a third guy. When they invited me to be that third man, I leaped at the opportunity.

It was a wonderful adventure. We drove Land Rovers across the sand dunes; visited the primitive tribe, the Dogons, whose mythology and traditions linked back to the ancient Egyptians; ate delicious fresh pigeon that we learned post-prandially had been fattened on human remains; and danced with the natives. Doing the Watusi at Le Club in New York was never like this. We then took a rusty and rickety *African Queen*–style riverboat five hundred miles down the River Niger and went to fabled Timbuktu, which was the pinnacle of African Islam in the fifteenth and sixteenth centuries and retained all of that history and mystery. Diamonds never crossed my mind the entire trip. Here, I wasn't Harry Winston's son; I was the African explorer. I couldn't share my exhilaration, my joy of freedom, with my fellow travelers. I didn't want them to know what I was running away from.

I had never felt more alive, even when I almost died in a plane crash in a little single-engine Czech-made craft I had chartered to get from Bamako to Dakar and on to Paris and New York and work, which I dreaded more than death itself. The little craft, flown by tribesmen in bib overalls and run on a low-octane fuel that was weaker than Vitalis hair tonic, nearly crashed into a Sahara mountainside on one of our anemic ascents. Only when on our next landing did I find huge clumps of desert vegetation stuck to the bottom of the plane did I realize how close I had come to perishing, as we had actually scraped the peak we were struggling so mightily to fly over. All I could think about was not my own safety but my father's unimaginable grief at losing me, the legacy of his diamond dynasty.

Finally back in Manhattan, I briefed Dad on my trip, telling him all about his investment in the Kéniéba exploration site, describing it in every unsanitary detail. He was happy not to have gone, just as he was happy not traveling to Saudi Arabia. After all, Dad was over seventy now. I told him a little about the safari, leaving out the death-plane part. I also shielded him from my excitement at being out in the world, exploring the Sahara and Timbuktu and loving the nondiamond life. As I told my stories over dinners at the Colony and Quo Vadis, my mother seemed strangely unresponsive, almost mute. She had begun to act bizarrely before I had left. Once, she, Dad, and I were returning to Scarsdale from a baseball game at Yankee Stadium when Mother began hallucinating and reacting hysterically to a large pack of nonexistent rats following our car along the side of the road.

Things got even worse when one warm spring evening in May, I'd had dinner with my parents at their Fifth Avenue apartment, then gone for a walk along the edge of Central Park across the street to savor the first cherry blossoms of the season. I came home to my walk-up and fell fast asleep. At three in the morning, the phone rang. Mother was on the line. "My darling Ronnie," she said. "You called me."

"No, Mother. I didn't," I replied in a haze.

"But you needed me. You're in trouble," she pressed.

"Please, Mother, go to sleep. I'm fine, just fine," I reassured her. "I'll see you in the morning for breakfast, if you're up." I said goodbye and tried to fall back to sleep. I was distressed by the call.

Fifteen minutes later, the intercom buzzer jolted me out of bed. "It's your mother," the voice crackled. I buzzed her in and rushed out to meet her. When I opened my apartment door, I received an even greater shock. There, climbing the stairs, was my mother in a diaphanous nightgown and slippers. She didn't even have a bathrobe on. "Ronnie, you're deeply troubled," she said.

That was the understatement of all time. "Mother, you've had a bad dream," I said, putting my arm around her and bringing her into my place. I got her one of my Burberrys and put it over her nightgown. "I'll walk you back." She took my hand like a child, and we walked home through that tragically perfect balmy spring night, the beginning of a season and the beginning of the end for my poor mother. Somehow I kept thinking of the Wordsworth quote: "The child is the father of the man." At some point we become parents to our parents. That point had suddenly and sadly arrived. I took Mother up to her bedroom, tucked her in, kissed her forehead, and turned off the light. Returning home, I could not sleep a wink. She wasn't even seventy. She was beautiful. She was rich. She had it all. I prayed she would be fine.

In the morning I told Dad the story over breakfast. Mother was still sleeping, as usual. Dad seemed worried, but, as with my draft notice, he didn't have a clue what to do. With diamonds, he was Houdini. With everything else, he was like everyone else. Recently my mother had had some plastic surgery, which was still in its infancy but still the secret addiction of rich women. Some would go for a three-week holiday in Rio, which was code for a visit to Dr. Ivo Pitanguy, the world-renown pioneer of face-lifts and body-lifts and a one-man fountain of youth. But Mother didn't go to Brazil. Dad needed her too much, so she settled for one of New York's own face men. Being Mrs. Harry Winston meant always being on the cutting edge of beauty, and I guess Mother took this literally. Diamonds, couture, beauty, glamour—these were all part of the same continuum. I worried that the anesthesia my mother had endured in the name of beauty and the name of Harry Winston might have somehow damaged her brain.

I took it upon myself to call on my mother's psychiatrist. He didn't seem to know about the plastic surgery. If he did, he avoided the subject. It turned out the shrink had been trying to treat Mother for her ongoing confusion, but, again oddly enough, had never discussed her condition with my father. "Your mother," he said with all the warmth of a mortician, "probably has presenile dementia. In any case, there's nothing to be done." Those were the days before the public learned about the scourge and horror of Alzheimer's. But I had studied a lot of medicine, and in this doctor's diagnosis I could hear the dirgelike chords that smacked of death and decay. My mother was very, very sick, and our family would never be the same.

CHAPTER FOURTEEN

Succession

I always felt I beat the sixties to the punch. By the time I graduated from Harvard in 1963, I had already been in the vanguard of psychedelia with my teachers Leary and Alpert. In that year I went from the glamour of *Camelot* to the horrors of Dallas. By the time the real sixties got started in Liverpool and London, then moved to Haight Ashbury and culminated in Woodstock, I had already, in the parlance of the times, "sold out" by going to work for my father.

My brother Bruce might have been considered the embodiment of sixties youth. In vast contrast to my driven and intense father, Bruce was as laid back as any California surfer.

Although Bruce, who was three years younger, had followed me to Riverdale, he did not follow me to Harvard. While he did not blow up the chemistry lab as I had, neither did he set the school on fire academically. The closest he got to Harvard was American International College in Springfield, Massachusetts, a small school founded by a group of ministers in the late nineteenth century for émigré French Protestants. He sometimes came to visit me on weekends, but he wasn't interested in visiting Boston's museums. What he liked to do was to "bird dog," in the argot of the Everly Brothers, whatever women I was dating.

Bruce didn't last long in college. He soon decamped for Europe, first for Antwerp, to learn the diamond trade at its ancient heart. Uninspired, he then crossed the Channel to London, which, thanks to the emergence of Beatlemania, was becoming the hippest world city of the sixties, a fun place to be for a rich boy who had everything except focus. To that end of anomie Bruce found his own supershrink in London, an austere South African who had taken his practice there. In what may have been a part of this therapy, Bruce became a kind of summer camp counselor at the famous Gordonstoun School in Scotland, the alma mater of Princes Charles and Andrew, as well as the Duke of Edinburgh and Lord Mountbatten. The Gordonstoun program, called Active Revision, was similar to the American Outward Bound program. Bruce, who had attended several summer sessions, now was honored by being hired as an instructor. On one of his early walkabouts in the Scottish highlands, Bruce decided he was too tired to proceed. He sent his dozen or so charges on ahead to base, wherever that was, and promptly fell asleep on a rock in the middle of nowhere. His campers managed to find their way to civilization and reported their leader was missing in action.

The next day, the British papers reported the diamond heir was lost in the mountains and that RAF planes had been dispatched on rescue sorties. Luckily Bruce, a very sound sleeper, slept until dawn, undevoured by wolves. He made his way back to Gordonstoun and soon to "Swinging London," where, surely inspired by the Antonioni film *Blow-Up*, he took up the indoor sport of photography, dating the sleek ballet dancers he took pictures of. Eventually he fell in love with one of these budding ballerinas and proposed to her.

My future sister-in-law was named Annabel Jane King, the daughter of a retired general in the British Army Artillery. My mother and father flew to England to meet the couple and couldn't have been more thrilled. Annabel was blonde, lithe, and charming. The engagement was a tonic for Mother. She had been depressed since her beloved father, and my beloved grandfather, died of pneumonia in the summer of 1960. Mother had relocated him from his old-world apartment on East 88th Street, where he read his endless books, chain-smoked unfiltered cigarettes, and was cosseted by his house-keeper and his girlfriend. Mother thought she was doing him a favor by relocating him next door to us in Scarsdale. Alas, her "hothouse flower," as she called him, could not handle being uprooted. He died within ten days of the move. Mother never could forgive herself.

The prospect of a Winston "royal wedding" in England, with grandchildren to follow, energized my mother like noth-ing in her life before. She decided this would be the occasion not only for a psychological makeover but a physical one as well, occasioning the plastic surgery that may have triggered the disturbing nocturnal episode where she showed up at my apartment in her nightgown. Mother, who had always been vain, was most critical of the flap under her chin. "I hate my neck," she would exclaim, joining a chorus of millions. "I'm going to have a face-lift for Bruce's wedding," she announced one day to Harry. "I want to look my best."

"Edna, you're nuts," Dad replied. "It's new-fangled and dangerous." Mother refuted him with a long list of her friends who had survived the process with flying colors. Despite his initial protestations, Harry bought into her program, and she went under the knife in New York with no instantly apparent ill effects. "Edna, you looked beautiful. You didn't have to do it," he said, proceeding to tell her how much more beautiful she was now. In sum, when she healed, the consensus was that she had erased ten years from her face.

I think part of the joy Mother found in planning Bruce's big wedding was not just for her son but also as a self-vindication for her own aborted nuptial celebration in rejecting Ben Kaufman to elope with Harry Winston. As a retired British officer, General King did not have the resources to provide for the elaborate wedding my mother wanted, so she and Dad graciously stepped up to the plate. In actuality, most of the planning for the celebration that would take place at Claridge's, the Winstons' home away from home in London, had been done by Dad's office.

Alas, no sooner had we all checked in to the hotel, Mother began acting erratically, changing her mind on elements of the fete that had long ago been decided. More troubling to me was that Mother seemed angry and irascible, a mood she had never evinced before. A very bad incident occurred on a telephone call between Mother in her suite and Bruce, in Annabel's London flat. Without telling Mother that Annabel was listening on a separate extension, Bruce began baiting Mother as to why more of Annabel's extended family had not been invited.

Mother quickly snapped, "Your father and I are paying for all of it. Her family's coming. I don't want to hear one more thing on the subject. That little Annabel doesn't have a pot to pee in. She should be glad she's marrying you." Bruce, furious, hung up on Mother. Annabel hung up too and conveyed the unfortunate conversation to her father. A few hours later, I, the Best Man to Be, received a call from General King. "You may know what has transpired," he said in a very soft voice. "Annabel wishes to withdraw from the marriage."

I had not been expecting this marriage to provoke an international incident. Summoning all my inchoate diplomatic skills, I beseeched the general not to act hastily and invited him to coffee the next morning.

The commander seemed mortally wounded. "General," I pleaded with him. "Please don't call it off."

"Why shouldn't I?" he replied in a near whisper.

"I don't know why," I answered, "but my mother's not well. She's acting very strangely." The general stared at me, not saying a word. "General, you know what it means to have a sick wife. Please don't do this to my father."

Still not speaking, the general stood up. He was tall, maybe six feet four. I instinctively stood to meet him. He reached out and shook my hand. "You're a gentleman,' he said. That was all.

In the end, all went beautifully—the ceremony, the reception. Holding Mother's hand, Dad worked the crowd from De Beers, from Lloyd's, from Burke's Peerage. He was at the height of his amazing career. His business had never been better. His prodigal son was getting married. His wife had survived her surgery. I was garnering kudos for my work by his side. I thought of Robert Browning's "Pippa's Song": "God's in His heaven, / All's right with the world!" Bruce and Annabel departed for their honeymoon. I'm not sure they told us where they were going. I knew better than to ask. Eventually they returned to live in New York, which delighted my parents.

Meanwhile, Mother's presenile dementia, or whatever the psychiatrist thought it may be, was getting worse. I had a sit-down with Dad about Mom's condition. He didn't like dealing with it. He held his hand over his eyes as he did in his private elevator, before facing each new day in the office. The King of Diamonds simply dreaded ascending his throne, all the glory and fortune notwithstanding. Now at home, he just winced with his eyes closed. "Poor Edna," he moaned. "Poor, poor Edna."

"Dad, we have to find the best medical talent possible to get to the bottom of this," I urged, knowing he had all the connections in the world.

Dad took courage with three fingers of Haig & Haig. He was inspired to call Harold Gelb, a Scarsdale friend who was a major benefactor of Mount Sinai, still considered New York's finest medical center. It wasn't an easy call, because my father could never forget the trauma, in 1910 when he was thirteen, of seeing Sinai, then, as now, a redoubt of German-Jewish wealth, turn away his dying mother, Jennie. But there was no time for pride now. Mother had to be saved. We seemed to need a miracle, and we couldn't be fussy where it was performed.

Now, with money no object where Harry Winston was concerned, we found ourselves welcomed into the bosom of Mount Sinai, under the care of the chief of neurosurgery, Leonard Malis, whose very name seemed to remind Dad of his initial boyhood impression of the forbidding institution. Brain-imaging technology in the late 1960s was primitive at best. MRIs had not been developed. Instead, Mother was subjected to an upside-down brain X-ray procedure known as pneumoencephalography that seemed as if it had been inspired by the Spanish Inquisition. Air was injected into her spinal column while her head was down and her feet were up. Then she was rotated to the sitting position to allow the air bubbles to rise up the spine into the brain. Mother wailed and cried throughout the torturous procedure.

It wasn't worth the pain and suffering. What was found were two enormous blood clots, subdural hematomas that usually were caused by a bad fall or other blunt trauma, such as her plastic surgery, or "lifting." Brain surgery, we were informed, was the only resort but was unlikely to provide a happy ending. Back home on Fifth Avenue, there were not enough fingers of Haig & Haig on any of our hands to calm Dad, who, after finishing three quarters of the bottle, sobbed his way to sleep on the tiny love seat in the library.

I don't recall Bruce being at the hospital during all this turmoil, though at a family meeting at 927 Fifth he seemed completely detached, which I wrote off as bewilderment rather than indifference. This was his mother. He had to care. Annabel seemed to better comprehend the gravity of her new mother-in-law's predicament. Eventually, armed with all the information of my self-directed crash course in comparative anatomy, Dad and I had a summit with all the top brains of Mount Sinai in the hospital's glassed-in, sun-dappled Klingenstein Pavilion overlooking Central Park. The goal was making a command decision, but these geniuses could not agree on anything. Dad, who may not have been a man of science, was definitely a man of action. He gave an unforgettable peroration to the assembled doctors, comparing his work to theirs. Both brain surgery and diamonds were about cutting. "I thought when we studied a huge and hugely valuable rough diamond in order to determine how to cut it, it was normal to have a number of different opinions. But I never thought with all you learned doctors there would be such a difference of opinion."

Dr. Malis replied, "I understand this must be terribly difficult, Mr. Winston. This operation, if there is to be an operation, is not without risk. No one can guarantee your wife will regain her mental capacity."

Every day I visited Mother, she seemed to slide more and more under the waves. This was not some big stone to be cut, I thought. This was my mother. Sometimes she would reach out her hand to me across the bedsheets, with a little smile, as if to say, "I know it's going to be all right, Ronnie."

Eventually Dad and I decided to roll the dice and do the operation. Dad insisted Bruce come over and be part of the process. "He hasn't exactly been in the front line of all this, but I want him to understand."

Bruce came over. We sat around the seventeenth-century Dutch dining table with the Barberini corkscrew legs. "How's Mother?" he asked, too casually to be believed.

Dad was as tolerant as any father could ever be. He didn't lose his temper. "The doctors have recommended brain surgery. There seems to be no other choice."

"Oh, when?" Bruce asked.

"A week from today," Dad said.

"Can't we change it?" Bruce asked, pained by the prospect.

"Change it?" Dad replied, confused by Bruce's request. "Your mother is going downhill."

"In a week? Well, that's no good. That's the day I'm going to Greece. That's my vacation."

"Bruce, you can't be serious," Dad said. I again held my tongue.

"I am so serious. I'm not going to cancel my vacation."

"But your whole life is a vacation." Dad said it for me. All I could do was shrug my shoulders. On the day of the surgery, Bruce, true to his vow, left for Greece with his new bride.

Meanwhile, Dad and I sat at Mount Sinai while Mother was in surgery. It seemed like an eternity. Eventually, Dr. Malis came into the room to speak with Dad and me. "Mrs. Winston tolerated the operation very well," he said, devoid of emotion. We more than made up for the emotion he lacked, elated that she had survived.

"Will she be able to speak?" Dad pressed on. The doctor was, as usual, noncommittal.

We had to wait until she came out of anesthesia. He told us he had removed the blood clots from her brain, which was auspicious, but her brain, which had been pressed down by the clots and was an explanation for her loss of function, did not spring back into the space in her skull.

Twelve hours later, Mother came out of intensive care to her room with a large mummy-style wrapping on her head. We finally went home to get some sleep. When we returned the next morning, Mother was awake, sitting up, sipping orange juice. We were elated. Dad leaned over and kissed her cheek, or what he could find amid the bandages. His lips trembled.

Mother took his hand and held it. Then she spoke. "Well, Harry, "she said, "you have your wife back again." They were the greatest words I have ever heard. The moment was so intimate and touching that after I kissed Mother, I left the room. I wanted them to be alone together. Mother was speaking. It was a miracle, a genuine miracle.

I went to the office to call Bruce with the amazing news. He had grudgingly left me a number on the island of Mykonos. The phone rang. A Greek picked up. He spoke English. The phone was in a tavern. "Mister Winston climbing mountain. Maybe back tonight."

"Please tell him his brother called," I said.

The next day the message must have gotten through. Bruce was on the line. I barely said hello, when he began screaming at me on the line. "You're such a jerk."

"Whatever," was all I could say, shocked by his rage at me for invading his holiday, given our family crisis.

"No! You're a real jerk. You have the duty to keep me informed."

That's what I thought I was doing. Why was he so furious? "Bruce, there's one phone in this village. Don't you want to know how your mother is?"

"Yes," he conceded. There was no apology for his anger.

"She survived the operation and seems to be better. Goodbye." I slammed down the phone.

Tended by a couple we hired, Mother went home to Scarsdale to regain her strength and rejoin the world she loved so much. Alas, she became steadily mute all over again. She also gradually lost her ability to walk. By 1971 she was completely confined to her bedroom. I would often visit, but I found myself weeping at her bedside. It was much worse for Dad to be there with her. In 1972 he sold our massive fifteen-room cooperative at 927 Fifth and bought a smaller apartment back in the Sherry-Netherland.

Mother would be visited in Scarsdale periodically by one of Mount Sinai's star neurologists, Morris Bender. No progress ever occurred. However, Dr. Bender thought he could assuage Dad's grief by having him endow something called the Harry Winston Imaging Center at the hospital. The pitch was that, with so many new and advanced imaging devices coming to market, perhaps someone other than my mother might be saved. Dad was so shell-shocked from the loss of Edna that, if only to prove his deep love for her, he donated $300,000 ($2.15

million in 2023 money) to create such a center. Two years later, he had heard nothing further from Dr. Bender or the hospital. He dispatched me to try to get an answer from Sinai.

I was invited to lunch with the same group of superstar doctors whom Dad had called on the carpet, in his polite way, for not having a shared vision of how to treat his wife. What they told me about the Winston Center was as unclear as Mother's diagnosis. In the end, they never built a Winston Center, and they never gave back Dad's money. Three black marks for Mount Sinai: the heartless, snobbish rejection of my terminally ill grandmother; the failure to adequately diagnose and treat my mother; and, finally an act of extreme bad faith in asking for my father's money but never following through and building the proposed Harry Winston Imaging Center, a play on my father's raw sensibilities. Dad refused to seek restitution. He was as dedicated to realpolitik as Metternich. "I won't sue Sinai," he told me. "I have too many good friends and clients there." To this day, I have no idea what Mount Sinai Hospital did with my father's gift.

Dr. Bender, who came to Scarsdale to monitor Mother, basically gave her six months to live. "They don't really do that well in this semivegetative state," he intoned one day, using the third person plural to divorce himself from failure. Nonetheless, I couldn't accept losing my mother and vowed to do everything possible to keep her alive and comfortable. To that end, in the winter of 1972 I suggested to Dad that we take Mother to Florida, which she always adored as the perfect escape from snowy New York. We rented a house on Key Biscayne next door to President Nixon, who was vacationing after his landslide victory for a second term, which would end with the Watergate scandal. The hotline to Russia passed right under our lawn; the Secret Service was always checking it. The Nixon setter frolicked in our backyard. One day the president came over to retrieve him. Mother was sitting mute in her wheelchair taking the sun with Dad. Nixon walked over, patted her on the head, as in a benediction, and papally pronounced, "She'll be all right. I know it." As we learned, the president wasn't always right. Soon Nixon would be gone, but Mother endured, albeit not improved, for more than another decade.

Mother's incapacity was taking a terrible toll on my father. Here was the light of his life, the only woman he ever loved, the anchor of his existence, here but not here. The grim six months prognosis of the Sinai wizards had come and gone. She had beat the odds, but to what end? My father, who had beaten all the odds of life, had always been an optimist, a true believer in the American Dream. He was living next door to the president, that's how close he was to the top. But he saw Nixon go down and Edna go down, and he understood in his heart and gut how ephemeral all this was. Back in New York, whenever the private phone rang in his office, he would buzz for his secretary to pick it up. "Please. I hope it's not about Edna," he would say.

In his office in Geneva, where Harry spent more and more time, he would be even more trepidatious. His supersalesman Albano Bochatay, the star of Arabia, would come into Dad's beautiful salon with its French boiserie and freestanding showcase to show Dad some of his latest treasures. Sometimes he would announce to Dad, "Mr. Winston, New York's on the phone."

Dad would grimace, expecting the worst. "Is it about my wife?" was his first response. "No, no, it's Jerry Schultz,"

Bochatay would reassure him. That drama would repeat itself at least three times a day, from 3:30 p.m. when the New York office began gearing up for its day until 6:30, when Dad would leave. Bochatay would often drive him in one of his latest red Ferraris to the luxe hotel Le Richemond, across the lake from the office. Even though it was at most a five-minute ride, Bochatay would do it as if he were Juan Fangio at the grand prix in Le Mans. Getting out, Dad would admire the car he basically had bought for Bochatay. "It's very beautiful," Dad would say, conjuring up his own boyhood fascination with autocars. "But it's a selfish car," he would joke. "Only two people can ride in it."

When Bochatay was off in the Middle East making millions, Francine Del Rieux, Dad's towering office assistant, would walk him to the hotel. Francine was slender and over six feet tall, which appealed to Dad. He admired big men and college men, and he admired big women. Often Dad would celebrate the close of the day by having a drink of Scotch from a bottle he kept in the safe. Francine's task was to keep him steady as they crossed the lake bridge. Sometimes she gently placed her hand under his shoulder blade. Other times she took his elbow as they walked into the brilliant evening sunset. The notion of anything more than a walk was completely out of character. He was a married man, deeply in love with a wife who was in a terrible limbo. He could never dishonor her.

Francine would install Dad at the tiny, intimate bar at the hotel's Le Gentilhomme restaurant and make her polite exit. The wealth and resources of the famous enterprise created by this tiny man all by himself was not lost on the glamorous ladies of the evening who often dropped by Le Gentilhomme.

If there were propositions, Dad rebuffed them, just as he never invited Francine to join him for a cocktail. Dad drank alone. He liked the Lilliputian scale of Le Gentilhomme, which fit his own small scale: the low, tiny green leather chairs, which resembled those of Harry's Bar in Venice; the bar that only seated five; the parquet dance floor, which was no wider than two tables. Harry Winston did not dance. After two stiff drinks he began to relax. Something approaching a happy glow suffused him. He forgot the present and in this doll's house of a bar seemingly designed for a child-scale world. Dad perhaps became a little boy again, a carefree little boy, sipping milk next to his parents, Jacob and Jennie, who looked after him the way he now had the enormous responsibility of looking after his wife, his sons, his extended family, his empire of jewels.

Although the seat and soul of that empire may have been New York, in many ways the heart of Harry Winston was in Geneva. And if not the heart, certainly the vault. What made Geneva the Fort Knox of Harry Winston was that it was our firm's center for the sale of rough diamonds, or uncut stones. The source of rough, which was controlled by De Beers, was the Skeleton Coast of the former German colony then known as South West Africa, soon to be renamed Namibia. This forbidding Atlantic shoreline, which was a graveyard for ships, was a Garden of Eden for diamonds that had flowed down over the centuries from the Orange River. A day at the beach collecting stones from the sand could easily turn a beachboy into a millionaire.

De Beers had cornered this market for the last forty years, protecting it with an overlay of explosive mines, men, and dogs, sucking up gems in giant vacuum cleaners that looked like something from outer space. Through his "arrangement" with the De Beers syndicate, Harry Winston saw 22 percent of this torrent of rough stones flow into his coffers. From the early 1960s to the mid-1970s, this rough provided much of the company's profits, profits sheltered by Jerry Schultz's ingenious tax concepts. The lower the taxes, legitimately avoided, the more rough diamonds Dad could buy; he turned a 25 percent profit every six weeks on the sale of the rough, which, more than the Hope or the Vargas or the name gems that made him famous, really deserve the credit for making Harry Winston the Croesus of Carbon.

The best of these Namibian stones became Harry Winston treasures, artfully designed, cut and set by artisans in the company's Fifth Avenue workrooms. These were the diamonds that were a girl's best friend, the jewels Marilyn Monroe wanted to talk to Harry Winston about. What nobody talked about were the masses of poorer-quality gems that were cut in Israel or India and found a home in the commercial designs that Harry Winston manufactured and sold to JCPenney, Sears, Zales, and others. The Winston provenance was a deep secret. These mass market jewels were never marked or labeled with our fabled name.

Between these high and low ends, there was a middle tier of diamonds that Dad did not cut but sold as rough directly to various dealers throughout the world who came to Geneva to do their shopping. Dad's specialist there was Nathan "Nick" Akselrod, a third-generation diamond maven who had worked his way up from being a cutter's apprentice on 47th Street. Most of Dad's large diamond surplus was sold in Geneva rather than New York; the Swiss paradise was closer to the main European market in Antwerp, whose top Orthodox dealers, having celebrated Shabbat, flew to Switzerland on

Sunday to be welcomed by Serge Fradkoff, who spoke their language and treated them like kings.

Dad loved Serge's Sunday souks, held in the Winston grand salon. There were no staff on Sunday, so no dreaded calls about Edna. Even Harry Winston deserved a day off from worry. He and Serge would host, handle, and *hondel* the visiting dealers from the Low Countries. They came in droves, savoring the idea of bypassing De Beers, which were shamelessly anti-Semitic toward its more traditional brethren. These buyers reminded Dad of his early days in the trade. They made him feel young again.

Serge Fradkoff had about as much use for me as De Beers had for the Antwerp Hasidim. Geneva's favorite rumor, that Serge was Harry Winston's out-of-wedlock son, was assiduously cultivated by the Tunisian. Nothing, in his mind, could have been more flattering. Dad did like Serge, for his rapier mathematical mind and his overweening obsession with diamonds, an obsession he would have liked to see replicated in both his sons. What he didn't like was, beginning in the mid-1970s, Serge's obsession with his own publicity. Stories about him began appearing in English, French, and Swiss papers about the "young genius" with nary a mention of the "old genius," the genuine one who was his boss and mentor. Much was made of Serge's segue from being a bridge champion to the Prince of Diamonds.

But it wasn't just gems that Serge was associated with. With the fortune he earned through Harry Winston, Serge had begun buying racehorses, hobnobbing at Longchamp and Epsom with the Rothschilds, the Hunts of Texas, the Aga Khan. When he came to New York to see his steeds compete in the Belmont Stakes, Harry Winston was not even mentioned.

Harry Winston was the man who forbade any photographs of himself. He was the antithesis of a publicity seeker.

Harry felt betrayed by Serge, outraged by his flamboyant narcissism. He never shared his misgivings with me, but I could sense it. He did share his bruised feelings with Nick Akselrod and his wife Sue on a gastronomic road trip to Auberge du Père Bise, a three–Michelin star temple where the *poulet a l'estragon* was one of Dad's favorite dishes. Relaxed by this foodie road trip across the French border, Dad let his hair down. He told Nick and Sue that Serge was "the biggest disappointment of his life," which was really saying something in a ruthless business where betrayal was the rule rather than the exception. I was pained as Nick described the tears shining on Dad's cheeks under the streetlights of Geneva.

When I arrived in Geneva a few weeks later, Dad told me that he and Serge were going to part company. I warned Dad that Serge was the mainspring of his business at this point and privy to a great many secrets. I didn't tell Dad that, at age seventy-nine, he needed Serge, but I did attempt to intervene and effect a rapprochement. To that end, I asked to meet Serge. He invited me to his apartment, filled with Chagalls and a jumble of French reproductions and heavy antique Swiss furniture. When I told him I felt any dispute between him and my father was unnecessary and destructive, Serge feigned shock. What dispute? He then began weeping. I felt it was a show more appropriate for the Yiddish theater than for the serious big business we were in; those crocodile tears belonged in the reptile house.

Between sobs, Serge related how much he adored Dad. I suggested that he had made too much of a public show of his success. To stop the flood of tears, I told him how fond of him

Dad was and urged him to do all he could to patch things up. My diplomacy seemed to have worked. A few days later, Dad told me that Serge would stay. The PR onslaught stopped. Still, Dad began spending more of his evenings with Bochatay than with Serge. I never had a relationship with Serge and did not start one then.

Later in the summer of 1975, Dad decamped, once again across the Swiss border, to the idyllic French spa town of Évian-les-Bains on the shores of Lake Geneva. Settling into a luxury hotel on the lake, Dad, who was invigorated by cold water, went for polar bear swims every morning, then called New York for several hours. There was no bad news regarding Mother, and, relieved that matters with Fradkoff had been resolved, Dad told me on the phone that the stay in Évian was doing him, as he put it, "a world of good."

His peace of mind would sadly prove to be short-lived. In mid-July, Dad's main man in London, Gerald Rothschild of Hennig, the leading rough diamond brokers who was his intermediary with De Beers, received an urgent call from Monty Charles, the scary Darth Vader of the syndicate. Without explaining why, Charles had told Rothschild that Harry Oppenheimer, head of De Beers, needed to speak to Rothschild "straightaway." That translated into an order for Rothschild to fly to Johannesburg, which he did the following morning.

What Oppenheimer told Rothschild was that Harry Winston had to go. It didn't matter that Harry was the best customer of the CSO (Central Selling Organization). Geopolitics were at play. There was a guerrilla war going on against South Africa by the liberation forces that would eventually "free" South West Africa and change its name to Namibia. The resistance, or SWAPO (South West Africa People's Organization), was divided into two factions, one communist, the other capitalist and pro-West. Oppenheimer feared that if the Communists prevailed, the country's incredibly rich diamond resources would be nationalized and De Beers destroyed.

The worst thing would be for the new government to learn that its diamond patrimony, the asset that would make Namibia rich and support it, had been sold out and shipped out of the country to Harry Winston at a staggering profit to De Beers that did not benefit the country. Oppenheimer told Rothschild that all future sales to Harry Winston, including one two weeks hence, had to be canceled. The fifteen-year Pax Africana between Winston and De Beers was thus abrogated. Oppenheimer told Rothschild he would try to "make up the shortfall in other ways." Rothschild knew better than to hold his breath.

Rothschild was in turmoil on the long flight back to London. He loved my father. How could he tell him? However, he had to do it, and fast. The first call he made back on the ground was to Harry to set up a meeting. Dad was confused. Why now? Rothschild, without sharing details, insisted. Dad told him to come to Évian and to arrive by 7:00 p.m. to join a dinner party he was hosting. Alas, a freak thunderstorm arose, something out of Shakespeare's *The Tempest*, and delayed the ferry Rothschild was on.

Rothschild finally arrived at the Évian hotel at 11:00 p.m. He knew Harry went to bed early, and he didn't want to disturb him, but this was too big to wait. He woke my father and told him that Harry Winston would no longer be able to buy Namibian diamonds. All Dad could do was stare at him.

"Then he abruptly bid me goodnight," was how Rothschild put it to me in his understated, British way.

"Bastards," was how Dad described it to me when I met him the next month for his annual August trip to the Hôtel du Cap-Eden-Roc on the French Riviera. "I should never have trusted them. I had no contract. I should never have trusted them."

I thought to myself what might have happened if Rothschild had waited until the next morning, when Dad was wide awake and at the top of his faculties, to break the treacherous news. Maybe he would have called his lawyers and fought back against De Beers. Maybe the result would have been different. But De Beers knew what it was doing; it wanted all the profits and none of the risk. It was the master calculator, and it figured that Harry Winston, nearing eighty, lacked whatever it took to mount a campaign of retribution against the diamond cartel. He simply no longer had the strength to go up against de Beers.

How fragile my father was became apparent when he went to London for his big stone sight at the end of July, after Rothschild's brutal visit at Évian. He still needed de Beers, if not for rough, from which he now had been cut off, but for the big stones. This was a bridge he could not afford to burn. Nick Akselrod met him there at Claridge's and reported to me that he was not his usual self. They had dinner together, but Harry never mentioned the loss of Namibia.

At 3:00 a.m., Nick was awakened by a call. "Nick, where are you? I'm in the lobby waiting. We're going to be late for the syndicate and our sight."

"But, Mr. Winston, it's the middle of the night."

"No, Nick, it's not. Get down here."

Nick dressed as fast as a fireman went down to the lobby, where my father was pacing the black-and-white marble floor, perfectly dressed in his three-piece pinstriped suit and white, starched dickey. Nick took Dad to the front door, where the limousine had been called and was waiting. They drove through the empty streets of London through Piccadilly Circus, Trafalgar Square, down Fleet Street to Charterhouse Street. It was 4:00 a.m. The drive took fifteen minutes. It normally took fifty. Nick pleaded with Dad to let him get out first to see if there were people there to receive him. Dad would have none of it. "We don't want to be late. You know how punctual the English are." Dad emerged from the limo and went up to the bulding and began banging on the giant, locked doors. No one was there. Not even a night watchman. Eventually, Dad turned to look at Nick, realizing the state of his disorientation. "I guess you're right, Nick. We should go back."

They drove back to Claridge's. The incident was never mentioned, except to me by Nick.

My time to take the helm of Harry Winston was coming sooner than I thought. The nocturnal perambulations of my mother and now my father signaled that their decline was accelerating, that old age was coming for them. Nick and I tried to persuade Dad that he needed a companion on all his trips abroad, but he wouldn't hear of it. At the Hôtel du Cap-Eden-Roc, he walked more slowly, and he had the bellhop ferry him via golf cart from his cabana by the pool to the hotel, which was up a steep hill and which he used to climb like a mountain goat. He was, however, still able to enjoy a cocktail and regale his friends with stories about his life.

Back in New York, he continued to do business. In 1974 Richard Nixon resigned, and Gerald Ford replaced him. Ford was not a crook, but he was anything but inspiring, and the country was suffering from recession and the new phenomenon known as "stagflation." Nonetheless, people were still buying diamonds, and by the end of 1975, a worldwide diamond buying frenzy began that was to last six years. Perhaps people were stocking up on diamonds, as a hedge against the economic turmoil of the times.

In the Fifth Avenue carriage trade, Harry Winston had no real competition. Tiffany was busy going down-market, having been taken over by Avon, which had turned selling makeup into a Tupperware party. Tiffany, an odd fit in the "Avon Calling" empire, now started selling stationery and china, along with diamonds. Van Cleef & Arpels, the firm Dad had helped when it fled the Nazis for the American market, seemed a one-trick pony, imprisoned by its innovation of the "invisible setting," a technique that allowed the appearance of big gems but were in reality an amalgam of many small stones held together by pressure.

Cartier had been gutted by a series of divestitures that left the British and French stores standing alone as separate companies. Bulgari had just arrived on these shores and set up shop in the Pierre, specializing in a stylish flat-link gold chain of newly minted ancient Roman coins. But there were no great gems there, or anywhere else, making Harry Winston the only game in town, and the world.

Whatever feeling Dad had toward De Beers, he still did business, big business with it.

In late 1975 he purchased, sight unseen by him but in reliance on the eyes of Nick Akselrod, a 204-carat rough diamond for the price of $10,000 per carat, which was the highest price ever paid for an uncut stone. Dad cabled $2,040,000 to De

Beers, and the stone was shipped to New York in the traditional cardboard box with the heavy blue wrapping paper and red wax seal. The diamond was cut in early 1976 and topped out at a perfect pear shape of 75.52 carats. With its weight rounded off to seventy-six carats, I named it the Star of Independence in honor of the American bicentennial.

Who bought these treasures? Lots of extremely rich people, like the Patiños, the tin kings of Bolivia; Charles Engelhard, the Platinum King of New Jersey, who owned a big piece of De Beers; Imelda Marcos, of the Philippines; the Shah of Iran. However, the vast majority of Dad's biggest customers, whom he called "privates," were not household names, kings, or stars. There was a "silent majority" of simply rich people who loved beautiful jewelry. Yes, the very act of wearing a million dollars around your neck may seem ostentatious, but in reality Dad's superbuyers were largely quietly rich and wore these items only on very special occasions.

In March 1976 Harry Winston turned eighty. I threw a private family birthday dinner at Café Nicholson, an eccentric, antique-filled Sutton Place restaurant with a wonderful Black southern chef and an artsy celebrity clientele that included people like Tennessee Williams, Gore Vidal, and Dad's client, Elizabeth Taylor. The celebration was less a bash than a sober reminder of the march of time. Dad's ascetic, recluse sister Dora, the bag lady of the Barbizon, arrived looking sad, which was her default mien. Dad had showered Dora with a lifetime of gifts, but she never opened any of the boxes. Brother Stanley, always jovial, was a necessary counterweight to Dora's gloom.

When the massive, flaming birthday cake arrived, Stanley, who had traveled in vaudeville with the Marx Brothers, leaned over to blow out the eighty candles and said, "For me!" But then, with a magisterial wave of his hand, let the cake be passed to Harry. Both brothers shared a moment of laughter. There would not be many more. By the end of 1977, both Dora and Stanley had passed on, buried beside their parents and brother Charles in the bleak family plot in Queens.

When Stanley died, he left his antique and chandelier business to his nephew John, continuing the family tradition there. I wondered about our family business. Dad simply did not confide in me, and there were too many details about the business I didn't know. If something was to happen to Dad, or more realistically, when something happened, what would I do? I felt miserably unprepared for the daunting task ahead, which was to keep the business going and also pay what would be a 60 percent death tax, which would be levied when both of my parents had passed away. These thoughts and fears often woke me at four in the morning, the hour of the wolf.

Yet Dad carried on. The summer of 1978 brought Dad, Bruce, and me together for our last holiday at the Hôtel du Cap-Eden-Roc. Bruce and Annabel were divorced by then. She had once complained to me, "He doesn't do anything." The endless vacation was too much for her. Mother was languishing in Scarsdale. Her absence hung heavy in the scented Riviera air. Dad enjoyed his daily swim, splashing in the sea with the likes of movie mogul Darryl F. Zanuck. "I'm getting my health back," he would call out to me. Sometimes he would exhort himself, "Harry, darling. Find diamonds! Find diamonds!" The three of us would dine together every night, often at the nearby fish restaurants Dad fancied, the Maison des Pêcheurs in Juan-les-Pins, or Tetou, in Golfe-Juan, the world's most expensive fish shack, where Aristotle Onassis might be at one table and Frank Sinatra another.

But our most unforgettable dinner occurred at the Eden-Roc, the hotel's spectacular dining room perched on the rocks above the Mediterranean. The waiters fluttered around us like doves. Harry Winston was a legend at the hotel, one of the top customers in a roster of legends. The sun cast long shadows across the white tablecloth. As I sipped my white wine, I reflected on Dad's leonine good looks. Even at eighty-two, he was still a handsome man with a full head of graying black hair, a luminescent tan, and a regal bearing belying his short stature. He may have been tiny, but he seemed huge. We discussed all the many business prospects that stemmed from our annual August jewel exhibition at the Carlton hotel in Cannes. Suddenly, Bruce stopped Dad in midsentence, saying that he had to raise a very important subject.

"Yes, Bruce, what is it?"

"Dad, when you're dead, Ron will control everything."

Dad simply nodded.

"I don't intend to work," Bruce continued in a defiant way. He was stating the obvious.

I don't think there was ever a day when my father expected his younger son to join the family business. Then Bruce lowered the boom. "I want to make sure now that my brother gives me money so I can live the way I want."

Silence. Dead silence. That silence could be heard in Cannes, far across the bay. Dad looked at me. He shook his head. I could tell he was extremely agitated.

"I'm not dead yet," Harry Winston said.

I was engulfed by a terrible wave of sadness. How could Bruce say such a thing? How could he be so cruel? The flaming sunset sky went black to me. I knew I was going to cry.

Excusing myself, I left the table and walked out of the dining room. I stood on the rocks over the sea. Not normally given to tears, I found myself weeping uncontrollably. I felt like Dick Diver in Fitzgerald's novel *Tender Is the Night*.

Having composed myself, I returned to the table. Bruce had settled down into a state of petulant silence. Dad was drinking a double whiskey. Nothing about business, or succession, or money was uttered. The dinner ended. Dad proclaimed his weariness and asked for the chauffeur service. A golf cart arrived and took him up the hill to the hotel.

The next day, I bought a tape recorder. Through the long summer afternoons in the cabana, I began interviewing Dad about his life and his memories. We played a little game. I kept the recorder hidden, and he pretended he didn't know it was on. However, one evening at one of our exhibitions, he told Bochatay, "Ronnie's interviewing me and taping it. I'm not supposed to know about the recording." But he never let on to me, and that was our compact. Many of these recorded stories became the basis for this book.

The fall of 1978 was a blur. I went to Europe in late November after Thanksgiving for a short business trip. I took the Concorde. I planned to return on December 8. I spoke to Dad the night before I left. I told him I loved him. When I was gone, I learned from Jerry Schultz, Dad came into the office later than usual. The normally impeccable Harry seemed uncharacteristically disheveled. After going through the mail with Jerry, Harry simply sat by his window, gazing out at Fifth Avenue and the pre-Christmas crowds making their way through a rainstorm. His secretary, Elinor Wurtzel, told him he didn't look well. She warned him that a flu was going around and that he should go home and rest. Dad didn't seem to be listening. "I should sell everything. I'm going to get out," he mused to himself as he watched the shoppers on the street. Then he turned to Elinor, "Please call the car. I'll have my manicure and head home." He did.

He died in his bed that night, December 8, 1978. He was eighty-two. His houseman discovered his body that next morning. It was concluded that the cause of death was a heart attack.

I was on the Concorde flying back to New York. I had no idea. When I arrived at my apartment on 73rd Street, Nick Akselrod and Elinor Wurtzel, aware of my travel plans, were in the lobby waiting for me with the horrible news. It was like being hit by an ax. Dad's body was in a coffin at Frank E. Campbell on Madison, the mortuary of Manhattan's elite. There would be a memorial in two days. I called Bruce, who said he had dressed Harry for the coffin and put his favorite gold cufflinks, one with sapphires and gold and the other with rubies and gold, in his death shirt. I knew they would be stolen, but I didn't have the strength or the heart to bring it up. Nor did I have the stomach to go see Dad lying in state.

The next few days were a blur. Campbell's was packed with a who's who of the diamond world, as well as dealers from 47th Street, who held Harry Winston in the highest esteem; he was "one of them" who had become the king. The Geneva Sales Trio of Horowitz, Bochatay, and Fradkoff had flown over to pay their respects to the man who made them rich. The main speaker was Dad's longtime lawyer, Harry Torczyner. No lawyer in the world knew more about the diamond trade, and no lawyer loved his client more than this Harry loved that Harry. Torczyner gave a eulogy about my Dad and the cycle of life, but again, I was in the fog of loss. Our funeral procession of black cars made the long, sad drive out to Queens to lay my father to rest along side his sister, his brothers, and his parents. Outside, in the tattered graveyard, if you craned your neck, you could see the Empire State Building. My beloved father, Harry Winston, the undisputed king of the diamond trade, had, at last, come home to his humble roots.

CHAPTER FIFTEEN

The Taxman Cometh

Benjamin Franklin had it right when he said nothing is certain except death and taxes. In the months and years after the death of Harry Winston, those two immutable forces totally dominated my new role as the captain of the great ship my father had built. My main hope was to prevent it from becoming another *Titanic*. For the first few weeks after laying Dad to rest, I kept nagging myself that I might have somehow saved him had I not been in Europe. I soon found out that Dad had visited his doctor, Max Trubeck, who warned him of severe cardiac issues. But nobody told me, starting with Dad, who would never admit to being mortal, and not Dr. Trubeck, who conveyed his warning to Bruce, who never thought to call me in Europe and inform me. I would have come home immediately and insisted on further workups, not that Dad would have agreed to them. Still, I beat myself up time and again for not being there for him.

That was death. Then there were taxes, which I had been haunted by once I saw Dad's increasing frailty two years before his passing. Given my mother's brutal incapacitation, I never imagined that my father would predecease her. Now she was all alone, but she didn't even know where she was. Like my father, I had been dreading for years that I would get the call telling me she had died. It actually took eight more years, until 1986, for that call to come. But both Harry Torczyner and Jerry Schultz, Dad's brain trust, not to mention his powerful Park Avenue corporate law firm of Rogers & Wells, which represented Harry Winston, Inc., had instilled in me the fear of God and of the Internal Revenue Service.

Jerry Schultz and I had numerous meetings with the Rogers & Wells firm, whose senior partner, William Rogers, had been Richard Nixon's secretary of state. I'm not sure whether Dad met Rogers when Nixon was our Florida neighbor, but we only dealt with his underlings, not with him. I'm not sure which of these Ivy Leaguers wrote Dad's will, but it was a time bomb waiting to explode. Under its terms, I inherited the business, which I was to run "in trust" for Bruce, who had made his disinterest very painfully clear to our father. I was to be paid an annual salary of $400,000 for my efforts, which were Herculean, given the challenges the business faced. Bruce would be paid an annual stiped of $200,000 for doing nothing, which is precisely what he demanded of Dad that tragic night at the Hôtel du Cap-Eden-Roc.

Per the will, Bruce and I would divide all future profits, which put an extra burden on me. Harry Winston had always been extremely profitable; however, the huge impending tax bill would eat up decades of profits and then some.

My father, who kept everything inside his brilliant head, in a business that was arcane and secretive to begin with, had not fully trained me to step smoothly into his shoes. After a month that had to be the bleakest Christmas season of my life, at the beginning of 1979, I flew off to the snows of Switzerland on my first mission at the helm of Harry Winston. That mission was to fire Serge Fradkoff, who was about to destroy Harry Winston before I could even have a fair chance to run it.

In 1978 Serge had gotten involved with his new horse-world billionaire pals, the Hunt brothers of Texas, in their quest to corner the market on silver. In the first half of January 1979, the price of silver jumped from six dollars a troy ounce to nearly fifty dollars. The Hunts controlled a third of the world market, to the great dismay of those who wanted silver but were now priced out of the market. One of those silver seekers, our rival Tiffany's, was so rattled that it took out a full-page ad in the *New York Times* denouncing the greed of the Hunts, who had borrowed heavily from Wall Street and beyond in their speculations. When I was in Geneva, I found out that a key financier of the Hunts' silver play was Serge Fradkoff, who was betting the farm using Harry Winston funds. Seeing not only a high crime but a major disaster in the making, I immediately dismissed Serge, demanding full restitution of our money. Otherwise, I threatened to go to the *fiscs*, as the French called the financial authorities.

With silver still sky high, Serge paid us back in full, reversing his thievery. It was just in the nick of time. On "Silver Thursday," March 27, 1980, the silver market crashed, dropping over 50 percent, nearly dragging Wall Street into a crash with it and losing the Hunts over a billion dollars. The weak Carter administration was able to step in and stem the tide with a $1 billion loan to bail out the Hunts, who in 1988 were found guilty of civil conspiracy to corner the market. Serge escaped legally unscathed and continued to trade diamonds, and whatever else he could speculate in, but now on his own dime.

The other big decision I made was to liquidate Harry Winston's entire stock of large diamonds—that is, everything over five carats. In his bitter end with Harry Winston, Serge Fradkoff was not widely missed. Selling our big stones was another matter, a command decision, one that almost everyone inside the company and throughout the industry thought was insane, a crazy move by a thirty-eight-year-old whom the old diamond hands thought was "just a kid."

I took solace knowing that Jerry Schultz, our financial genius in residence and mentor to me, agreed with this decision. He found it to be logical: there had been an amazing diamond boom since 1975. With the post-Nixon economy in shambles, people looked to top quality, Harry Winston–level diamonds as a hedge against inflation in a possibly imploding world. This frenzy over diamonds soon became a global phenomenon, with people far less wealthy than our typical customer buying lesser, lower-carat stones for investment purposes. Prices quickly began spiraling upward, and so-called diamond investment firms sprang up all over America and Europe, issuing certificates of authenticity that often were not worth the paper they were printed on. The *Wall Street Journal* began listing diamond prices every week, further giving these baubles street cred as an investment vehicle. Now was the time to sell our big stones, while the market was climbing.

Just as the Hunts, abetted by Serge Fradkoff and unknowingly by us, were creating a silver rush, the leader of the pack in this diamond rush was the state of Israel. Harry Winston had a presence in Israel for years, with a diamond-cutting operation in the Tel Aviv suburb of Ramat Gan, where post–World War II émigré artisans from Antwerp plied their craft in the warmth and safety of the Holy Land. The Israeli government was very eager to welcome these craftsmen and to promote the diamond trade because of its vast potential to enhance the new country's gross national product. Israeli banks aided and abetted this boom by offering huge amounts of money at shockingly low interest rates to diamond manufacturers and dealers. By then, Israel was suffering from runaway inflation of 400 percent. Speculation in diamonds was thus a bet many high rollers were excited to take.

In March 1978 De Beers began imposing onerous surcharges on sight holders, the first one being 40 percent. In effect the Johannesburg octopus was cutting itself in on these dealers' speculations. By August 1978 De Beers's Central Selling Office inflicted another hard-to-swallow 30 percent surcharge. The result of these body blows was that the Israeli diamond market began to crumble. In 1979, for the first time in thirty years, the value of the country's diamond exports fell. Employment in diamond manufacturing dropped by one third. I saw the handwriting on the wall, and I heeded it, much to the dismay of my firm and its salesmen.

I am not a gloater, but I was quickly proved correct. In 1980 the diamond market totally collapsed, as did America's consumer confidence. Our consumer spending plunged to record lows. The prices of top diamonds, like the ones I unloaded at top dollar, dropped by 50 percent. Many diamond dealers and manufacturers declared bankruptcy. For once in my life as a diamond man, I was hailed as a "boy genius," a true chip off the old block. It felt good, though not as much as having the money in the bank to pay our inheritance taxes when that dreaded day arrived.

Meanwhile, while I had sold high, I strategically bought back low. I, for one, knew that diamonds were indeed forever. As it turned out I bought back, at the bottom of the market in the early eighties, so Harry Winston was ready to reap the benefits of the glitz and glamour of the Reagan presidency.

Meanwhile, I stepped into my father's office on Fifth Avenue, working to reassure his long-time customers that they were loved and that I would take care of them, just as my father had. But this wasn't always easy to do. Phyllis McGuire, the lead singer of the legendary McGuire Sisters, and the one-time mistress of the late Sam Giancana, the most powerful mobster in America, was one of my father's most important clients.

Phyllis was the queen bee of Las Vegas and the leader of society there, such as it was. In her gated mansion in the desert, Francophile Phyllis had a miniature Arc de Triomphe that led into a vast living room that had its own forty-four-foot-tall replica of the Eiffel Tower. She had a lake full of black swans; twenty-eight household employees, including numerous armed bodyguards; and bulletproof steel shutters that covered, at the flick of a switch, every window and door of the ersatz palace. She could never forget how Giancana met his end in Chicago in 1975, riddled with bullets while cooking Italian sausage and peppers in his basement. Still, her gangland associations paled next to those of her dear friend and fellow Vegas darling Frank Sinatra.

I thought Phyllis was a real lady until she hit me and the firm with a $60 million federal lawsuit for conversion, fraud, and breach of contract, filed by the highest-profile lawyer in

America, San Francisco's Melvin Belli. Belli, known as the King of Torts, had represented everyone from Zsa Zsa Gabor to Errol Flynn to the Rolling Stones, after the Hells Angels murder in Altamont, to Jack Ruby, after his assassination of Lee Harvey Oswald. In her case Phyllis claimed that we had substituted synthetic stones for the $10 million in gems she had brought in for cleaning in the fall of 1979. Phyllis wanted $10 million for the jewels and $50 million in punitive damages.

The corporate response, through our PR man, was that Harry Winston had "been in business for 50 years and had tens of thousands of satisfied clients. There's no way we could stay in business if that was the way we did business." We had to protest, but we didn't want to protest too much, acknowledging the popular wisdom that "the guilty dog barks."

Belli, who fought his legal battles less in the courtroom than in the press, had a typically pithy retort. "I've always bought stones for my gals at Woolworth's and I knew what I was paying for," he said. "After this, Woolworth's will be taking Winston over."

This surreal situation, I always believed, had been created by a surreal character, the successor to Giancana as Phyllis's lover, a ruthlessly ambitious, profane oilman named "Tiger" Mike Davis, a high school dropout who had risen from the lower depths to become one of America's most successful ladies' men. Davis's ticket to heaven was his job "driving Miss Daisy" for Denver's richest and most influential woman, the Rocky Mountain heiress Helen Bonfils who owned the *Denver Post*. Ironically, Helen Bonfils, like Phyllis McGuire, had been, with her older sister May Bonfils Stanton, one of Harry Winston's biggest customers. May was the proud owner of two of Harry's biggest rocks, the El Libertador and the Idol's Eye.

Like May, Helen had impeccable taste, except in men. She married Davis when she was sixty-nine, he twenty-eight. The marriage lasted, surprisingly, thirteen years until 1971. Davis took a huge divorce settlement and went into the oil business, starting a company called Tiger Oil, where he was often cited as "America's Meanest Boss." Phyllis, who obviously had a soft spot for tough guys, soon fell for him. Part of his allure was the criminal ingenuity that led to masterminding her lawsuit against us, which impelled the normally refined Harry Torczyner to rechristen the beloved songbird SiPhyllis.

Tiger Mike may have also been motivated by Tiger Oil's impending bankruptcy. Sixty million dollars would have solved a lot of his problems. Davis had access to Phyllis's safe-deposit box at the Pierre, where the jewels were kept. It would have been easy for him to make the switch, leaving his girlfriend as the innocent victim betrayed by Harry Winston, the merchant she trusted above all others. Tiger Mike showed up at our offices in his polyester dinner jacket and more jewelry on his fingers than Ringo Starr, to meet with me and the two salesmen who had catered to Phyllis. After abusing us with a jeremiad of profanity, he pulled out a pistol and laid it in front of us on a silver platter. "Now let's talk business," he declared.

As the preeminent luxury jeweler, Harry Winston, like Caesar's wife, had to be above suspicion. Nobody would pay much heed to Tiger Mike, but Phyllis McGuire, as one of America's sweethearts notwithstanding her dubious consorts, was another story. And no one was better at getting publicity than Melvin Belli. Once his inflammatory accusations showed up in the *New York Times*, we decided we couldn't fight fire with fire but had to extinguish the flames. Luckily, we had a $300 million insurance policy with Lloyd's of London. I called our agent in London, Teddy Denman, to discuss the matter. "Not over the phone," warned Teddy, a close friend of Prime Minister Edward Heath.

Teddy was a great character who loved to drink. We would go to Le Cirque for dinners that would end with his eating the flower displays. I'll never forget Teddy with a pansy in his mouth. But he was a great insurance man. I took the next Concorde to London to meet with him and the Lloyd's adjusters to address what was categorized—and covered—as a "mysterious disappearance." In the end, Torczyner and Belli worked out a deal whereby we would replace and reset $2.5 million worth of roughly equivalent big stones. Mike Davis never got his $50 million in punitive damages, though he did profit by the millions he must have reaped from the stolen jewels. And Phyllis was all charm, willing to kiss and make up. She even had me as her front-row guest for her big show with her sisters at the Plaza, and I went to visit her when I opened our branch at Caesars Palace in 2004. Sometimes, diamonds, like love, can conquer all.

Having made something of a killing by, in effect, shorting the diamond market, I felt comfortable in having enough of a reserve pay our estate taxes. Then, Harry Winston could get back to its trademark business of selling big stones. The problem was where to get them. The natural and obvious source was De Beers. Jocelyn Hambro, an eminent banker and horse breeder in London who had befriended Dad during the war, advised me that I needed to forge my own relationship with De Beers and Harry Oppenheimer, notwithstanding the way they had treated Dad. "You must show your colors," the old warrior insisted. However, because of the way they had, I believed, broke the heart that ultimately gave out on him, I was loath to eat the humble pie of dealing with them again. In time I realized that pride might be fine for scientists, but it really could have no place in a big business controlled by a monopoly. So, in 1982 I began making efforts to rebuild our bridge to Johannesburg by contacting the self-effacing, no-nonsense Bridget Oppenheimer, with whom I had remained cordial, if distant, over two decades.

Bridget was kind, welcoming, and all-encouraging for the grand return of a Winston to South Africa and hopefully a new entente cordiale that could prove profitable to both families. We came up with the idea of creating a Harry Winston jewelry exhibition that would benefit one of the Oppenheimers' favorite charities, the African Children's Feeding Scheme. Aided by my in-house PR whiz Jill Ciraldo, we spent a year planning a gala show.

We ended up bringing ten of our top people, including the smooth-as-silk Bochatay and $200 million worth of amazing jewels, to the Carlton hotel in the then-pristine and booming downtown Johannesburg, decades before racial unrest turned the area into a no-fly combat zone. For two days and nights we put on a great show, raising over $400,000 for the Scheme.

After this success, I was granted my audience with Harry Oppenheimer in his clubby office, almost identical to the one in London, in the modern downtown skyscraper that was the home of the Anglo American Corporation. Harry was now around seventy-five and still looked the same as he had decades before, as small and regal as ever. He retained his unique way of tilting his head like a sparrow to hear your every word, making a great show of how interested he was in what I had to say. But I knew from Dad's experience that behind your back he was sharpening the stiletto to spear you with.

As I sat with Harry O., I felt a deep loss and nostalgia for my father, the American Harry whom this South African Harry had done so wrong. I suppressed those thoughts. Let's start anew. I was willing to give Harry O. a second chance. We had lunch at a long table in the boardroom. I was in the center. At one end was Harry O., at the other his Anglo right hand Julian Ogilvie Thompson, who was two heads taller than the big boss. Like Harry Winston, Harry Oppenheimer had a respect for big college men, of which Thompson was a prime example.

Finally, I said I wanted to buy big diamonds from De Beers, just as my father had. Harry O. looked down the endless table to Thompson, then shook his head. "So terribly sorry, Ronnie," Harry O. said in his plummy Charterhouse–Christ Church British accent. "We haven't got a thing, Ronnie. Do we, Julian?" Julian shook his head. I knew instantly they were lying. And it hurt me. De Beers not having diamonds was like McDonald's not having burgers. Still, it was a valuable lesson in the cruelty of this business and of Harry Oppenheimer. It was dog-eat-dog, no matter whether they were greyhounds or pit bulls. I went back to New York empty-handed, but at least I knew where I stood, which was outside the syndicate.

I would have to get my big stones elsewhere. There was always the great diamond Bourse, or market, in Antwerp, where many great stones were sold. But to show how extra hard we were willing to try, Harry Winston soon opened ten separate offices in different African diamond-producing countries, so we could snap up the best big stones before they even got to Antwerp. Soon we would have active bureaus in Ivory Coast, Congo, Sierra Leone, Togo, Central African Republic, Ghana, Liberia, and Lesotho. With the New York–based Jolis brothers, we became partners in two South African mines that never yielded great fruit but still managed to make De Beers nervous that we were prospecting in its own back-yard. The idea was to leave no stone unturned, and that's just what we did.

Another colorful challenge for me as the head of Harry Winston was getting us off the Arab League blacklist of firms that did business with Israel. This was in the same spirit of the OPEC blacklist that created the brutal Arab oil embargo of 1973, which threw a giant monkey wrench into the world economy, not to mention creating the epic endless gas lines. Until the oil-rich, spend-everything Sultan of Brunei entered the scene in the late 1980s, the most coveted clients in the world were the Saudi royal family. Harry Winston had dominated this market for decades, but with Dad gone, we now found ourselves on a blacklist, not because we were Jewish, but because of our diamond factories in Israel. We were out in the cold, with the taxman circling the door like a vulture. We needed that Saudi business more than ever.

When Dad died, all the Saudi business was being conducted not via Harry Winston, but though Albano Bochatay, who was superficially trading on his own account and then paying us back in Switzerland. The problem with Bochatay is that there was no way to check on him, and he could be as devious as he was charming. I wanted the buck to stop directly with me. To that end, I found a very reliable New York–based intermediary named Riad El Azim who said he could get Harry Winston off the blacklist. Very western-ized, Riad was more an Ivy Leaguer than an Arab Leaguer. Between 1980 and 1981, Riad went for us to the Arab League boycott office in Damascus and charmed his way into getting us off the blacklist. This took Bochatay by great surprise, and as much as he professed to enjoy my company, I'm not sure how much he appreciated it when I began traveling with him to Riyadh and Jedda to sell our wares.

The Saudis did a lot of their diamond buying at our exhibitions at the Hôtel de Paris Monte-Carlo during their summer sojourns on the French Riviera. After the oil crisis in the early 1970s, when their wealth gave them the keys to the world of luxury, they seemed to make Paris their second home. My parents were crazy about Paris long before that, and in the mid-1950s, encouraged by our man in Paris, La La Adout, Dad opened a Paris salon in a stunning, chateau-esque *hôtel particulier* right next door to the Hôtel Plaza Athénée. Rather than going head-to-head with the likes of Cartier and Van Cleef, whom he called the "Place Vendôme Mafia," Dad staked out the newer Eighth Arrondissement of the Champs-Élysées instead of the traditional venue of exclusivity that was the First Arrondissement.

Bochatay, who was a natural showman, was very effective in making the Paris salon a hot spot; not the least of his efforts was hiring, in 1979, as our French director of publicity one of the most gorgeous women in Europe, Marie-Claude Parnaud, a Casablanca-born six-foot blonde and voluptuous Amazon. Marie-Claude, who could draw an elite crowd, was the frequent subject of a favorite Paris guessing game: was she or wasn't she a former protégé of Madame Claude, the world's most exclusive madam, whose own headquarters

336

were a few blocks away on the Rue de Marignan? There was nothing dishonorable about having worked for Claude, who was more of a matchmaker than a procuress; many top models and actresses met their rich, titled, and famous husbands through her. Marie-Claude, who ran with the same jet set of Agnellis, Thyssens, Krupps, Rothschilds, and Ruspolis as did Fred Horowitz, worked for us for a decade before marrying the brother of the Portuguese Duc de Braganza, one of the oldest titles in Europe.

As for me, in 1982 I shifted my focus from the Old World and the Arab world to the new world that was Japan, where in time I was able to open the country for Harry Winston in the spirit of Commodore Perry, who opened it for trade with the United States a century before. By the early 1980s the country had developed a serious obsession with diamonds. The phenomenon had been seeded in the 1960s when De Beers took its fabulously successful "A Diamond Is Forever" campaign to Japan, where matrimonial conventions and arranged marriages remained basically feudal. There was no tradition of courtship or romance that a diamond had come to symbolize in the West. De Beers enlisted the agency J. Walter Thompson to create a campaign using Western models in Western settings, riding bikes, camping, sunbathing, going to football games, dressing in Brooks Brothers button-down shirts and driving Chevrolets, things that were alien to Japan. Japan, it turned out, embraced the alien. When the campaign began in 1967, only 5 percent of engaged Japanese women received diamond engagement rings. By 1981, 60 percent of Japanese brides were sporting diamonds. I quickly saw the market possibilities for Harry Winston were infinitely expansive there.

In 1982, when I first went to Japan, I saw that its elegance and taste were a perfect match for Harry Winston. Dad, who had never been there, would have loved it. I immediately wanted to open a branch in Tokyo. To that end, I connected with Bernie Krisher, the German-born former Tokyo bureau chief of *Newsweek* and a leader of the Tokyo Press Club who made endless connections for me. Following the Thomas Jefferson philosophy in foreign affairs of "no entangling alliances," I vowed to avoid taking a traditional local trading partner.

To become self-sufficient, I began making multiple trips to Japan, learning the language and making new friends in high places, like the designer Hanae Mori, who had similar ambitions for New York, and with the Seiko watch family.

After five years of learning and networking, I was finally ready to roll. I found a space in the elegant Hotel Seiyo Ginza, which had a serene mezzanine space where Harry Winston would not be overwhelmed or overlooked. In 1989 we opened the salon, a mini version of our Fifth Avenue flagship, with a ribbon cutting by Brooke Shields, our "Miss Harry Winston." Eventually, I would open five successful Harry Winstons in Tokyo and Osaka.

In 1984, five years before our first Tokyo outpost opened, we had a trial run for a similar operation right across Fifth Avenue, on the mezzanine of the new Trump Tower, which, given the personality of the developer, was one of the most ballyhooed new skyscrapers in the history of Manhattan commerce. I was loath to forgive Trump for ruining the Harry Winston view by tearing down the elegant Bonwit Teller building in favor of an edifice that, putting it politely, was no Chrysler Building. However, short on prestige tenants for his

Tower's ground floor shopping emporium, Donald, through one of our salesmen who was his golfing partner, approached me with an offer he felt I could not refuse. In his early thirties, he had just married Ivana and was the self-crowned king of the tabloids. As one brand name to another, Donald Trump clearly loved the name Harry Winston. His pitch to me was that we were too expensive for the tourists he hoped would fill his atrium. Instead, I should follow the lead of Tiffany and Cartier and sell the brand of Harry Winston, not the diamonds, by opening a boutique that would offer affordable gifts, from stationery to leather goods to scarves and lesser jewelry, all bearing the Harry Winston logo.

Trump loved the idea more than I did and wouldn't give up. He took me and the woman I would later marry out to dinner at Il Mulino, then the hardest reservation to score in New York. He shamelessly flattered her, and me, by saying, over fried calamari, "You have hooked a giant!" as if I were a monster squid out of Jules Verne. Whatever he said, the rent he offered was appealing, and it would give me the opportunity to try out our take on the Cartier model. I designed an elegant salon with New York's premier restaurant designer Adam Tihany (Le Cirque—Daniel), which was intended as a welcome respite from the Vegas glitz of Trump Tower and installed my cousin Nicole Winston, granddaughter of my Uncle Charles, to run the operation. It would last a decade.

Back at the high end, in the mid-1980s I began experimenting with colored pearls, which had been one of my father's great obsessions. If Harry Winston was the King of Diamonds, his friend Salvador Assael was the King of Pearls, and in particular black pearls from Tahiti. Black pearls had enjoyed a vogue in the mid-nineteenth century, when they were worn by the French Empress Eugénie, the wife of Napoleon III. In the 1970s Assael created a new vogue for grand clients like Elizabeth Taylor, Nancy Reagan, Brooke Astor, and Margaret Thatcher who could pay over $100,000 for a strand of Assael black pearls. I began working with Assael to create beautiful settings, Winston settings, more like diamond jewelry than pearl strands. They became a huge hit for us.

Assael was the son of a Sephardic Jewish diamond dealer who had fled Mussolini's Italy for New York, before the outbreak of World War II. He made his first fortune after the war selling Swiss watches in Japan. Then he became an expert in oyster breeding and created a vast empire of pearl farms in the South Pacific that yielded giant white pearls that exceeded twenty millimeters in circumference, as well as sublime black ones. I began creating my own oyster beds in the Marshall Islands. It was on one of these pearl trips that, overnighting in Honolulu, I received the terrible but long-anticipated and dreaded news that my mother had died in Florida. I flew directly back to New York, where my mother's body was brought to be interred next to my father at the Queens family plot. She died on January 13, 1986, which was Bruce's forty-fifth birthday. Instead of mourning, Bruce just complained. "Her final gift to me," he grumbled, as if she had spoiled yet another vacation.

Because she had been ill for over fifteen years, there were no friends left to attend the memorial at Frank Campbell. I hired the actress Celeste Holm, who had won an Oscar for *Gentleman's Agreement* and was considered the quintessence of sophisticated New York , to deliver, in her beautiful dulcet voice, a eulogy to a wonderful woman whom she never knew. She opened by saying "I want to tell you about a woman who has been in bed for eighteen years and has now passed away."

But there would be no period of mourning. The IRS, which is not known for its sentimentality, sent a tax bill immediately. It was vastly more than we had estimated when my father died, mostly because no one dreamed Mother would survive so long. Despite pulling off a very smart move in dodging the bullet of the diamond crash of the early 1980s, my Harry Winston was, to be painfully frank, not doing as well as the Harry Winston of Harry Winston.

Notwithstanding the boom of celluloid glamour in the Reagan years that generally led to more diamonds on more cleavage, 1986 was a terrible year. Held back by a crippling trade deficit, the US economy grew by a very anemic rate of 2.5 percent. The outlook for the next year was equally bleak.

"I've got just the person for you," said Salvador Assael, coming to Harry Winston's rescue. Because we showcased his pearls, he wanted us to thrive. "He's a marketing genius," Assael assured me. The wizard in question was a Frenchman named Claude Saujet, who in the 1970s had been president of Van Cleef and from 1980 to 1985 of the French Cartier, which was doing much better than the New York branch. Saujet, who was around my age, was a slick character. He bragged about his hair implants and told me I would look much better if I followed suit. A diplomat he was not. However, given his résumé, and Assael's glowing recommendation, I accepted the possibility that looks can be deceiving and the only look that mattered was Harry Winston's bottom line. I should have followed my instincts. Within a year of his arrival, Saujet was already trying to sell my company out from under me. I finally reached the end of my rope and fired him in 1991.

But before that sorry end, we went on an expansion tear, one that enabled us to pay the tax bill in what seemed like record time of three and a half years. In the process, I inaugurated the outposts not only in Japan but also in Beverly Hills and in Las Vegas, which was opened, poetically, by the singer Jewel. Before we eventually moved to a large store on Rodeo Drive, our Beverly Hills operation began in the Beverly Hills Hotel. Running the operation was another friend of Assael, the Milanese count, Enrico "Chico" Carimati, a motorcycle-racing playboy who, with his by then equally glamorous ex-wife, had run his own jewelry boutique on Madison Avenue.

Chico was open to new adventures, and he took on the challenge of introducing Harry Winston to the moguls and stars in Beverly Hills. He also connected me to the Reagan Kitchen Cabinet and the exploding Persian diaspora, which had followed the exiled Shah's mother to Beverly Hills (Tehrangeles) and beyond. He bought a jazzy red Alfa Romeo Spider and somehow encouraged me to acquire a matching model. There the similarities ended. After five years of building our Beverly Hills profile, Chico nearly unmade it when he was set up by an ambitious salesgirl who sued us for $100,000, claiming Chico raped her on an office desk. Despite being an unrepentant lady's man, Chico proclaimed his innocence. To make the case go away, we settled for $75,000. A short time later, the alleged victim had the audacity to show up at the store waving a check. "Ha! Ha!" she gloated. "I got your money! He never raped me." Chico's reputation had taken a vicious hit, but he carried on.

When I wasn't in the air shuttling between our branches on three continents, I spent a great deal of my time in New York doing what my father had done, giving our customers the best service in the business. One was Ross Perot, the homespun Texas computer tycoon whose independent candidacy was instrumental in splitting a vote that put George H. W. Bush out of the White House in 1992 and ushered in the age of Clinton. Ross loved diamonds and not just for his wife. He walked into the Fifth Avenue store one day and mistook my cousin Richard Winston for my father, who had been dead for years. With Ross, who was a very literal, precise man of science, Richard got us into trouble by overpromising the quality of a $1.5 million pair of emerald drop earrings he was trying to sell to Ross. "I said they were the greatest emeralds that ever existed," Richard told me. "Please, Ronnie, please call Ross and say they are really the greatest. He's hesitating."

I got on the phone to Texas to try to close a deal Richard's exuberance may have jeopardized. "How are things up there in the North?" Ross greeted me in his Texarkana drawl, then cut to the chase. "Are they or aren't they? The finest on earth?" Ross pressed me. I assured him they were indeed great, but great wasn't enough. "Just send me a letter that they are the greatest, and I'll buy them."

"I can't do that, Ross," I told him, then appealed to him in a language I felt he might understand, the language of faith. "We just don't know what the good Lord will bring us tomorrow. But what I can say is that these are the finest emeralds I've ever seen." That worked. Best for me was best for Ross. That closed the deal.

As with Sharon Stone, most stars were not "customers" in the sense that they *bought* jewelry from us. Being a star meant never having to pay for luxury goods, not when your celebrity image could be traded for them. Take Michael Jackson. Once I was summoned to Jacko's suite at the Plaza Hotel. "I'm sad," he told me. "Sad for the poor children in Serbia. I want to do something special for them. I want to buy jewelry, but I don't want anybody to see or to know." I assumed he wanted to auction an array of baubles for charity.

A Michael Jackson wish was a merchant's command. After six, I opened the Fifth Avenue store for him, his second wife, and his two kids. The kids played on the Aubusson carpet while Michael spent hours examining jewels. He picked out well over $1 million worth of items. It was clear to me it wasn't for the orphans of Serbia but for himself. I had the jewels delivered to him at the Plaza. Six months went by. He never paid. Then, when I was in Los Angeles, I saw Michael at the Ivy Restaurant, surrounded by a retinue of very pretty boys, resplendent in the Winston finery. I had one of our bookkeepers call Michael about paying his bill. Six more months went by and radio silence. Then, after a year, he sent the jewelry back.

The Hollywood story is always the same: the stars never bought, or if they did, they rarely paid. And they didn't have to be film stars. Take Mike Tyson, who walked into the salon one day wearing jeans and a torn T-shirt. We had never met, but he called me "Ron" right away. He said he was going to a funeral and needed some jewelry to wear. I brought out a tray of treasures. Mike ripped off the T-shirt and, standing bare chested, flaunting his amazing physique, he ordered, "Put them on me." I had never adorned an undressed heavyweight champion, but I rose to the occasion.

Tyson took the gems. After a few days, he sent them back. Another one of our lend-but-no-lease star clients I liked immensely was Whoopi Goldberg, to whom I lent jewelry to wear at three Academy Awards shows. Once when she was being fitted, a diamond fell down her back. Our head of security, Frank Barone, was assigned to fish it out. "Do you feel anything?" she asked Frank. "I feel lots," he replied, "but no diamond," bringing down the house.

The one superstar client who had purchased from us, or to be precise, had her famous spouses buy for her, was Elizabeth Taylor. But like any star, Liz was perfectly happy borrowing, as she did for a festival for the queen of Thailand. Showing her a selection at the Plaza Hotel, I was bold enough to blurt out a quid pro quo: "Maybe I'll come with you." Liz, all charm, said, but of course. Off I went to Bangkok to meet the queen at a lavish fashion show featuring a small army of bejeweled ladies-in-waiting. However, at the moment of truth, Elizabeth appeared not wearing any of the gems we had lent her, or any gems at all. Instead she was wearing orchids, nothing but orchids. Orchids in Thailand were like bananas in Guatemala, hot dogs in Coney Island. I was disappointed yet relieved when Liz returned the jewels, yet without an explanation or apology for not wearing them.

Whatever I did at Harry Winston, I was always inspired by my father. How could I not be? One such inspiration was his donation of the Hope Diamond to the Smithsonian and the creation of the Harry Winston Court of Jewels. Given that Nancy Reagan and her best friend Betsy Bloomingdale were both customers, I decided on pitching the new and gem-loving First Lady on creating what I called the "White House Jewel Collection" that would be a natural extension of the Court of Jewels at the Smithsonian. To broach the idea, I made a gift to Nancy of some beautiful diamond earrings. She loved the earrings and the idea and invited me to the White House to discuss the matter. I recall being there with her in a room next to the Oval Office where President Reagan was discussing the future of communism with Mikhail Gorbachev. Unfortunately, a *New York Post* reporter got wind of this meeting and the earrings, and penned a headline to the effect of "Bribery at the White House." The First Lady promptly returned the earrings, and the White House Jewel Collection went up in carbon smoke.

Speaking of Gorbachev, I, accompanied by Nick Akselrod, took numerous trips to Russia, which had great reserves of superb rough diamonds in Siberia. We went to explore creating another diamond front in our ongoing undeclared war with De Beers. Working with the Russians was no easy matter. They used us as a stalking horse against De Beers, further infuriating Harry Oppenheimer and making it impossible to achieve any truce that could get us the millionaire-quality big stones we sought. The level of tension on these trips in those days was intense. We were spied on constantly, our bags would disappear, and there was always the chance that we might be detained and possibly sent to Siberia, not to do a diamond deal, but to be imprisoned in a gulag for a manufactured crime against the state.

Speaking of manufactured crimes, this brings me to my brother, who had basically been missing in action, or inaction, since Dad passed away. When Mother died, I added Bruce to the Harry Winston board of directors, making my own effort to posthumously please Dad by getting Bruce involved in the company. To inspire him, I set up a trip for us to Brazil to purchase some rough diamonds that had been mined in the country's interior. We flew down to Rio together and stayed at the Copacabana. However, after a few days of relaxation and bikini-gazing and before we could actually see the diamonds, Bruce announced that he had to go back to New York. Why, I asked him. We have business to do, gems to see. "This is more important," he said gravely. "I have to feed my cats."

"Your maid can feed them," I countered.

"No!" he declared. "If the maid feeds them, they will be very upset with me." And off he ran.

Bruce and Harry Winston made no sense. Bruce sailed his sailboat, he drove his collection of sports cars, he traveled the world and dated lots of women. But he couldn't bring himself to spend five minutes showing any interest in the business.

His best friend was a man named Ed Wohl, a graying, disheveled lawyer who had handled Bruce's divorce from Annabel Jane King. Even though the slightly portly Wohl did not look like an athlete, he became Bruce's squash partner, and they played several times a week at the Harvard Club, where Bruce was able to use my membership. I had increased Bruce's annual draw from the company to $350,000 a year, not to mention the six-figure rents we both drew from the company's occupancy of the Fifth Avenue building, which we owned jointly. Because I had engineered the rapid payoff of the IRS, I assumed that it would finally be smooth sailing for both Harry Winston and the Winston brothers.

So I was taken aback when Bruce called me in October 1989, announcing, with a sense of urgency, "We have to meet." Because, the royal "we" for Bruce included his lawyer Ed Wohl, I called Harry Torczyner, who insisted that something must be afoot and that I should not meet without counsel.

We assembled in the walnut paneled library of my new town house on East 74th Street. Bruce sat quietly with a Cheshire cat grin that signaled nothing but trouble. Ed Wohl did all the talking. His message was simple but severe. "We want to sell the company. We want to redeem the stock. And we want to do it fast."

"I do not make instant coffee," was Harry Torczyner's trademark reply. But once Bruce and Wohl departed, Torczyner was anything but placid. "He's going to sue you," he told me with a gravity that implied that what lay ahead was going to be a very big, complex, and miserable war of litigation. At first I didn't believe it. I tried to figure out a way to defuse his rage, or greed, or whatever it was. What did Bruce really want, and why did he want it now?

In 1990 Ed Wohl formally demanded a full accounting of the value of Harry Winston, Inc. What followed was an irrational volley of claims against me by my younger brother. Jay Lewin, a dear lawyer friend of mine who knew and advised Bruce on sundry matters for many years, decided to try to help make peace in 1991, after Wohl had filed suit against me for a list of brotherly wrongs that would have made Cain and Abel blush. I was being blamed for not making Bruce even richer than he was. Dad naming me as Bruce's trustee created a fiduciary duty upon me to maximize the profits of Harry Winston for my brother's benefit. What Wohl charged was that the only benefit I was concerned with was my own; that I had exploited Bruce's fiscal innocence and naivete; that I had overpaid myself for running the company while underpaying Bruce to run with the wolves; that I had usurped business opportunities for my private gain, not sharing them with Bruce; that I used the business to pay my personal expenses and for my lavish residences, Concorde flights, three-star Michelin meals. All of these ridiculous claims were just the tip of the iceberg; the others were far more sinister and personal.

Jay called a meeting at his Connecticut home that he hoped would do for the brothers Winston what the Paris Peace talks had done for the Americans and Vietnamese. Wohl was not invited, but there to back up Bruce was his new wife, who was tough enough to make Roy Cohn tremble.

Blessed peacemaker that he was, Jay set up a lavish buffet in his lovely, landscaped garden and got to the point of the meeting. The question on the table was something out of Sigmund Freud: "What does Bruce Winston really want?" Bruce flipped out at the very impudence of the query. "How dare you ask him that?" his wife defended her husband as if he were being asked to confess to a capital offense. All I could say is, "Bruce, I can't read your mind." I pressed him, "What is it that you want? Let's work this out." He just glared at me, refusing to answer, then he and his wife got up to walk out. Jay beseeched them to sit down, eat, drink, be cordial. But Bruce wouldn't have it. A new suburban French restaurant that had won raves in the *New York Times* had just opened nearby. They had to eat there. Blood, it seems, was not thicker than vichyssoise.

The reality here was that Bruce couldn't have hit me and the company with this massive lawsuit at a worse time. Yes, we had paid our tax bill, but that bill had depleted the Harry Winston coffers. Furthermore, the Japanese boom of the late 1980s, when the country bought everything American from Columbia Pictures to Pebble Beach, had turned into a massive global bust. I knew what I was facing, and I knew I had to fill our treasury not only for the looming national fiscal crisis ahead, but to defend myself against claims that I hadn't made my fiduciary ward Bruce Winston enough money.

Despite all our efforts, we had never gotten over being cut off by De Beers from the fortune we had made on their Namibian rough diamonds. The only source that could approach that was Portugal's African colony Angola, where my father had dreamed of turning the mines into his own diamond source in the 1950s. In 1975, battered by a Marxist-versus-capitalist tribal civil war of independence and greed, aided and abetted by Cubans, Russians, Chinese, and South Africans as well as sub rosa Americans, Portugal withdrew from its African colony. By the early 1980s the newly independent powder keg Angola withdrew from the CSO (De Beers Central Selling Organization) and abrogated De Beers's long contract to manage the country's diamond mines and sell its production. Angola was now, where its diamonds were concerned, both a free agent and a wild card.

Here in this gaping power vacuum, I perceived a superb opportunity for Harry Winston to make itself whole, if not flush. Motivated by the twin desires of making Harry Winston whole and making Bruce Winston happy, I was literally putting my life on the line for my father's memory and my brother's indolence.

CHAPTER SIXTEEN

My Bleak House

My greatest wish for my brother was that he would have been more of a reader. I know school wasn't his thing, but I cannot recall his reading even comic books, *Uncle Scrooge,* or *Mad* magazine, much less Shakespeare or Dickens, despite his living in England and having a British wife. He simply wasn't curious about literature, or anything intellectual, just as he wasn't curious about our family business. He had his boat and his cars and his girls, and that seemed to be enough for him. But if there was a single book I could have persuaded him to read, it would have been Charles Dickens's novel *Bleak House,* published from 1852 to 1853 as a twenty-installment serialization that is considered the ultimate satire of the excesses and pomposities of the English legal system.

It's the story of a bitter fictional inheritance battle, *Jarndyce v. Jarndyce,* that goes on for decades. The book was so influential that it precipitated a major legal reform movement in the 1870s. Dickens himself cited numerous real-life precedents, including one case in which a will that was first read in 1797 was never finally settled until 1859. Welcome to my world. *Winston v. Winston* became Bruce's and my *Jarndyce v. Jarndyce.* The ill will Bruce was litigating dated back to our father's will, which was read after his death in 1978. The case itself started in 1989 and was not settled until 2000, with the court-decreed sale of Harry Winston, Inc. Even then, Bruce, whom the law could never seem to satisfy, continued his litigation by suing our father's trustee, Bankers Trust, and then its successor, Deutsche Bank, until a New York appellate court finally held in the bank's favor and put an end to Bruce's legal follies. By that point, I calculated that Bruce had spent $43 million in legal fees, and, more significantly, nearly half of his adult life in court. A long weekend reading Dickens might have saved Bruce a fortune and precious time.

The loss of the beautiful business my father had built from nothing was heartbreaking for me. How tragic it was that his only two sons, both of whom were ambivalent about the business when young, couldn't unite and fight together to keep Harry Winston's legacy alive.

Harry Winston's last will and testament on its surface gave both of his sons everything he had every reason to believe we each wanted. But Bruce had made it so painfully clear at that tragic summer dinner at the Hôtel du Cap-Eden-Roc that all he wanted was money, an unreasonable amount of money, and the source of that money—Harry Winston—be damned. Despite this direct insult to my father's life's work, Dad left Bruce half of his estate, which was valued at the time of his death at $150 million. It was to be distributed to Bruce in four five-year tranches of 25 percent over the next twenty years. My father was, in effect, trying to protect his younger son from his own extravagance.

It was ironic that Bruce expressed no desire whatsoever to join me in the business, whose continuing annual profits, which would be my responsibility, would be the source of the future fortunes of both of us. Dad assumed he had inculcated me with his passion for gems, that I loved what I was doing, and that this love would translate into great success for both me and Bruce. Having been named trustee, and therefore my brother's keeper, I had the double duty of running the business successfully and keeping my brother in the high style to which our father's success had made him accustomed.

What was most devastating, in the end, wasn't losing the business, but it was having to accept the fact that my brother didn't love me; he only loved himself and money. His irrational anger frightened and saddened me more than any other aspect of the whole sordid affair. The day he came over to Stonwin in a blind rage and told me that I wasn't going to be living in my father's house much longer, because I would be in jail, signaled the end of our always fragile fraternal bond.

Only two years before, in 1988, Bruce had come to me cordially wanting me to buy out his share of Stonwin, which needed a small fortune in repairs and renovations that he wasn't keen on footing. At the time, he had moved into Aristotle Onassis's Olympic Tower on Fifth Avenue, above St. Patrick's Cathedral and next door to Dad's first town house office on 51st Street. Bruce was living in urban high-style, and had no use for the rustic charms of Stonwin, nor any nostalgia for our early days there. I asked him to name his price, which was $1.7 million, surely calculated by Ed Wohl, and I secured a loan and gave it to him without any negotiation. Like giving him a seat on the Harry Winston board, I hoped it would be a show of good faith and would keep the peace. I was wrong.

I was just as wrong in taking Jerry Schultz's blessed-are-the-peacemakers advice of having the firm pay all of Ed Wohl's initial legal bills for commencing Bruce's lawsuit against us. Talk about turning the other cheek. "Throw him a *kuvit*," which was diamond-ese for "throw him a bone," Jerry urged me. It would make Wohl happy, and he would have Bruce call off the dogs. So we threw Wohl a bone of $100,000, which only whetted Wohl's appetite. Soon he sent us another legal bill for $150,000, which we did not pay.

Once, I sat in Harry Torczyner's office, surrounded by his Magrittes and his George Segals, and broke down in tears, despairing that this ordeal would never end. Harry Torczyner couldn't stand it either. A man of peace, not war, Harry was a negotiator, not a litigator. Accordingly, he delegated the task to his designated "pit bull," Ken Stein, who was one of the city's smartest and most pugnacious young courtroom wizards. Ken had a huge ego, a great trait in a trial lawyer. He once paid me what was for him a supreme compliment, namely, that I was "reasonably intelligent." What he thought of my brother I dared not ask.

However, after seven years of Bruce's endless legal accusations, even Ken had had enough. There were no hard feelings. I sensed that Ken was vastly relieved to see the last of Bruce. I replaced my pit bull with an Irish setter named Kevin Plunkett, a charming former Holy Cross basketball star and a politically savvy Westchester litigator who saw the case to its tragic end.

Meanwhile, Bruce had opened a second front in his war on me. This was in Florida's Broward County, site of our mother's last residence and sad demise and where her will was probated. I felt my life was being eaten up by the case, shuttling between Scarsdale and Miami some weeks, then off to Paris, London, Japan, and Africa on others, stoking, nurturing, and expanding a business that my brother was hell-bent on destroying.

The presiding Florida judge, W. Clayton Johnson, trying to break the standoff, hired a very devout Jewish lawyer to be a referee in the case. This orthodox counsel took a very unorthodox approach. He called a meeting and presented Bruce and me with a dreidel, the spinning top used as a Hanukkah game. It also has deep religious symbolism, unknown to Bruce and me, neither of us having ever been bar mitzvahed. In any event, the referee said, "This is your bond" and then, "I want you to stand up and shake hands." I acceded to the order of the court, stood up, and prepared to do the referee's bidding. Bruce waited a long time. Then he jumped up and gave me a most perfunctory handshake. But he spoiled the effect by blurting out, "I did it, only for you, judge, and only because you wanted it. But I didn't mean it at all." The referee was at a loss for words.

The dreidel did not bring good luck. Judge Johnson next ordered the sale of Mom's unique and remarkable jewelry collection, something she had implored us to keep intact "for the ages." But Bruce, who was anything but sentimental, wanted money, and he wanted it now, perhaps to defray his gargantuan legal bills. Accordingly, Sotheby's was selected over Christie's to do the auction, which netted over $8 million.

Nineteen ninety-six was a big year for a change of lawyers, for me as well as for Bruce. Ed Wohl had lots of help, hiring from a who's who of the most prestigious, high-profile lawyers in New York and Florida. It was hard to imagine Wohl's newfound power. Here was an attorney who, before he found

Bruce, supplemented his legal income by renting carrels to Hasidic lawyers in a dingy building near the 47th Street diamond district. Now he was subcontracting Bruce's case to the likes of Rosenman & Colin, which had served Franklin Roosevelt; Phillips Nizer, which was Manhattan's legal link to the Hollywood studios; Shea & Gould, which had represented both the Mets and the Yankees, in addition to Aristotle Onassis and Reverend Moon. Bruce had every reason to gloat that he was in the best legal hands money could buy.

Wohl then bagged the biggest legal trophy in the city from New York's preeminent law firm Cravath, Swaine & Moore, which has seemingly represented every American mogul from J. P. Morgan to Warren Buffett. Cravath's superstar was David Boies, who was just about to leave the great firm to start his own. Boies, a famously dyslexic graduate of Yale Law School, made his name suing Bill Gates and Microsoft for the Justice Department and defending CBS in the General William Westmoreland libel case. In the future he would lose big cases for Al Gore in the 2000 election and for Harvey Weinstein in the #MeToo scandals of 2019, not to mention his being involved in the Jeffrey Epstein sex trafficking litigation, where *everyone* lost. But now his big fish was Bruce Winston, and his targets were me and Harry Winston, Inc.

Notwithstanding Boies's stellar reputation as a pillar of the New York Bar, the conduct of our trial often seemed like something out of Al Capone's Chicago. For example, one day I came to my office and found that my computer was missing. I asked my secretary where it was. "I sold it." She said.

"You sold it?" I asked her. "Why would you do that?"

"It was old," she said.

"Who did you sell it to?" I asked.

"Oh, er, Bruce," she replied. I was speechless for a long while.

"Did you wipe it clean?" I asked her.

"Er . . . no. Was I supposed to?" She was not long for the office.

Far worse was the incident with an assistant I trusted enough to send to Japan to help set up our offices there. She had seemed very reliable. Was I ever wrong! Boies and Wohl somehow got to her and induced her to sign an elaborate agreement to provide "assistance" to Bruce "to help him understand the business practices of the company. (Harry Winston, Inc.)." Her compensation was $25,000 for her first fifty hours of "assistance," plus a potential "bonus" ranging between $100,000 and over $1,000,000, depending on "the usefulness of the information provided," payable after a "culmination event" by which "Bruce would have received some relief against Ronald." After that event, she would continue to be paid $500 per hour for more information.

When this venal quid pro quo was exposed, Wohl contended the financial arrangements reflected that she was a "consultant" to Bruce's legal team. However, because she had been listed as a possible witness in the case by both sides, she was determined to be not a consultant but rather a "fact witness." Bribing such a witness was a violation of the law in Broward County, and elsewhere, and Wohl's law license (but not Boies's) was suspended. The suspension lasted ninety days, and Wohl was required to do ethical rehab in a "Practice and Professionalism Enhancement Program." Reflecting how slowly the wheels of justice could turn, I found out about the breach in 1998. It took until 2001 for the Florida Bar to censure Wohl and until 2003, three years after the *Winston v. Winston* was settled, for the Florida Supreme Court to affirm Wohl's brief but bitter punishment, a scarlet letter upon his legal license that could not be expunged.

The shocking matter of my assitant's witness tampering seemed to have brought our case to a head. Enough was enough. In early 1998 David Boies made the shocking admission to the Westchester Surrogate Court that he could not find any proof of any misdeeds on my part. Judging by the way Bruce and his wife reacted in the courtroom when Boies dropped this bomb, it appeared this was the first time their superlawyer was letting them know that he was not the magician they were paying him to be. It all ended with Judge Emanuelli issuing a decree that Harry Winston, Inc. be sold to the highest bidder.

With an auction on, all sorts of characters came out of the woodwork, including Serge Fradkoff in Geneva, who put together an investment group that, to my surprise, did not include Bruce. Since Fradkoff's shtick was that he was the secret son of Harry Winston, he didn't want to have a brother casting a shadow on his claim. A lot of tycoons and corporate raider types, like Nelson Peltz and Marvin Davis, expressed interest, but they all had, as a sine qua non, that I, Ronald Winston, not be part of their acquisition.

However, no one wanted Harry Winston more than I did. I had been fighting a decade for my honor and for my father and for the opportunity to continue the business I was blessed to be born into. Nearing sixty, I didn't want to go into nine figures of eternal debt for the rest of my life. I needed a backer, and in 2000 I found one in Peter Lamm, a Columbia MBA, who headed a relatively new private equity concern called Fenway Partners, so named in nostalgia for Lamm's happy college years at Boston University. Fenway paid $50 million for a 51 percent ownership stake in Harry Winston, then valued at around $100 million based on gross sales. It kept me on as chairman of the company, and it kept paying my salary of $400,000, which seemed like a relative bargain in those days of exploding executive compensation. Most important, it paid Bruce $54.1 million to settle, at long last, our Dickensian case. Bruce and I still shared ownership of our Fifth Avenue headquarters, one of the prime retail spots in the world.

Of course, Bruce and Wohl were anything but satisfied. No sooner had the ink dried on the settlement than Bruce filed a $1.3 billion lawsuit (which would grow to $2 billion) for mismanagement against Deutsche Bank, which had purchased Bankers Trust in 1999 for $10.1 billion, making it the largest bank in the world. DB was a perfect target for Bruce, who contended that a $700 million treasure trove of rubies, diamonds, and emeralds had been siphoned off from the bank, which managed the Harry Winston trust, over the two and a half decades since my father had died. Bruce declared to the press with great fanfare that DB/BT had used his father's estate "like a personal piggy bank." That suit would continue until 2007, when it was finally dismissed. Finally, it seemed, I was out of my brother's line of fire.

"We love complicated, messy dysfunctional-family stories," said Peter Lamm at the closing. The *New York Times* made much of the differences between my style and Lamm's, underscoring my "elegant" office and my attire in "suit and Gucci loafers" in contrast to Lamm's "jeans, sweater and cowboy boots." It also noted that Fenway had never played the luxury game before, citing its previous acquisitions of Simmons mattresses and Aunt Jemima pancakes. All I could do was hope that Fenway would find Harry Winston a new superpartner, one that would save the company and my father's legacy.

Lamm immediately began hyping the market about Harry Winston's vast untapped potential. With an eye toward selling us to one of the engulf-and-devour luxury conglomerateurs, like the French François Pinault or Bernard Arnault, Lamm predicted that the Fenway-Winston partnership could increase the value of the business "fivefold"—to $500 million—over the next five years. To accelerate that process, while retaining me as chairman, Lamm installed a "caretaker" president, a fortyish Christie's executive named Patty Hambrecht.

On paper, Patty looked like she had the right stuff. She had grown up in New Orleans in a family of antique dealers and had traveled the world with her parents. She had degrees from Yale and Harvard Law School. When I took her to Japan to introduce her to our operations there, she brought enough expensive luggage for an around the world cruise, and I became her designated bellboy and bag wrangler.

The potential buyers that Lamm corralled did not inspire any more confidence than Patty Hambrecht. There were the Hong Kong fashion investors Lawrence Stroll and Silas Chou. Stroll, originally from Montreal, had made his billions when he brought both Pierre Cardin and Ralph Lauren to Canada. Chou was born into his billions from his family's knitting mills, among the largest in the world. Stroll and Chou had teamed up to buy Tommy Hilfiger, which they would flip in 2006 for $1.6 billion. Fenway felt that they could do something similar with Harry Winston. Luckily, I had the occasion to see how they interacted with Hilfiger, when they ordered him to bring them espresso—which he dutifully did. If Patty Hambrecht was turning me into her bellboy, Stroll and Chou were turning Hilfiger into their butler. "I can't work with those people," I told Peter Lamm.

Finally, in the fall of 2003, Lamm made a match. The company was Aber, a Canadian mining concern that had a huge new diamond mine, the biggest on the continent, which began construction in 2001. Outside of Yellowknife, in the Northwest Territories, the Diavik Diamond Mine, as it was known, was being touted as the next Kimberley, with stones of the highest quality, and its owner Robert Gannicott, the Cecil Rhodes of the subarctic. Although Fifth Avenue and Yellowknife may have seemed like an odd pairing, it was conceivably a brilliant one that fully integrated the diamond process from the pit to the palace.

The deal took six months or so but resulted in Aber paying $85 million to me and Fenway for a 51 percent controlling share of the company, with an option to buy the remaining stock in six years. The trade press made a big deal of this marriage of producer and retailer and its seemingly enormous upside. All I could do was join the cheers. "This is a great day in the 70 year history of Harry Winston," I told the press. "Aber's investment in our company and the relationships it brings will allow us to expand to new markets and introduce new product offerings. It fulfills my father's dream of creating a company that extends from the mine to the finished jewel."

Soon after the deal was done, I flew to Yellowknife, which was as desolate as its name, to get to know my new partner Robert Gannicott. Gannicott looked the part of the old prospector—balding, bearded, big, burly, with a beer gut that overhung his trousers. He told me a story of his prospecting days, riding through the barren icy tundra of the north country on Skidoos with his partner, who he described matter-of-factly as having frozen to death on one of their ventures. Without shedding a tear, Gannicott recounted throwing the poor man's body over his handlebars and continuing on until the job was done, then riding back to base camp with his partner's frozen corpse in tow.

Gannicott had grown up in Somerset, in England's West Country. His father was an engineer and submarine officer in the Royal Navy in World War II. Gannicott's childhood hobby had been "caving," exploring underground caverns. He dropped out of a mining program at the University of Nottingham and went to Canada to work in the fields outside Yellowknife, then spent over a decade prospecting in Greenland. He loved the wilderness and its isolation the way I loved Paris. He had made Canada the third-largest rough diamond producer on earth and made himself one of the country's richest men. Calling him confident was an understatement.

After the endless journey to inspect the Diavik mine, Gannicott informed me that he couldn't show me the diamonds, or much of anything else. What was he talking about? We were partners now. Or weren't we? He confessed, he had a bigger partner in the Diavik mine, the colossal Anglo American Rio Tinto Corporation, the world's second-largest mining concern. Rio Tinto owned 60 percent of Diavik to Aber's 40 percent, and so it pulled rank. It didn't want Ron Winston snooping around its mine. Maybe the Oppenheimers in South Africa warned Rio Tinto of my father's challenges to them in Angola and in Namibia. Whatever, I never got to see the diamonds, which were the chief reason for selling Harry Winston to Aber.

It went downhill from there. Even though my contract saw me retained as chairman of Harry Winston, Gannicott dismissed Patty Hambrecht and put in his own designated overseer as CEO. This was Tom O'Neill, a very conventional "face man" whom Gannicott lured from the presidency of Burberry. O'Neill had a jewelry background, having served as vice president of Tiffany, and the jewelry division of LVMH. Gannicott mumbled his name to sound like "Toenail," so that's what we called him on Fifth Avenue. O'Neill and I barely spoke, and my influence over the company I chaired waned. Having started the company's new and highly profitable watch division in Geneva during the Bruce wars, I had lots of ideas for the company's newly deep pockets, but O'Neill had no interest in hearing them.

At a dinner in New York at the late Osteria del Circo, the nostalgic Italian restaurant owned by Le Cirque's late Sirio Maccioni, I made my case to Gannicott that I was being paid a lot of money that was being wasted because no one was listening to me.

"I've got the perfect solution," Gannicott said. "We'll pay you a lot less money."

A few months later, in 2007, O'Neill left a sealed letter with my secretary. Inside was a note of dismissal, ordering me to clean out my office by the following day. There were no testimonials, no goodbyes, no thanks. I was sixty-six years old, and I was fired. Sometime later that year, adding insult to injury, Aber changed its corporate name to the Harry Winston Diamond Corporation. Every diamond that came out of the Diavik mine that I was forbidden to see would now be designated a "Harry Winston Diamond." "It was Harry Winston's dream to own a mine," O'Neill told the press, without ever mentioning my name or my dreams. My only reward was being paid $157 million for my remaining share of the company. Gannicott got a far bigger reward in 2013, when, bored that the posh retail business lacked the thrill of the chase in the Arctic wilds, he sold the Harry Winston's Diamond Corp's retail jewelry arm and (my) watch division to Swatch, the low-budget Swiss watch colossus, for $1 billion. He then dropped the Harry Winston name and renamed his mining company Dominion Diamond Corporation.

All that remained of Harry Winston, Inc. were the retail spaces that bore his name. My father would be as aghast as I was if he knew that his name had ultimately been used as a bargaining chip in a high-stakes game of corporate jockeying, with the net result being his son's dismissal from the family firm and his company name being buried by an unscrupulous diamond mining outfit.

But so powerful was my father's genius and his lifetime of hard work that the world at large, beyond the boardrooms and banks, will always equate Harry Winston, the man, with the most precious diamonds in the world.

So it is that Harry Winston, like a diamond, is forever.

Epilogue

It's true that for most of my youth, I was determined not to join the family business. I had always loved my father, and I had always admired him. I just didn't know back then that I, too, loved diamonds.

But my father was nothing if not persistent, so in 1968, when I was twenty-seven years old, I joined the family firm. For the first two years, I worked as an unpaid intern, literally sitting silently at my father's elbow while he conducted business. This was excruciatingly boring for me, and I kept begging him to give me something meaningful to do. He'd simply look at me, as though being in his presence ought to be enough. But he wasn't sharing his thought processes with me. He wasn't explaining why he did things this way, rather than that. It was beyond frustrating, so I finally gave myself an assignment and threw myself into the deep end of the international side of the business. I just followed my gut, and I made it up as I went along. Ironically, this is also how my father had learned the trade and had grown his empire.

I don't know if this was his strategy from the get-go, but I found myself in a sink or swim environment, which was challenging, frustrating, at times even dangerous. And I liked it.

Lo and behold, I fell in love with Harry Winston, Inc. and I became an important member of my father's executive team, bringing a vital younger point of view to the company, which complimented my father's old-world ways. Eventually, as my father aged, I took on more and more responsibility and, after his passing, I took the reins of Harry Winston, Inc., expanded its reach and scale, securing its position as the pantheon of the luxury gem stone trade. Harry Winston was and remained synonymous with impeccable, rare taste under my watch and care. I had a fantastic forty year run and am proud to say that I enhanced the beautiful legacy begun by my father.

My love of diamonds is, in all honesty, my love for my father. And my dear mother. They're eternally intertwined not just in my mind, but in my heart, and I know that they are proud of the way I not only held on to the company but also navigated through the death tax debacle, managed to uphold the brand's integrity throughout myriad unscrupulous business dealings, and grew the brand in the ways my father had most hoped, building it into the world-class brand of his (and also my) dreams.

I know that he and my mother, wherever they may be, are eternally grateful to me for my hard work (I learned from the best) and my dedication to their vision. Together, the three of us built a magnificent company, a company that transcends the world of business and has become, and will remain, the symbol of absolute luxury.

Today, I live a beautiful life in California with my wife and son, and I've returned to my first love: science. I established a biomedical foundation, with the remarkable Dr. Cynthia

Bristow, where we are working on a new class of drugs for treating and eradicating cancer. Our work is still in the early stages, but we're onto something quite promising. I feel quite hopeful that we'll help revolutionize successful cancer treatment during my lifetime.

I've also been working with a team of rocket scientists on a new hybrid rocket, which will, we hope, lead to an important satellite mission.

All these things keep me busy and happy.

It's something to realize that my life's work has taken me from diamonds to the stars. I'm an incredibly grateful and lucky man.

—Ronald Winston, 2023

Acknowledgments

To say that writing this book has been a labor of love is an understatement. I've had the pleasure of working with an extraordinary team of people over the past several decades to tell my father's remarkable story.

Chief among them is my collaborator, William Stadiem. Bill became my devoted partner in this project and helped me find the words to bring my father's life, and the world of diamonds, vividly alive.

Mort Janklow, agent and dear friend, believed this story was worth publishing. Since his passing, his son Luke Janklow, and his able team at Janklow & Nesbit, especially the wonderful Claire Dippel, have championed this book and were instrumental in the publication process.

At Skyhorse, Mark Gompertz and Caroline Russomanno shepherded this through production admirably.

My chosen team of editor Emily Heckman, designer Elizabeth Demeter, and PR guru Megan Beatie have elevated the project and made publishing this a complete joy. I am grateful to this triumvirate, affectionately known as "Team Ron."

The women running my New York office, Gabriella Klett-Greenway, Naho Wilkerson, and Nancy Zhang, anchor everything, and I am eternally grateful to them.

I'd also like to thank Ryan Fox, who joined us to provide legal oversight and secure photo permissions.

I've worked with a remarkable team of historians, researchers, transcriptionists, and other professionals whose contributions anchored this book in fact and historical detail, especially Hannah Gill, Mathew Negru, Carol Winston, and Ann Sonstelie. I'd also like to thank colleagues Brigitte Devine Delaney, Melody Newberry, Laurence Krashes, Goli Parstabar, Erin Jensen, Kevin Plunkett, and Dr. Jeffrey Post.

Additionally, I've had a tremendous circle of friends and family supporting me in this endeavor, including Nathan Akselrod, Louise Arias, Jessica Burstein, Dr. Tommy Garvey, Richard Holkar, Dr. Robert Holtzman, Gordon Jacobson, Ed Kelley, Jane Lewin, Usha Malhotra, Jerry Schultz, Jackie Simon, John Lahr, Sally Mann, and Whoopi Goldberg.

This book has been in the works for nearly two decades, so to those who helped who are not named here, I thank you.

Lastly, I'd like to thank my mother and my father, for bringing me into the world of Harry Winston, and to my wife and son, for giving me such a wonderful life.

Index